FINDING YOUR LEADING MAN

JUNKIE · PAL AND PARTY BOY · PARTY BOY AND PERENNIAL CLOS
· SHY SNOB AND THERAPY JUNKIE · BLUE COLLAR GUY AND DIS
IMINATING SHOPPER AND MISFIT · HYPER-ROMANTIC AND NICE
SET CASE · PARTY BOY AND SEXPOT · PERENNIAL CLOSET CASE
ER-ROMANTIC · CREATURE OF HABIT AND MISFIT · DISCRIMINATIN
TY BOY · NICE BOY AND PERENNIAL CLOSET CASE · PAL AND SE
JUNKIE · CREATURE OF HABIT AND SEXPOT · DISCRIMINATING S
AND MISFIT · MISFIT AND NICE BOY · NICE BOY AND PAL · PAL AN
SET CASE AND SEXPOT · SEXPOT AND SHY SNOB · SHY SNOB AN
ATURE OF HABIT AND HYPER-ROMANTIC · DISCRIMINATING SHOP
E BOY AND PERENNIAL CLOSET CASE · PARTY BOY AND SEXPOT
· BLUE COLLAR GUY AND HYPER-ROMANTIC · CREATURE OF HABI
MANTIC AND PAL • MISFIT AND PARTY BOY · NICE BOY AND PERE
ENNIAL CLOSET CASE AND THERAPY JUNKIE · SHY SNOB AND S
E COLLAR GUY AND HYPER-ROMANTIC · CREATURE OF HABIT AN
MANTIC AND PAL · MISFIT AND PARTY BOY · NICE BOY AND PERE
ENNIAL CLOSET CASE AND THERAPY JUNKIE · CREATURE OF HA
ATURE OF HABIT AND MISFIT · DISCRIMINATING SHOPPER AND N
ENNIAL CLOSET CASE · PAL AND SEXPOT · PARTY BOY AND SHY
D HYPER-ROMANTIC · CREATURE OF HABIT AND MISFIT · DISCRIMI
MANTIC · NICE BOY AND MISFIT · HYPER-ROMANTIC AND PAL · MIS
AND SEXPOT · CREATURE OF HABIT AND SEXPOT · DISCRIMINAT
AND MISFIT · PAL AND PARTY BOY · PARTY BOY AND SEXPOT · PA
LAR GUY AND CREATURE OF HABIT · CREATURE OF HABIT AN DIS
· HYPER-ROMANTIC AND MISFIT · MISFIT AND NICE BOY · NICE BO
RAPY JUNKIE · PAL AND PARTY BOY · PARTY BOY AND CREATURE
· SNOB · SHY SNOB AND THERAPY JUNKIE · BLUE COLLAR GUY A
MANTIC · DISCRIMINATING SHOPPER AND MISFIT · HYPER-ROMAN
D PERENNIAL CLOSET CASE · PARTY BOY AND SEXPOT · PERENNI
LAR GUY AND HYPER-ROMANTIC · CREATURE OF HABIT AND MISI
· MISFIT AND PARTY BOY · NICE BOY AND PERENNIAL CLOSET C
E AND THERAPY JUNKIE · CREATURE OF HABIT AND SEXPOT · DI
ER-ROMANTIC AND MISFIT · MISFIT AND NICE BOY · NICE BOY AN
ENNIAL CLOSET CASE AND SEXPOT · SEXPOT AND SHY SNOB · S
PPER · CREATURE OF HABIT AND HYPER-ROMANTIC · DISCRIMIN
D PAL · NICE BOY AND PERENNIAL CLOSET CASE · PARTY BOY AN
RAPY JUNKIE · BLUE COLLAR GUY AND HYPER-ROMANTIC · CREA
ER-ROMANTIC AND PAL · MISFIT AND PARTY BOY · NICE BOY AND
JB · PERENNIAL CLOSET CASE AND THERAPY JUNKIE · PARTY BO
KIE · BLUE COLLAR GUY AND HYPER-ROMANTIC · CREATURE OF
MANTIC AND PAL · MISFIT AND PARTY BOY · NICE BOY AND PERE
ENNIAL CLOSET CASE AND THERAPY JUNKIE · CREATURE OF HA
ATURE OF HABIT AND MISFIT · DISCRIMINATING SHOPPER AND N
D PERENNIAL CLOSET CASE · PAL AND SEXPOT · PARTY BOY AND
D HYPER-ROMANTIC · CREATURE OF HABIT AND MISFIT · DISCRIM

FINDING YOUR LEADING MAN

HOW TO CREATE MALE-TO-MALE
INTIMACY AND MAKE YOUR
RELATIONSHIP A BLOCKBUSTER

• • •

JON P. BLOCH, PH.D.

ST. MARTIN'S GRIFFIN
NEW YORK

www.stmartins.com

Book design by Casey Hampton

ISBN 0-312-26736-3

First Edition: December 2000

10 9 8 7 6 5 4 3 2 1

CONTENTS

■ ■ ■

PART 2: MALE MATCHMAKING

PART 3: MALE BONDING

ACKNOWLEDGMENTS

■ ■ ■

Two people in particular made this book happen. My agent, June Clark, of the Peter Rubie Literary Agency, offered—and continues to offer—invaluable guidance and support. If she weren't such a great agent, she could make a lucrative living as a rent-a-mom. My editor, Keith Kahla, understood immediately what I wanted to accomplish with this book, and his enthusiasm made it all fun and easy. He also is a perfect gentleman.

My oldest friend, Pat, has always believed in me and made life magical. Bruce, Dave, Jack, Jim, Michael, and Robert have been there for me and then some over the years. Memories of so many men no longer living help sustain me, including Alan, David, and Paul. In fact, I wish to thank all the gay men who have enriched my life and whose diverse ways of living and loving have taught me so much about the gay experience—and of course about myself.

INTRODUCTION
NEWS FLASH: GAY MEN ARE MEN

■ ■ ■

MEN AND WOMEN ARE DIFFERENT.
How many millions of times have you heard someone say this? And
we all know what it means. Women want intimacy, men want instant gratification. Women want men to open up emotionally, and
men want to do this about as much as they want to experience adult
circumcision without anesthesia.

But what if you're lesbian or gay? Do lesbians *also* seek intimacy?
Do gay men *also* try to avoid it? The lesbian question I'll leave to
someone better qualified to answer. But I am here to tell you that
gay men are . . . well, *men*. And as men, we often find it difficult
(to put it mildly) to be intimate with another person.

A lot of books have been written on the subject of how gay men
can find that Special Someone. And many of them have worthwhile
suggestions. But most of them assume that as a gay man you're
totally ready for intimacy. It's only a matter of meeting the right
guy, and then playing your cards just so.

But it gets more complicated than that, doesn't it? Sometimes
you meet a special guy, and you do all the "right things." And for
two weeks here or six months there, you think you're onto something. Maybe you even move in together. But we all know what
happens next: "It just didn't work out." "The chemistry just wasn't
right." "He wasn't giving me enough space." "I wasn't giving him
enough space."

And so on.

So many gay men have a "favorite" movie that's all about un-requited love. How Person A did *not* get Person B in the end. And, unfortunately, we take that script into our real-life dramas. We come to expect feeling all alone.

Why do so many gay men want intimacy yet shy away from it? Some say it has to do with growing up in an antigay society. And certainly that's part of it. Sometimes I'm amazed that most of us gay guys turn out as well as we do. Yet studies show that lesbian rela-tionships often are more stable than straight ones. So maybe it has more to do with being male. Maybe it isn't our gay genes so much as our male Levi's.

Are men and women born different? Some say yes, some say no. But certainly we're taught to be different. From the moment of birth, boy babies and girl babies are not only dressed in different colors. Boys are taught to be independent. To take action. To set aside their feelings for "more important" goals. Girls are taught to need other people. To nurture. To express themselves emotionally.

Of course, no one learns these lessons to perfection. Straight or gay, males and females occasionally break the rules and act like the other sex. However, straight or gay, males and females also learn to conform to many of the expectations set before them. As a gay man, you obviously didn't do everything you were taught about how to be male. But you probably do many things very much the way a straight man would. Studies show that gay men sometimes are more like women than like straight men. But overall, gay men still are *more* like straight men than they are like women.

I'm not saying we're exactly the same as straight men. Our fear of intimacy is different in two important ways:

Gay male partnering is man-to-man. You might be thinking, "Well, duh!" But in a funny way, we forget this when we're dating. You may think that you're Barbie to his Ken. But to him, *you're* the Ken. Why? Because in more ways than you realize, you *act* like Ken. I have a news flash for you and hope you're sitting down: When the relationship fails, it's not all his fault. You, my friend, are also to blame. You, amigo, also fear intimacy. You, mine kinsman, are also hard to get to know.

Humming a show tune or thinking boxing is icky doth not a nonmale make. If you don't believe me, try this simple experiment. Make a list of all the guys that wrote you off in their guy-type way. Now make a list of all the guys that *you* avoided because of false pride, fear of rejection, or because he called you twice in a row so you felt "suffocated." I'll bet that second list is not exactly short. (I know mine isn't.)

"There's no way to tell if a man is gay." "A gay man can be just as masculine as a straight man." "I'm a regular guy who just happens to be gay." We hear these statements all the time. And the thing is, they're *true*. That's the good news. But it's also the bad news. As a gay man myself, I've had to deal with the fact that I'm attracted to men. I don't just mean all the homophobic crap. What I mean is, I'm attracted to *men*. You remember?—those creatures who keep busy all the time to avoid their feelings. The ones whose pride and egos prevent them from connecting emotionally. The ones who want a quick sexual fix. The ones afraid of closeness and commitment. However . . .

Unlike straight men, gay men hide their fear of intimacy. Straight men actually *brag* about how much they don't want to get close to people. "Make my day," says Clint, blasting the other guy with bullets. Talk about avoiding intimacy. *"Hasta la vista,"* says Arnold, to similar end. But we gay guys grow up learning to disguise who we are and what we want. It's too bad the CIA doesn't like to hire gays, because your average gay man is a natural secret agent who effortlessly conceals a hundred different mysteries at once. The problem is, we're *too good* at keeping secrets. We're overly cautious when it comes to trusting others.

Who can forget the story of Red Riding Hood, especially the part where Wolfie does drag? Well, in a way, that's what a gay man does. He may *seem* "sensitive" and "in touch with his feminine side." But he sure is good at saying, *"Hasta la vista,"* isn't he? He can growl and bite with the best of them. Just think about the last guy you dated, and what you *thought* he was like at first, versus what you *knew* he was like after two weeks or six months or whatever.

As a gay man, you've learned to hide your fear of intimacy behind a performance you give to the outside world. And just like that movie star you always wanted to be, you're a good actor. If they gave out Oscars for acting in the real world, you would probably have won a few by now. C'mon, admit it. Don't be modest.

In fact, there's a whole series of performances that gay men feature, each with its own personality traits and bedroom behavior. Sort of like having an astrological sign. I call it a gay man's *Oscar-Winning Typecast Appearance*—OWTA, for short.

- It's *Oscar-Winning* because you know how to give a good performance.
- But you're *Typecast* in this one role. You know what "typecast" means—someone becomes so strongly identified with one performance, they never get to play something different. Yes, it even happens to Oscar winners. Look at Liza Minnelli after *Cabaret*. Look at Louise Fletcher after *Cuckoo's Nest*. Being typecast in the real world means that you're so good at this one shtick that you never break free of it.
- So this *Appearance* that you adopt for the outside world is just that—it's a show, a disguise, aimed at keeping people from getting too close.

Does any of this sound familiar?

If it does, then you've come to the right place. This is a book for the gay man who wants to do one or both of the following:

Overcome his own fear of intimacy. In straight relationships, a woman sometimes works around the man's reluctance to connect. But in a gay relationship, at least one of the men has to get past his *own* fears and hang-ups if it's going to last.

Achieve intimacy with another man. Even if you're one of those lucky gay men ready for intimacy, it doesn't mean *he* is. Connecting to a man—not to mention holding on to him—takes effort. Not only that, it takes knowledge. Knowing what to say and when to say it. Books written for straights can offer ideas about how a woman gets a man to open up. But in this book you'll learn how *another man* can do it.

Yes, Virginia, gay relationships are complicated. Not impossible, just complicated. And like most complicated things, there are ways of making it simple. That's why this book is organized into three simple parts: "Finding Your Inner Male," "Male Matchmaking," and "Male Bonding."

A word of caution: If you're looking for a book that says, "This is exactly how you should live your life," you've come to the wrong place. For example, I'm not going to insist that monogamy is right for everyone. Sometimes people stay in monogamous relationships to *avoid* intimacy. They're afraid to face how lonely or unhappy they are, and they hide their feelings from themselves and their partner. Doesn't sound very intimate, does it? Sometimes open relationships are extremely honest and intimate; in other instances, additional sex partners signal a fear of intimacy.

I'm also not going to say it's right or wrong to have sex on the first date, or how long you should know someone before moving in together. All that's up to you. Sometimes couples who go All the Way in the first five minutes end up living happily ever after. For that matter, some people genuinely are happier living single than with another person.

The point isn't *what* you do, but *why* you're doing it. Whether you're single or married, whether you're monogamous or not, are you trying to connect to other people, or are you trying to avoid connecting to them? Are you striving to be true to yourself, or are you trying to make certain parts of yourself go away? These are the issues I can help you with—how to be the best possible you while engaging in romance and lovemaking and all that other stuff.

Are you ready to become the Leading Man in a totally new movie—one that has a happy ending? And are you ready to find the right Leading Man to play opposite you? Great. First, let's figure out what type of Inner Male you are—and what type he is, too.

PART ONE

. . .

FINDING YOUR
INNER
MALE

LIKE STRAIGHT MEN, GAY MEN HAVE A lot of hang-ups about getting close to people. But like women, gay men often feel they haven't the right to assert themselves. Put it all together, and you have a gay man with a typical male fear of intimacy that he camouflages behind a disguise. As I just got done explaining, this is his Oscar-Winning Typecast Appearance, or OWTA.

Just like the twelve signs of the zodiac, there are twelve basic OWTAs: the Blue Collar Guy, the Creature of Habit, the Discriminating Shopper, the Hyper-Romantic, the Misfit, the Nice Boy, the Pal, the Party Boy, the Perennial Closet Case, the Sexpot, the Shy Snob, and the Therapy Junkie. But unlike in astrology, these twelve personality types are not fixed for life. You can change over time from one type to another. But what is more important is that you can overcome being *any* of these types at all. Here's how:

- First, recognize your OWTA type. You need to get out of denial.
- Second, embrace your OWTA for the good things it's done for you. It's hard being a gay man in our society, and it's nice that you found a way of coping. If your OWTA were all bad, you wouldn't keep doing it. So get a little spiritual and acknowledge the gifts it's brought you.

- Third, you need to overcome those aspects of your OWTA that are holding you back. Yeah, yeah, yeah, the universe is bliss. But you're not all *that* happy, are you? So after noting what's good about your OWTA, start overcoming the bad stuff about it. This is one time when it's good to be Clint or Arnold. Take out that imaginary gun (or whatever) and blast away that wall holding you back. Just as you came out as gay, get outta the trap of your OWTA. Learn to be intimate instead of OWTA-mate.

A final word before we get going: When you're reading about the OWTAs, you might think, "Wow, this one type really applies to me." But what if you end up thinking you're two or three different types? Or what if you think, "In my last relationship, I was this type, but now I feel more like this other type"? Does this mean you're Sybil? Not at all. Some people change quite a lot from one phase of their life to the next—or from one relationship to the next. If you find useful suggestions in more than one OWTA, that's great. Still, see if you can concentrate on one OWTA at a time. In your gut, in your heart of hearts, when it comes to intimacy *now*, which *one* of the twelve OWTAs are you? That's your OWTA. Which *one* is the man in your life? That's his OWTA. First and foremost, follow the information for the OWTA that you are, first and foremost.

THE BLUE COLLAR GUY

. . .

PERSONALITY

One of the most popular types of OWTAs is the frankly masculine
Blue Collar Guy. There's nothing wrong with being blue-collar.
Plumbers, carpenters, and police officers are essential to society—
more so, if you think about it, than political science professors or
dance critics. So if you're blue-collar, I say all the more power to
you.

However, blue collar can be a state of mind as much as a statement of fact. Guys with white-collar jobs can still have a blue-collar
personality. Just the other night, I asked this flannel-shirted guy in
a bar what he did for a living. "I fuckin' teach art history at a
finishing school, man," he informed me, butchly slamming his Bud
on the counter. Come to find out he grew up in a blue-collar family.
Even though he wore a shirt and tie to work and had all these
yuppie diversified stock portfolios (among other assets), he had the
same salt-of-the-earth ideas about life as his father.

You Blue Collar Guys have a lot of great qualities. For one thing,
you're sexy when you sweat. For another, you're sincere. Some gay
men mask their emotions behind clever words, but Blue Collar Guys
shoot straight from the hip. Your directness is refreshing, especially
for men who are burned out on flippant bar talk. When you like
someone as a friend or love him as a lover, you really let him know
it. You are warm and affectionate and full of passion.

Not only that, but you have values and standards. Some people say that the gay world doesn't have enough role models or road maps to teach us how to live. So a lot of gay men are attracted to your having principles to live by. Regardless of how your family feels about your being gay, you maintain the ideals and beliefs you were taught. Things like hard work, perseverance, and honesty mean a lot to you. You very much want a partner to settle down with, so that your relationship can resemble a conventional marriage as much as possible.

In choosing friends, it's more important that they share your simple, honest values than whether they are gay or straight. Whether fishing with your buddies or helping your brother-in-law put up a new fence, you enjoy feeling like one of the guys. And so just by living your life, you help familiarize straight people with the gay experience.

About the most traumatic thing that can happen to you is having your family reject you for being gay. Obviously, that's never easy for any gay man to deal with. But some gay men relish the opportunity to reinvent themselves. They're glad to get out of Podunk (or wherever they came from) and make a whole new world for themselves in New York or San Francisco. But it's different for you Blue Collar Guys. They can take you out of Podunk, but they can't take the Podunk out of you. Since you lack the imagination to envision a different type of life for yourself, you stubbornly cling to the lifestyle you were taught to live—with a slight variation, of course. If your childhood was unhappy, you probably have a great deal of difficulty admitting that it was, because such an admission would be disrespectful to your family.

Specifically, you have extremely rigid ideas about men and women. While it's great that you help shatter stereotypes about gay men, it's at the cost of being extremely defensive and self-righteous about your masculinity. You sell yourself short in the intimacy department rather than saying or doing something that would give the impression that you aren't butch. As long as you can "pass" for "one of the guys," you'll do things you don't really enjoy, even staying in an unhappy relationship. Even in a potentially happy one, you'll hold back those parts of yourself that might be labeled "feminine," and so the relationship won't be as close as it could be.

BEDROOM BEHAVIOR

Since you often use your muscles on the job, you Blue Collar Guys don't go the gym route as much as other types of men. After lifting and bending all day long, who wants to work out? (Even if you work behind a desk, you are probably more inclined to hike or landscape the yard than aerobicize). So for the man who wants a nice, big cuddly bear to snuggle up to on those cold winter nights, you're just the ticket. You make him feel loved and protected in your arms. You want lots of touching and kissing and hugging. Because fancy words are not your specialty, the physical path is primarily how you express your needs and feelings. For your partner, things could certainly be worse.

As affectionate as you are, you change when you get purely sexual. You like to feel like you're a "real man." So you want to call the shots in bed. If you take the bottom role, you explain it or justify it somehow. You need to feel that you're still a man—or maybe *the* man. You may *enjoy* treating your partner like a mere object that exists to satisfy whichever role you're taking. There is always the danger that you'll alienate him over time by your need to be in control.

Because commitment is important to you, you won't necessarily leave if the sex lessens over time. But you'll start to feel unloved, because you view sex as a primary way of demonstrating love. You may start looking elsewhere for sex, yet you'll expect your partner to remain faithful. Some of your ideas about partnering go back to outmoded traditions where the wife was considered the husband's "property," and you feel jealous and threatened if your lover seems even remotely interested in someone else.

INTIMACY BLOCKERS

You have black-and-white ideas about what it means to be a man or a woman. And you get self-righteous about defending your masculinity. You avoid any part of yourself that might be seen as "feminine." You refuse yourself permission to enjoy an umbrella drink or a Babs movie. Let alone permission to seem weak or afraid.

But by hiding who you are, you aren't really present. And if you aren't present, you aren't getting close to people. You're just giving a performance.

Also, there's a flip side to making your feelings known. Just as you let others know when you like them, you *really* let them know when you don't. You are hung up on getting your own way. Compromising is seldom an option. You'll say or do whatever it takes to win the argument. And since you're not as verbally skillful as other types of gay men, you'll resort to lies, insults, sulking, shouting, slamming the door, leaving the house—maybe even violence—to have your way.

You're technically "expressing your feelings" when you're angry or threatened. But ironically, these feelings are expressed to push the other man away. Either that, or to control him. And control is another way of avoiding intimacy. If you need to control another person, it's because you're afraid to share who you really are and let things unfold naturally.

POSITIVE ASPECTS OF THE BLUE COLLAR GUY
Sincerity, warmth, affection, loyalty.

CHALLENGES TO BE OVERCOME
Fear of the feminine, bossiness, jealousy, fear of losing.

HOW TO CHANGE
First, acknowledge the many wonderful memories you've given to the people you care about. No doubt people treasure the kindness and caring that can come only from you. But now, my Blue Collar friend, comes the fun part . . .

Discover that "male" and "female" are not opposites. Physiologically, men and women have *some* differences, but they are more alike than they are different. Yet many of us (yourself included) are taught to concentrate more on the differences than the similarities. We stereotype men and women. We notice what we want to notice about each sex's behavior and ignore what we choose to ignore, so that these stereotypes will be confirmed. ("Of course she's emotional—she's a woman." "Of course he's a grouch—he's a man." Like there are no emotional men or grouchy women?)

Make a list of three qualities you consider "male" and three you consider "female." Then think of some women you know and see if they don't have some of those "male" qualities. Next, think of some men you know—yes, even straight men—and see if they don't have some of those "female" qualities.

Finally, think about a woman you admire—in real life, the movies, whatever. List three qualities she has that you like. Ask yourself how your life could be enriched by taking on these qualities yourself.

Come out of the closet over your "feminine" interests. (And don't tell me you don't have *any*. I wasn't born yesterday.) If you secretly want to buy a Judy Garland CD, do it. And walk down the street holding it proudly for all the world to see. Don't hide it in a bag or tell the salesclerk it's for a friend. Relax. Let a little flamboyance in. Buy that Hawaiian shirt. Ask the guy in the supermarket where the portobello mushrooms are. And if he figures out you're gay? *Hello?!* And where were you last Saturday night? Besides, maybe he's gay, too.

Drop the G. I. Joe routine. First, you need to realize that it's okay to be afraid. Nature gives us the fear instinct for a reason. Fear tells us when to be cautious. If we never felt fear, we'd all be dead. Fear is a good thing. If you feel afraid of someone or something, it shows that you're a strong, functioning being.

In a given week, tell one other person about someone or something you're afraid of, and why. Study the other person's reaction. I'll bet they don't think any less of you. In fact, they might even have more respect for you for being so honest.

You also need to learn to ask for help. In the animal world, many of the mightiest beasts do things in packs or prides or herds. These male wolves, lions, or elephants are fully confident in their masculinity. But they also know that they can't do everything by themselves. So in a given week, ask one other person to help you with something that you'd normally struggle with by yourself.

Stop having to "win." No one *always* wins. No one *always* gets his own way. Everyone has to answer to other people. Everyone has to bite his tongue sometimes and go with the program. Look at Bill Clinton, the leader of the free world. So stop thinking that you're going to be the big exception, okay?

Make a list of three instances when you *didn't* get your own way. Then think about what happened instead. What it really as bad as all that? Did *no* good come of it whatsoever?

Stop expecting a man to be your "wife." He's your *partner* and deserves to be treated as an equal. (In fact, wives also deserve to be treated as equals, but that's a topic for another book.) By throwing your weight around, you are *not* winning your boyfriend's respect. You are *losing* it.

Once a week, do *one thing* completely the way your boyfriend wants to do it. Let him plan the entire evening. The movie *and* the restaurant. Let him get things going in bed. Let him set the mood. Let him name the fantasy. Let nature take its course. No complaints are allowed. Just go with the flow. Notice how it doesn't kill you to let go.

If there's a disagreement between you and your man, get in the habit of immediately saying, "Let's compromise." *Even if* he's the one being impossible. Don't feel you have to win at all costs. Remember—you can win the battle, but lose the war. You can drive that man right out of your life, even though you've "won" the argument. A wise man chooses his battles carefully.

After a month or so of doing all these things, see how you feel. More important, share how you feel with the man in your life.

FINAL THOUGHTS

We are all made of many things. Stop worrying so much about proving you're a man. Look, you're a man, okay? If you have any doubts, try this: unbutton your 501s and feel what's inside. I rest my case. No one mistakes you for a woman.

Anyway, the people who care most about that macho stuff are antigay. You'll never please them, anyway. So you might as well stop trying. Do what makes *you* happy, and the right man will come into your life.

THE CREATURE
OF HABIT

. . .

PERSONALITY

Outsiders who criticize the gay world for being superficial or flighty should spend a day around the Creature of Habit. If you are one of these entities, you are *very* stable. You might be just what the doctor ordered for the gay man who feels he's stayed too long at the orgy. Your ordered, disciplined, and thoughtful way of life just might rub off on him in a positive way.

Additionally, you make a loyal friend whom others can count on to remember their birthdays or help them make it through those long, lonely nights. In fact, certain friends might become part of your routine—Friday night means cribbage with Ed, and on Saturday night it's the leather harness with Tim.

Though Ed and Tim are both your good buddies (albeit in rather contrasting ways), it's possible they've never even met each other. Your sense of order dictates that your life be compartmentalized. Others might think you contradict yourself from one activity to the next, but as far as you're concerned, your life is unified. Because your need for independence and privacy is at the center of everything you do.

You probably have at least one hobby that occupies a great deal of your time. If you garden, it's not a just a Saturday-afternoon enterprise. You own *hundreds* of plants. If the yard is completely landscaped, you change things around just to keep busy. You don't merely collect recordings of the music of your choice (whether opera or heavy metal), you scan dozens of Web sites and catalogs to add to your thousands of CDs.

You Creatures of Habit are found in all walks of gay life. You can be a city slicker or a country bumpkin. You can be a homebody or world traveler. Perhaps most important, you can be single or have a husband. In either case, you give the *impression* of being a bachelor. In fact, you are such a dyed-in-the-wool bachelor that you have virtually no interest in changing any of your daily, weekly, or lifetime routines.

Whether you're Oscar or Felix around the house, whether your comb is kept to the left or the right of your toothbrush—whatever your routine, that's *it,* and woe to the man who tries to change it. Not that you get violently angry—it makes no sense to spoil your day with emotional outbursts. But in your quiet, dignified way, you make your needs known and then some.

On the surface, you probably have a "pleasant" relationship with your family. Privately, you might wish you could talk to your relatives on a different level, but you aren't inclined to confront them with this. However you regard your past, you need to feel that your *present* is under control. You tend to say that you *used* to be angry at your parents or whomever, but you've worked through all that long ago. Or perhaps you'll insist that nothing's ever happened that bothered you. Dwelling too long on problems or unhappiness might spoil your routine. You won't be able to concentrate on your puppy farm or collection of *Life* magazines. You won't get your eight hours of sleep.

You are unlikely to be accused of being needy or clingy—and if you occasionally are, you are stern with yourself for being so foolish. You bruise but never crumble. Your theme song might well be "I Will Survive." In today's world of topsy-turvy relationships, your genius for self-sufficiency and constancy is laudable.

BEDROOM BEHAVIOR

As with other aspects of your life, you like it when sex can be compartmentalized. Maybe this means every Friday night at the baths; maybe it means having a weekend fuck buddy. But even if you have a husband, your partner suffers confusion over your ability to be making love one moment and balancing your checkbook the next. Whatever you're doing, you think you should give it your all. And if you're only 50 percent present during sex, you'd just as soon be doing something else. It's nothing personal against the man you're with, but he may have trouble understanding this.

You are more comfortable having him at your place than the other way around. You like being around familiar things and will have an easier time picking up your routine where you left it. (Probably you'll be impatient to have him leave in the morning.) It's disorienting to spend the night at his place—and you might "eat and run," so to speak, to rush back to the comforts of home. A neutral setting—such as the baths or a hotel—might be best of all. The sex is that much more compartmentalized, and you're spared the anxiety of letting him into your world, or letting yourself into his. (If you live with a man, you need to feel that the dwelling is first and foremost *your* place—as opposed to "our" place.)

You are as much a Creature of Habit sexually as in other ways. You like only what you like, *period*. Because you avoid messy scenes, you might technically agree to try some sexual practice that turns you off. But in your passive-aggressive manner, you'll find a way to get out of it.

INTIMACY BLOCKERS

Many people have a problem with being alone; you have the opposite problem. You are so good at keeping yourself company that you have difficulty being around people. Not that you're totally isolated. Probably you have a well-organized support network. You are highly selective in what you share with whom, but technically there are people in your life to ward off the blues. But what it all adds up to is trying to have complete control over the things that happen to you, and the ways that other people perceive you.

Even if you live with another man, you come across as a loner. You may travel all over the world, yet you seem like you never do anything. Why? Because you aren't connecting with anyone, so in a way you really *aren't* doing anything. You're merely keeping as busy as possible to avoid intimacy.

And busy you most certainly are. In fact, there probably wasn't an isolated moment in which you decided to become a Creature of Habit. Maybe you even mean to stop being this way one of these days. But between your job and all the other things you have going on, it just isn't possible right now. You make sure things stay that way, too. Suggestions on how you can streamline your time are not heeded, because even when you complain about being too busy, you have no intention of changing.

If there's a man in your life, probably he feels like the social director in the relationship, because it's up to him to plan new and exciting activities. Your self-preoccupied manner of living does not tend to bring out the most interesting aspects of another man's character, yet you often complain if a man doesn't seem "interesting" enough. What you fail to grasp is that watching you water the plants (or whatever) is not likely to make someone sparkle.

POSITIVE ASPECTS OF THE CREATURE OF HABIT
Stability, independence, resourcefulness, accomplishment.

CHALLENGES TO BE OVERCOME
Fear of change, fear of spontaneity, fear of appearing vulnerable, fear of being alone with your feelings.

HOW TO CHANGE
First, honor what a good job you've done taking care of yourself. You've taught yourself a lot about how to cope with disappointment, and to be your best friend. But now, my Creature of Habit, comes the challenging part . . .

Make change your new habit. You have to get over your *fear* of change in order *to* change. First, think of someone you've known whom you do *not* admire. Make a list of three qualities about this individual that have bothered you. Then take a good hard look in the mirror: Have you turned into this fuddy-duddy in your own way? Could

someone accuse you of having any or all of these same three qualities, and of being just as stubborn about changing them?

Now that you feel good and shaken up, think of someone you
do admire, and list three of their positive qualities. Think about how
you can become more like this person in your own way. Make it
part of your daily routine to do something each day to emulate one
or more of these qualities. Maybe you pick a different one each
day—whatever works for you. But in this way, make change become a part of your daily routine.

Admit that you hurt. Somewhere in your past, you became mistrust-
ful of other people. Moreover, you had a great deal of pride and
worried that others might think you were vulnerable or needy. So
you decided you needed to be perfect. That way, no one would try
to hurt you. And why let unhappiness stand in the way of your
goals?

True, if depression gets to where you can't eat or sleep or leave
the house, you have a problem (and should see a doctor). But you
use all that as an excuse. You say to yourself, "If I faced my sense
of loss, I won't be unable to function." But as you and I both know,
what you're *really* afraid of is being in pain. Sorrow is not what
makes people depressed—it's the *failure to face sorrow* that does.

Write three statements that begin "I feel pain because . . ." Think
of someone you can talk to about each of these situations—if possible, the person they involve. If that's impossible or not a good
idea, use a surrogate. Ask this person (corny as it sounds) to hold
your hand while you share. Talk only about your hurt and sorrow—
do not tell it as if you've already worked through it or learned some
big, profound lesson from it. Do not give it a positive spin. Also,
do not tell it in terms of anger. Often, anger is a way of putting
yourself "above" a situation. Share with another person your human
imperfections.

Go easy on the stamp collecting. There's nothing wrong with having
a hobby. But again, the key word is *moderation.* Put a six-month

moratorium on adding to your collection of whatever it is—you already have enough of it to last a lifetime. If your hobby requires ongoing care (such as plants), get rid of at least some of it. Sell what you can and spend the profits on something silly and frivolous—and utterly disposable.

People are more important than routines. Once each week, permit another person to interfere with your routine. Maybe it's something major, like letting a man do something sexually that you do not normally permit (though of course make sure you're being safe). Maybe it's something as small as letting a friend put his jacket or book bag where it doesn't belong, *and then letting it stay there.*

I know I've been saying you need to get more in touch with your feelings, but in this instance *don't.* Here's where all your rigor and discipline can come in handy. Ignore the creepiness you're experiencing. Pretend that you aren't feeling violated. "Fake it till you make it" goes an old saying, and here that's just what you need to do. Force yourself to believe that the other person has more value than your trivial routine.

Be a fool for love. Give at least one man the benefit of the doubt once in a while. Set aside the yard work or the bills for a few hours for the riskier adventure of intimacy. And if he stands you up or never calls? Then you, my friend, are a hero. That's right. You bravely took a risk. You were vulnerable and curious, despite life's disappointments. Which, if you think about it, is practically the point of being alive.

Go ahead and say things like "I want to see you again" or "I'm sad that we can't get together tonight"—even, yes, "It breaks my heart that you don't love me." Then try again with someone else. As long as you're being true to yourself, you won't suffer long-term depression over the loss. You might need to be out of commission for a few weeks while you nurse your wounds, but it's better than being out of commission for years because you refuse to take chances.

FINAL THOUGHTS

My Old World grandmother used to say that men who didn't get married got "kind of funny" after a while. I used to think that she meant gay. Now I think she meant something else. Gay or straight, men (or for that matter women) who don't connect with others get overly absorbed in their own way of doing things. Other people are good for us. Sometimes it's healthy to be forced out of our limiting routines.

As a Creature of Habit, you confuse keeping people at arm's length with freedom. But true freedom means being able to connect with others and still be yourself.

THE DISCRIMINATING SHOPPER

■ ■ ■

PERSONALITY

You not only want a man in your life, you want a very specific man. Society gives us little permission to express our gay sexuality, so some men feel forced to take whatever comes along. But not you. You know exactly what you want and are determined to get it. Despite all the ways we're put down for being gay, somehow you acquired a great deal of self-respect. You see no reason to settle for second best.

The personal ads are full of you Discriminating Shoppers. The specifics vary a great deal. One man must meet someone between the ages of twenty-one and twenty-four. The next man wants someone who's clean-shaven—the next, with a beard. Smooth chests versus hairy chests. And so on. Your type can also be spotted in bars. More times than not, you leave alone, a seemingly unapproachable man of mystery.

It's not as though men never come on to you. To afford the luxury of being a Discriminating Shopper, you probably are no slouch in the looks department. Even if you don't have classic GQ looks, seeming to be unavailable gives you an aura of desirability. But if a man is not exactly your type, you're not about to waste his time or yours.

In truth, you're idealistic and wistful. *If only,* you tell yourself (and possibly your friends), *if only I could meet Mr. Perfect.* It's a sign of integrity that you refuse to sell yourself short. After all, neither you nor the other man is going to be happy when you know he's wrong for you. Many people (gay or straight) lack the wisdom and foresight to do this.

You have high standards in all areas of your life—albeit rather superficial ones. Your motivation for getting ahead is largely driven by what others think of you. Though people may not realize it, you are very competitive. If you visit a home that is more interesting than yours, you'll want a home just like it—only nicer. If you do not have a "respectable" career or live in a low-status town, you probably suffer a great deal of restlessness and depression. "Happiness," for you, is getting a major promotion or buying something expensive. You drop friends like hot potatoes the first time they behave or dress in a manner you do not approve of.

When it comes to friends, lovers, or even your place of employment, your normally remote personality becomes animated with optimism. You think you've found *the* friend, lover, or job. But when you change your mind because the friend, lover, or job isn't perfect after all, your optimism becomes a kind of desperate, determined pessimism. You *must* get free of this situation at once, if you are to have a shred of integrity or pride left to your name. Unless something happened recently to humble you, you have little sympathy for the trail of hurt feelings you leave behind. It never quite dawns on you that these other people were responding to signals that you put out to them.

You aren't exactly thrilled at the prospect of remaining single. But since men express interest in you, you need not feel completely alone. Plus, whether it's through ads or social contacts, you're very much having dates and whatnot in your quest to meet Mr. Perfect. So loneliness doesn't often get the best of you. If it does, you may temporarily date a man you know isn't exactly right—or even move in with him. But in your heart, you're still a single man who's shopping around, and the relationship never feels permanent.

BEDROOM BEHAVIOR

You have an easy time differentiating between recreational sex and making love. The former is done when good old-fashioned horniness gets the better of you. (For all your idealism, this has been known to happen on occasion.) If your partner also has a casual approach to the encounter, you both can have a pretty good time. You might even decide to start a fuck-buddy type of thing—as long as it's mutually understood that nothing tumultuous is going to develop.

If the other man feels things you're not feeling, you do not indulge his fantasies. For his sake as much as yours, you'll nip things in the bud—or somewhere thereabouts. You'll be unresponsive and perhaps even call it quits in the middle of the night, rather than give a false impression. If you do politely say that you'll call, only the most inexperienced of gay men will think you mean it.

However, sometimes you think you've met capital-*H* Him. And when such is the case, you do not merely have sex—you make love. You become an utterly expressive—and monogamous—partner. Since sexual behavior might well be among your criteria for Mr. Perfect, you'll be extremely determined to please the potential candidate. In fact, you need to be careful that you don't do something unsafe—be it emotionally or physically. You have a hard time believing that Mr. Perfect could possibly bring any form of negativity into your life. And that can be dangerous on many levels.

At the same time, Mr. Potentially Perfect can become Mr. Yesterday's News if it turns out he doesn't like being a top—or shaves his pubic hairs or whatever it is that turns you off. When he turns out not to be exactly right, making love digresses into mere sex, and the inevitable good-bye that follows.

Since much of your attention is focused on the imperfections of others, you might not be cognizant of how hurtful and confusing your hot-to-cold routine can be. You all but hook up the other man to an IV of Viagra, then say to yourself something like "Gawd, he is getting *so* carried away. I just don't feel safe around his intensity. I mean, he *barely* knows me. He must be some kind of sicko to want me so bad." But *you,* my friend, were acting pretty wild and crazy but a moment ago yourself.

INTIMACY BLOCKERS

I have shocking news for you: Mr. Perfect does not exist. He's a figment of your imagination. Figments of imagination are *not* flesh-and-blood people. No, Virginia, there is no Santa Claus. Get the picture?

I hope so, because your quest for Mr. Perfect is keeping you from finding intimacy. No one is *ever* good enough for you. In having a permanent excuse to reject everyone, you mask your fear of getting close to people.

It's perfectly natural to have certain preferences. A man might feel he'd realistically be happier with a fellow Jew or Catholic, or a man with a similar income level. A smoker and a nonsmoker might have serious problems hitting it off. As more gay couples opt for parenthood, it's important to be with a man who also does or does not want children (and who shares similar ideas about how to raise them). But your standards for Mr. Perfect go way beyond practical considerations.

If your standards are based largely on appearance, you are being far more superficial than the average straight man (who might ogle a Budweiser babe, but who realistically settles for less). You also are extremely naive if you think a particular build or a certain kind of haircut will be enough to sustain a long-term relationship. When our looks inevitably change over time, the relationship will be in hot water—or should I say frigid water?—without anything to sustain it.

Seeking Mr. Perfect often means unfairly stereotyping people. I knew a man who rejected someone with whom he had a lot in common because the other man wore cologne. It seemed that Mr. Discriminating Shopper associated cologne with the "effeminate," whereby the other guy failed to live up to Shopper's macho ideal. Is it really *that* big of a deal if the other guy has an earring or not? In committed relationships, such issues are trivial.

POSITIVE ASPECTS OF
THE DISCRIMINATING SHOPPER

Idealism, discernment, self-possession, self-respect.

CHALLENGES TO BE OVERCOME

Naive expectations, overly critical nature, stereotyping, all-or-nothing thinking.

HOW TO CHANGE

First, give yourself a pat on the back for wanting the best for yourself, and for avoiding any number of Mr. Wrongs out there. But now, Discriminating Shopper, learn to be discriminating unto thyself . . .

Grow up. I wish there were a nicer way to say it, but there it is. Basing an attraction solely on someone's appearance (or other superficial details) is a fantasy that should be outgrown during adolescence. To some extent, it's not your fault. It's a prime example of how our society stunts the emotional growth of gay men. In your twenties or fifties you're going through what you should've gone through at age fourteen. But in the final analysis, it's up to you to get beyond it. You're functioning on the level of a teenaged girl going gaga over some boy because of his blond curls or liquid brown eyes. On a camp level, it can be fun to talk this way, but only if you're in on the joke.

Work on your symbolic meanings. To a large measure, we respond to the people and events in our lives on the basis of the symbolic meanings we assign them. It's not always a matter of something being intrinsically "good" or "bad" for us—it often has more to do with what we decide it means.

You need to realize that you exaggerate the importance of some relatively inconsequential detail about another man. Sometimes this means you underestimate him. Because he's bald or isn't bald, because he does or doesn't drive a motorcycle, you reject him for being less than perfect. Flipping the coin over, if for you Mr. Perfect has a shaved head and drives a Harley, you may decide that such a man has "everything you always wanted." You assign inflated symbolic meanings to technical details and think the man has qualities that he doesn't.

It's one thing to have a difference of opinion over what furniture to buy or whether he looks good with a mustache. It's another thing to decide that where he stands on such issues is symbolic of who he is as a person. Again, that's adolescent thinking. To start changing your symbolic practices, make a list of three men whom you misjudged based on some technical detail. List what the detail was and what you thought it would mean. Then list what the man actually was like. Get in the habit of catching yourself when you're about to make the same mistake again.

Mr. Imperfect is not necessarily Mr. Wrong. No, I'm not saying to get involved with any old schmuck who asks you. But just because he's not an artist or truck driver or has or hasn't heard of Judy Canova, don't automatically write him off. True, some differences in taste or opinion cause serious problems. Yes, if you truly *hate* his appearance, it's likely to keep bothering you. But leave a little room for compromise. Make a list of what you like about the man, and the ways in which he has the potential to make you happy. Then make a list of what you don't like. If the minuses truly outweigh the pluses, so be it. But if they don't, give him a chance. In fact . . .

Experience the middle. While you're giving Mr. Imperfect a chance, don't cut things too short. You often skip from the beginning of a relationship straight to the end. The slightest thing goes wrong, the smallest expectation is not met, and you decide that things will never work out. Give the relationship the opportunity to unfold. Experience the middle before jumping right to the end. Even if it doesn't last, you'll have some good memories and learn a thing or two about yourself.

Become your own Mr. Perfect. One advantage to having a same-sex orientation is that we can learn more directly about ourselves through our objects of desire. Since you're a man hung up on another man (albeit a fantasy man), it's easy to pose the question: What does he have that you feel is lacking in yourself? If you're attracted to qualities you associate with being "masculine," is there some hobby you can take up yourself that reflects this image? If you're attracted to more "feminine" types, is there an aspect of yourself that you're repressing? If your fantasy is to make it with a cop, volunteer at your local police station—and not just to get picked up, but to do something that you believe in. If you want a biker dude, be a biker dude yourself. I knew a Discriminating Shopper who had a big thing for guys who wore suspenders. Then one day he figured out he could wear suspenders himself. End of fantasy—beginning of genuine search for intimacy.

FINAL THOUGHTS

Straight couples have an obvious built-in contrast to keep things lively. In gay relationships, we must often consider more specific qualities to discover what meshes with our needs. To some extent, it's only natural that you're fussy about things that wouldn't matter to a straight couple. However, maintain standards about things that really matter: safer sex practices, parenting, politics and religion (if important to you), substance abuse, spending habits. If you want to live in rural Idaho and he wants to live in midtown Manhattan, you indeed have a problem. But since your perfect ideal doesn't exist, take a chance on *someone*. You may not find your fantasy, but you might just find happiness.

THE HYPER-ROMANTIC

. . .

PERSONALITY

Most gay men want to find that special someone, but for you the campaign is relentless. You aren't looking for Mr. Perfect—you're looking for Mr. Mister. To say you want a husband is like saying that the residents of the Castro are rumored not to have taken lifelong vows of celibacy. Marriage is what you *live* for, and when you have reason to hope, you all but sing and dance through your daily routine. You could get fired from your job, your house could burn down, but if you have a hot date coming up, all is well with the world.

When you tell your friends about your latest "one true love," they might teasingly say, "Who is it this week?" But actually, you probably keep them entertained with your relentless quest for a man. It's a real experience going husband-hunting with you at the bars, and watching you put all your calculated come-ons to work. Or hearing about your latest personal ad. Or about that guy you talked to in the checkout line at Super Kmart.

You are nothing if not resourceful. You have something approaching a genius for finding gay men. Whether in Timbuktu or at Toys "R" Us, you emerge with a phone number and a date for Saturday night. Virtually any interaction with a man has an element of flirtation—provided that you think he's cute. (Gay and single doesn't hurt, either.)

You're an eager and fun-loving optimist. You never stop trying.

Some men get cynical and withdrawn when scorned in love, but not you. When things fizzle out for the umpteenth time, you might suffer through a day or two of the doldrums. But there are plenty of other whales in the sea, and before long you're right back in the swim of things, splashing around with someone else's spout.

In today's emotionally complex, encounter-groupish world, you maintain simple and pure ideals. You want to give of yourself to another man. You want your love for each other to sustain you both through life. You want to go to sleep at night and wake up in the morning in each other's arms. There are worse things to want out of life, no?

Yet for all that is lively and engaging about your quest for a husband, you would seem to suffer from an urgent lack of love. Somewhere in your past, you came to believe that few if any people would care about you. Your being gay had at least something to do with it. You got the message that as a gay man you weren't entitled to the same degree of acceptance and belonging as other people. Now that you're accepting your gay nature, you want to make up for your past sense of rejection with a vengeance. You want to meet a man who makes all your pain of being alone go away with a single wave of his magic wand (or something like that). And since you easily feel rejected, you don't want the passion and intensity to let up for a second. After all, if you give the other guy a second to catch his breath, he's likely to think about what you're really like and dump you.

In truth, your feelings of being unwanted run extremely deep. It's highly unlikely that any one person's presence in your life will change the way you feel about yourself. In fact, as your insecurities manifest themselves, you're likely to actually turn the man off to you—and so your low self-image is reinforced. But what he rejected was the dishonest way you tried to control him, not the likable and lovable person you truly are.

BEDROOM BEHAVIOR

In carnal matters, you're like a cross between a car salesman and an auditioning chorus boy. On the one hand, you very much are trying to sell a product (yourself) and are quite aggressive in showing off your wares. On the other hand, you feel nervous and on the spot. You think the sex must be the greatest he's ever had or he'll never see you again—and you won't end up getting married. Sex with you is a bit of a roller coaster of starts and stops. There are intense physical gestures combined with awkward moments of uncertainty and boggled emotions. Premature ejaculation is less of a problem than premature declarations—of love, commitment, and other things that the other guy is not yet ready to hear.

Over time, you might force yourself to keep your trap shut— meaning your mouth. Meaning talking. (You know—about how you love him and so forth when you've only just met.) But however vocal you are in some ways, you hold back in others. Specifically, if he's doing things to you that aren't turning you on (or maybe even making you feel uncomfortable), you're reluctant to speak up about it. You consider sex to be the true testing ground from which eternal love and devotion will emerge. So you're not about to mess it all up by saying something like "Your elbow is hurting my armpit." As with certain other types of gay men, you must be careful not to compromise your standards of safer sexual behavior.

At the same time, since you want to demonstrate what a pleasure-giving partner you are, you go at his body something fierce— indeed, too much so. You give a *performance* more than you follow your instincts, so you may not be pleasuring him as much as you assume. In general, you tend to exaggerate the significance of it all. You respond to his touches or whatever with melodramatic grunts of ecstasy and kiss him back with a shade too much intensity for the moment. Unless he's feeling exceptionally horny or needy, he will probably decide that sex with you is a bit much.

INTIMACY BLOCKERS
You're so determined to connect that you don't connect—be it in bed, at a bar, or over breakfast. Though you talk about wanting intimacy, it's exactly what you don't want, because you keep the other man from knowing what you're really like. Instead, you pre-

sent an image of what you think you're *supposed* to be like in order to nab a husband. And that's called dishonesty, not intimacy.

Your impatience to have it all in the next five minutes if not sooner is another way you avoid intimacy. You wish to bypass all the communication glitches, difficult compromises, and inevitable disappointments that go into building a true, lasting relationship. Intimacy takes time. You can't just step up to the plate and slide into home, you have to hit the ball and round the bases. You might even have to swing the bat a few times first. (Are you following the metaphor?) By sidestepping complications and disappointment, you are avoiding reality—which is to say, avoiding intimacy.

By trying to manipulate the other man's responses, you make it impossible for him to get close to you. When the other man makes it known that he will not be pursuing you, you feel rejected. Yet however bad you feel, it's ironically the most honest, intimate moment you've shared with him.

POSITIVE ASPECTS OF THE HYPER-ROMANTIC
Optimism, endeavor, determination, purity of heart.

CHALLENGES TO BE OVERCOME
Impatience, fear of expressing needs, lack of discernment, inability to focus emotionally.

HOW TO CHANGE
First, have a well-deserved laugh on yourself for your many foibles and sexploits that make for such wonderful stories. But now, Hyper-Romantic, try composing a different story of your life . . .

A gay man is not a fairy. He does not have a magic wand that can abracadabra away all your unhappiness and insecurity. Other people do not make us happy; we make ourselves happy. I know that's a cliché you've heard a million times, but I'm afraid it's true. Other people can let us know they care and from time to time lighten our burdens. But ultimately, we must fight our own battles. You have unrealistic expectations if you think your newest date can magically change everything. And unrealistic expectations—since they're *un-realistic*—never come true.

Incidentally, it cuts both ways. You can't make him instantly happy, either. In fact, if you ever meet a man who thinks you can, you should run for your life. Here is a man who will make your life a living hell for his own unrealistic demands. He might even prove to be abusive. Because he sees you not as a human being, but as an object, a fix, a cure-all. Which you're not—just as he isn't for you.

Make a list of three important functions that your friends serve in your life. Then list three things about your life that your friends *cannot* fix. Add sex and a soupçon more intimacy and commitment, and that's what you can realistically expect from a life partner.

Express yourself. You simply have to let the man you're dating know the real you. Otherwise, he'll either sense that you're hiding yourself from him (and stop seeing you) or think you're someone you're not—in which case he'll eventually realize you've been deceiving him (and stop seeing you).

Yes, that's right. Try as you may, you cannot erase who you are to be exactly what you think he wants. Petty resentments will start to build as he ignores your real needs. Believe it or not, sometimes it's your own passive-aggressive nastiness that turns him off. And this nastiness is nothing more than your true self clawing to be let out of its cage.

Start speaking up *once* per encounter with every man you date. Maybe you tell him you'd rather not see a certain movie. Maybe you ask him to call back in a few minutes because you're watching something on TV. Or that you don't like it when he touches you a certain way.

One of two things will happen. He'll either feel closer to you or decide you're not for him. And if the latter happens, that's still a good thing. Better to know on the first or fourth date that things won't work than after one or four years of living together.

Enjoy singlehood. As a single man, you are sometimes lonely, unhappy, horny, and bored. Well, I've got news for you: as a married man, you'll sometimes be lonely, unhappy, horny, and bored. Having a partner doesn't permanently change everything. So while you're still single, enjoy it.

Make a list of at least three activities you enjoy that might realistically be compromised if you were in a relationship. For example, you might realistically have to see less of your friends. For all of your complaining, you might miss the anticipation of dating someone for the first time.

Until you enjoy being single, you won't enjoy being married. I know that sounds like a paradox, but it makes sense. If you're okay about being single, you won't approach your relationship with that desperate dishonesty you do so well. The relationship can be based on intimacy, instead of fake affection that masks your fear of being alone.

Cultivate mystery. Think about some of the men you've wanted. Weren't they always just a little unobtainable? Studies have shown that mystery and intrigue spice up attraction. So stop being available twenty-four hours a day, seven days a week. Be a little hard to get. *Don't* return his phone call immediately. Wait a couple of days. Make him beg for it.

I'm not saying to lie. I'm saying to be honest. In reality, you, like anyone else, *are* a little hard to get. The real you is *not* 100 percent available to someone you've just met. If you were planning on joining your friends for pizza on Friday, tell him as much. And if it turns out he can't make it Saturday? Well, he can try you again next week. Like you, the other man enjoys a bit of mystery and challenge.

You deserve the best. Don't sell yourself short. Just because a man asks you out, you don't have to accept. Just because he wants to see more of you, you don't have to agree to do so. Just because he offers to have sex, it doesn't mean you have to accept. Say no to men whom you don't want to date. Hold out for someone who shares your values and ideas about life.

What if you don't have any? Well, my Hyper-Romantic friend, you need to work on having some. Because until you know what you want out of life, no one will come along on the journey with you.

FINAL THOUGHTS

A couple can fantasize about someday buying their dream house, and that's intimate. They can engage in a sex fantasy, which can of course also be intimate. But when you secretly plot to turn a first date into a marriage proposal, it is a fantasy that has little to do with intimacy. Intimacy is about two people naturally unfolding before each other. Where there is manipulation, there is dishonesty—and no intimacy.

THE MISFIT

...

PERSONALITY

Some men come out as gay and think, "At long last! I've met my people." But for other men, it's not that simple. They come out as gay and don't feel they belong in the straight world *or* the gay world. If you're truly the Misfit type of OWTA, you are *not* one of those lucky souls who simply marches to his own drummer and is pleased with himself. Instead, you feel hurt and conflicted that a movement supposedly based on people finding their true selves so often gravitates toward conformity. Why should becoming your true self mean becoming just like everyone else?

Many of your complaints are worth listening to. After all, what's the point of having a movement aimed at people learning to express themselves if we censor each other? You don't understand why being gay has to mean that you listen to certain kinds of music, dress certain ways, and/or adopt certain worldviews. The movement could gain by listening to your diverse and dissenting point of view.

Moreover, as something of an outsider to both the gay and straight worlds, you have an interesting perspective to offer on the minority experience. It's never fun being on the outside looking in, but it's often a source of wisdom.

Hopefully, you have at least a few people in your life (gay or straight) whom you can open up to. No doubt they appreciate you for being a rare individual with a great deal to offer on many levels.

When you do have dates, the other guy notices how different you are. If he rejects you—as often happens—you think it's unfair that you're being dropped for trying to be your own person. But in truth, he may well feel intimidated by you. He may fear that he's too conventional for your unique perspective on life.

For all of your outspoken bravado and keen insights, you have a fair amount of internalized homophobia. It's hardly uncommon for a gay youth to be put down by straight kids. But in your case, you really did want to fit in with the "in" crowd. Even if the straight boys said all kinds of antigay things—and even if some of them teased you—something about their sensibility, privilege, and value system appealed to you. You *like* straight men, and as an adult you often feel that you fit in better with them—but for one minor detail, of course. Gay men often are frightened by you because you assume entitlement to a form of male arrogance that makes many gay men uncomfortable. Probably your taste in music and clothes and so on—whatever the specifics—is based largely on this straight-male orientation.

Yet there's something fey, creative, and sensitive about you, as well. So you often hide this part of yourself from straight men and express it more around gay men. You often feel like a "half-breed," torn between two worlds.

Yours is not an easy row to hoe. But with diligence, time will be on your side. As you mature through life, you can learn to integrate your many gifts. And as your peers mature as well, they may come to better appreciate what you have to offer. In particular, finding intimacy with another man may become easier—though it will still take effort.

BEDROOM BEHAVIOR

You seek deep and complex connections, so in the bedroom you want more than sex. If you've been picked up in a bar, the other man probably comments on how he's never met anyone like you before—someone he can talk to about art, spirituality, or the meaning of life. Alas, though he may appreciate these qualities, they weren't what he went out to the bar to find. All too often, you are disappointed that men seem to want one thing only.

It isn't that you have anything against sex. But your ideal sexual encounter would include a lot of other elements: interesting conversation, humor, adventure, looking for UFOs—all sorts of things. Unfortunately for you, many men (gay or straight) do not think in these terms.

You've had your moments of unbridled passion with other men. Sometimes horniness inhabits even the likes of you. But you tend to feel let down after sex. Since you go against the grain of gay stereotypes, you may not know or care for the Peggy Lee song "Is That All There Is?" But it speaks to how you all too often feel after pursuing a man sexually.

As a student of life, you're willing to try most anything once (though you probably keep your wits about you when it comes to playing safe). Still, experience has taught you that *gay* is not synonymous with *home*. Back in school, you might have been bullied by the popular kids, and now something similar happens with gay men. So you hold back on some level. You don't *quite* trust being with a man.

Also, since the gay status quo turns you off, you can lose interest in a man if he turns out to be "just like everyone else." Superficially, he seemed different from the crowd, but now under the covers he reveals a fondness for Bette Midler or campy/bitchy mannerisms. Your mind starts to wander, and that's pretty much that.

INTIMACY BLOCKERS

So you don't like show tunes. You can take or leave a lot of the usual gay icons. You like heavy metal, or the Celtic harp. Okay, next point. I mean, this hardly explains why you don't connect to gay men. Is dance club music *that* offensive to listen to? Does avoiding it justify shutting yourself off from the chance to meet new friends, maybe even meet a nice guy to date?

You're much harder on the gay world than the straight world. While some of your objections are valid, some might be coming from a place of internalized homophobia. Are there no straight morons? Do straight people always share your tastes in music?

It hurts your feelings when you perceive that gay men are shunning you. But at the same time, you shun them for not being as hip or intellectual (or whatever) as you are. For a man to like you, he has to feel that you're interested in getting to know him, too. If you're relentlessly communicating your own world, without giving him the chance to talk about his, you aren't really sharing. You're being controlling.

You take being "different" too far. You use it as an excuse. After all, it isn't *your* fault that no one understands you. But it is—if you stop trying to connect to people. You have high standards about what constitutes good communication. And when reality fails to measure up, you write off the whole experience as a failure. You become that much more convinced that you'll just never fit in. Which gives you the perfect alibi for keeping yourself ever more distant from other gay men.

POSITIVE ASPECTS OF THE MISFIT

Individuality, perceptiveness, introspection, critical capacity.

CHALLENGES TO BE OVERCOME

Egotism, internalized homophobia, fear of being misunderstood, dismissiveness.

HOW TO CHANGE

First, congratulate yourself. You've managed to create an identity for yourself without a lot of help from other people. But now, Misfit, it's time to give that identity some fine-tuning . . .

Examine yourself for homophobia. Being a man attracted to men does *not* physiologically predispose you to collect Liza Minnelli records. So, no, you don't have to start buying them. But since you value self-knowledge, you should ask yourself if your objections to Ms. Minnelli and her ilk are symptoms of internalized homophobia. Just because you don't like a certain type of music or way of dressing, why do you get so riled up when other gay men do? Why do your differences with gay men upset you so much more than the differences you experience in the straight world? If a straight man says something highly ignorant about the gay world, it might actually bother you less than when a gay man says, "Streisand is divine." Something about this double standard just isn't right.

Make a list of ten things about the gay world that annoy you. Then see if there's a straight equivalent that doesn't bother you in the same way. See what that tells you about your internalized guilt and shame over being gay. Are there singing acts that appeal to largely straight audiences that you also don't care for? If the gay world hasn't quite sorted through all the political, spiritual, and philosophical contradictions of contemporary society, do you mean to tell me that the straight world *has?*

Find common ground with gays. Maybe you don't think or dress the same as a lot of gay men. But to paraphrase Mae West, you get the general idea. There's probably any number of experiences you have in common with the "typical" gay men: childhood anxieties, your first moments of facing your sexuality, how it feels to be in love, how it feels to get dumped, what it's like to come out to people— the list goes on and on. Share with other gay men all that is similar between you. Which reminds me . . .

How different is different? If you *really* have a different belief system— if you think that the rings of Saturn are sending you special messages, for example—then I suppose you really are different. But consider the possibility that you might just be exaggerating the importance of some of your issues with the gay community. Things like clothes and music are pretty inconsequential, when you consider all you have in common with gay men. If you do think these are significant differences, then you're the one being superficial.

If you have spiritual, philosophical, or political differences, it's important to remember that you didn't get these ideas out of nowhere. Obviously, other people out there share some of these ideas with you. There are people you've listened to, books you've read, and so on that have shaped your consciousness. You're unique, but you're not *that* unique.

Accept people for who they are. Gay or straight, not everyone you meet is going to have your level of insights. But you can still appreciate people for what they have to offer. Perhaps—surprise, surprise—you can even learn from them if you give them a chance. But stop expecting people—especially gay people—to necessarily be as creative or intelligent or religious or whatever as you are. Don't expect coming out as gay to mean for other people what it meant for you. As you supposedly believe, everyone must be his or her own person.

Start a revolution. If you live in at least a fair-sized town, there's probably some sort of gay community out there. This means that it's possible to network with other gay men—through newspapers, switchboards, drop-in centers, and the Internet. And so you can make a concerted effort to meet other people like yourself. Start a group for gay Hindus or gay Bulgarian chanters—or ice hockey enthusiasts or whatever it is that you feel sets you apart from the crowd. Even if you meet just one other person who shares your interests, it will be worth the effort. One good, solid friend (or maybe even lover) is more than worth his weight in gold.

If you live in an extremely homophobic setting (and moving is not an option just now), there are still ways of networking with others. There's still the Internet. Or maybe there's a restaurant or café where you can introduce yourself to interesting people. Or you can start a sexually unspecified reading club—or some other activity that's likely to attract broad-minded people. And through these folks, you just might meet a fellow gay man—and an interesting one at that.

FINAL THOUGHTS

It's true that the gay movement hasn't always been as inclusive as it should be. But rest assured that you're not the only man who's ever felt excluded. Many gay men have had their share of differences with the community—personal differences, political differences, you name it.

Also, if you look through the popular gay media, you'll note that times are changing. More and more men from all walks of life (and from all corners of the world) are coming out as gay. There are all kinds of debates and disagreements between gay men. Difference is tolerated—sometimes even celebrated. Don't worry—there's a place for you in this exciting, ever-growing, and ever-changing brotherhood.

THE NICE BOY

. . .

PERSONALITY

Just like in the Disney or Shirley Temple movies you watched as a child, you believe the meanies and grouches of the world just need a little kindness and understanding. Yours is a life dedicated to conquering hate with love. You strive to look on the bright side. If someone says something negative, you try to point out something positive.

You steer clear of the petty squabbles that weigh down other people. You strongly believe that when people get upset, they're likely to say or do things they'll regret, so it's better to rise above these feelings. You feel it's wiser to let people lash out at you than to fight back. If they hurt your feelings or make you angry, you think there's nothing to be gained by confronting them. Instead, you try to say something nice.

Somewhere in your past, you got it in your head that you should never make trouble for anyone. People have enough to worry about without having to worry about you, so you put on a brave face to the world and insist that you're happy, even when you're not. Moreover, you have this way of insisting that *everyone's* happy. If someone expresses gloom and doom, you try to cheer him up. But if that doesn't work, you simply walk away from him or pretend not to hear what he's saying. Hopefully, there's a task handy that you can busy yourself with. If not, you can always stare down at the floor or do *something* other than confront the strong emotions threatening to bombard you.

You're something of a fair-weather friend, given your difficulty facing anything unpleasant. Moreover, you can be a fair-weather lover. If your partner confronts you with what he feels are problems in the relationship, you'll do what you can to avoid him—with a smile, if possible. Or maybe you'll put on your best kindergarten-teacher frown to scold him for his silliness. When your attitude makes him all the more angry, you'll be all the more frightened of facing him, and so it becomes a vicious cycle. You think the problem is all his fault, and you'll probably find some passive-aggressive way of letting him know this.

Your flight away from the unpleasant impacts in other ways how you express yourself. You are probably rather tepid in appearance. Even if you wear flamboyant colors, you come across as extremely nonthreatening. Men who want a relationship with a bit of sexy edginess will automatically scratch you off their lists. You have difficulty listening to music or watching a movie that isn't "nice." Since your belief system is based a lot on denial, it is extremely fragile and easily threatened, so like the famous trio of monkeys, you cover your eyes, ears, or mouth whenever necessary.

Regardless of your thoughts on religion, you consider yourself a spiritual person with a deep understanding of the emotional sacrifices involved in improving one's character. You strive to behave the way saints are depicted as behaving. Emotional entanglements that bring out the ire in others only compel you to grow ever more calm and reasonable. Like anyone else, you experience anger, fear, and sorrow. But you are an expert at keeping these emotions from interfering with the greater good you think you are achieving.

BEDROOM BEHAVIOR

You're a bit of a Jekyll/Hyde when it comes to sex. Mr. Nice takes a backseat as a more aggressive part of your personality takes over. Not that you approach sex as a free spirit. Some fundamentally reserved aspect of your nature thinks sex is naughty. So you go from being a Nice Boy to a naughty boy. Whether you're super-kinky or vanilla, you act as if what you're doing is as bacchanalian as can be.

Your voice, body language, and manner of speech suddenly change. Only moments ago you were talking about how wrong it is for someone to treat another person as a sex object. Now, however, the proverbial worm turns. You appear to favor all sorts of sexual objectifications of the human experience.

The greed and frustration you've been trying to ignore gets released during sex. Even you can exercise only so much control over your emotions—and during sex, emotions are difficult for most people to control. So other aspects of your personality are let out to play. It does not occur to you that you might be contradicting yourself. You do not dwell on ideas that might complicate the harmonious picture of life you have created.

Since you believe that everything should be nice, you do not deal well with bedroom conflicts. If your partner does not like the same things you do, you're not responsive to his needs. You might superficially agree to try things his way—unless you think it's something *too* naughty. But on the inside, you maintain that everything would be so much simpler if he could be like you in bed. Despite your alleged niceness, over time he will compromise sexually more than you do.

If you meet a man whose sexual habits are in sync with yours, you think that now everything will be nice. But when he expresses additional needs, you're perplexed as to why he's taking something so nice and spoiling it with complications.

INTIMACY BLOCKERS

You have an intense fear of anything unpleasant. Even if it costs you friends or lovers, you'll do anything to avoid an emotional scene. In other words, you use your surface niceness to avoid intimacy.

Most people learn to cope with a moderate amount of unpleasantness in their dealings with others. But you remain a child. You think that your feelings are more delicate than those of other people.

You're convinced that you can't cope with upsets the way other people can. Though you function from fear, you ironically suffer from a superiority complex. You think you're too refined to step off your pedestal and enter the muddle of humanity.

Your alleged niceness has cost you your share of loved ones. Probably you didn't make the connection. After all, you tried to quell the ugliness as best you could. What you never figured out was that the other person was angry at *you*. Yes, angry at your patronizing, condescending denial. They didn't want you to fix anything, they only wanted to let you know you were pissing them off.

It's been said that it's hard to be a good person when you're not being yourself. To an extent, it's laudable that you'd like to live in a world in which everything goes smoothly, and no one ever says or does anything too extreme. But life isn't like this, and by pretending that it *is,* you cut yourself off from the possibility of intimacy.

If you were a woman, you'd be called an iron butterfly. You are determined to be pleasant in a way that is finally unpleasant. It's not about helping people; it's about manipulating them so you don't have to say or do anything that makes you uncomfortable. And in the bargain, you'll exploit other people's problems to make yourself look superior.

POSITIVE ASPECTS OF THE NICE BOY

Positive outlook, cheerful disposition, desire for conflict resolution, ability to make lemonade out of a lemon.

CHALLENGES TO BE OVERCOME

Immaturity, denial, fear of emotions, iron-butterfly syndrome.

HOW TO CHANGE

Be proud of yourself for the times when someone reached out to you for emotional support and you were right there for them 100 percent. But now, Nice Boy, it is time to be nice to yourself in a new kind of way . . .

Redefine emotions. Though you act as if everything couldn't be more wonderful, probably something happened to make you fear emotions. There might have been one or more family members who were emotionally out of control. You determined never to be anything like that—and to avoid situations that reminded you of being back home.

However, *in moderation,* most emotions can be experienced positively. Since you enjoy seeing the good in everything, write down three emotions that you think are negative. Next to each one, write down something positive that could emerge from experiencing this emotion. Then take three types of emotional situations that you have trouble dealing with (such as confronting a lover). Next to each one, write down something positive that you could gain by facing this situation. Start to understand how good things can emerge from emotional complexities—not just for other people, but for *you.*

Join the human race. You fool neither yourself nor other people with your determination to be nice all the time. So you might as well start acknowledging all those ways of feeling that you wish would go away. In a given week, start spending just fifteen minutes experiencing a situation that makes you uncomfortable to think about. It can be from the past or the present. Write down how it makes you feel. Don't fix it or solve it—just get in touch with your imperfect human feelings.

Yes, some of these feelings are uncomfortable. Sometimes life as a human being is supposed to be uncomfortable. Some of these feelings make for complicated or unpleasant situations. Life is supposed to be complicated or unpleasant sometimes. Step down from your pedestal. Make a few mud pies with the rest of us.

Find an emotions role model. Ultimately, your problem is not that you are "too sensitive" for certain situations, but that you need more experience in how to handle them. Growing up, you learned that certain emotions simply were bad for the way they impacted all concerned. Hopefully, there is someone in your present environment who does a better job expressing emotions. Someone who expresses anger without giving the impression that he's going to kill someone. Someone who expresses sadness or disappointment without giving the impression that she's going to commit suicide. Study this person and start modeling your behavior on him or her. The next time you're in an emotionally challenging situation, think of how this person might handle it.

If you don't know anyone who handles their emotions well, you need to *seriously* reevaluate your social circle. There are people out there who do not give the impression of having a nervous breakdown every five minutes, and you deserve to know some of them. Try going into therapy or joining a support group. Or joining a reading circle or hiking club—do *something* to expand your social network so that you can meet healthy people.

Give others permission to be a mess. Life is messy. By trying to prevent people from stepping into messes, you are trying to stop them from partaking of life. Unless what they are about to do will cause obvious harm to themselves or someone else, let it be. You don't know everything. Despite what you think, quitting that job or accepting that invitation might be just what the person needs to do. So let them do it. They will, anyway. And you can spare the both of you a lot of unnecessary stress.

Give yourself permission to be a mess. I'm not saying you should make stupid mistakes on purpose. I'm saying you need to understand that life is never "perfect" (whatever that would mean), and if you're going to get close to people, you'll need to step into some of those messy moments yourself. There will be times when you say the wrong thing. Times when you take up an extra twenty minutes of his time because you really need to talk. Times when you need to tell him no, even though you know it will upset him. Times when he needs to do the same to you.

It all comes with the territory. As long as the good times

outweigh the bad, you have a pretty good deal going. A healthy relationship is not about avoiding messes, but learning how to face them as they arise.

In a given week, do one thing that risks making your life more complicated. It can be something relatively unimportant, such as sending back an unsatisfactory order at a restaurant or returning a shirt that's the wrong size. But it can also be something major, such as telling your current boyfriend that he did something that made you angry.

FINAL THOUGHTS

Conflict, anger, disappointment, and frustration are all part of life. In small doses, these states of being can spur one on to greater achievements or improve one's character. Disagreements can be intimate. Sometimes they're even necessary for intimacy to be maintained. In trying to hide from these "negative" states of being, you are hiding from life. Thus, you are hiding from honesty and intimacy.

THE PAL

■ ■ ■

PERSONALITY

You want to be everyone's best friend. You believe that people will like you if you do things for them. Whether someone needs their hedges trimmed, a ride to the airport, or sage advice, you are there to oblige. You quickly feel "close" to people—which means that even on a first meeting, you might buy them a drink, offer to help them move, or tell them how to improve their lives. Even just saying hi to someone on the street, you'll try to cheer them up with an entertaining story.

You get very involved in other people's comings and goings—particularly the former when dealing with gay men. At a bar, you play matchmaker, pointing out to your cute friends which guys are coming on to them. You probably host a number of social gatherings—some of which are fund-raisers—doing all the cooking and cleaning yourself. You tell campy jokes and refill glasses as you watch everyone else couple up.

You are regarded as a rather wry, absurd individual, and somehow the notion that you might want intimacy is a source of humor for all concerned—starting with yourself. When you have a crush on another guy, you often try to communicate it by offering to do him a favor. You'll help him paint his apartment or be "all ears" as he confides about a problem he's having. You'll call him a few days later to see how he's doing, whether or not he wanted you to do so. In other words, you'll do everything but be honest with him about your feelings.

If you do manage to find a partner, you play at being a kind of Ethel Mertz, begrudgingly tolerating your bargain-basement Fred. Single or coupled, your longings for romance and honest communication turn into a joke. In the drama of your own life, you cast yourself as a sort of good-natured second banana, rather than as the star. Even if you're married, you go through life feeling like the third wheel. When your partner talks to another gay man, you'll think you're being excluded. If a man comes over for dinner or stays as a houseguest, you extend this feeling. You might even start a fight with your partner about how he'd really rather be in bed with so-and-so—probably while you're chilling the bowls for the elaborate dessert you've made. Playing the odd man out is so familiar a role that you're afraid to let go of it.

This doesn't mean you are always a nice person to be around. Spending so much time concentrating on others (who often are "ungrateful" for all you do for them) can put you in some foul moods. But presumably, everyone should forgive you your emotional excesses, given all you do in return. In fact, if anyone criticizes you, you can always point to the thousands of things you've done to help him, whereby he has no right to be saying these things to you. People often seem to get tired of you, but there are always more people out there to help.

Underneath it all, you have little confidence in yourself. You worry that no one will ever like you for who you are. It becomes a vicious cycle: Because you feel unlovable, you do favors for people to get them to like you. But after a while, they see what you're doing, and since no one likes to feel manipulated, they decide that they *don't* like you—which confirms your original suspicion.

BEDROOM BEHAVIOR

Since you claim to get greater pleasure by pleasing your partner rather than letting him please you, you usually take a passive role in bed. If issues of top/bottom arise, you're probably the bottom—

not because you necessarily prefer it, but because you're afraid that otherwise no one will want you.

You want very much to please your partner—so much so that you pay little attention to what he actually enjoys. You want him to be so impressed with the massage (or whatever) that you're giving him, you have no idea how to act if he says he doesn't like it. You might respond defensively, rolling onto your side in a rather childish display of temper. Or maybe you try to obfuscate matters by submitting to whatever he wants. In either case, your own needs are not addressed.

That is, once you get yourself *into* the bedroom. You have difficulty concentrating on intimacy. If there's a man waiting in your bedroom, you come up with all kinds of excuses to avoid getting close to him. You'll order a pizza or call some friend of a friend to make sure he found a good dentist, rather than have to get close to someone.

When you do let down your guard, all the neediness that you've been trying to deny comes gushing out so forcefully, you're likely to say things—or do things—that you later regret. The other man (whether a stranger or a partner) feels overwhelmed by the extent of your insecurity. All he can think to do is keep a safe distance.

INTIMACY BLOCKERS

It's hard to feel close to people when deep down inside you assume that nobody will ever like you. You have a long list of reasons for why this is—which probably includes the fact that you don't think you're physically attractive. Even if other people do, you think it's because you somehow fooled them. How else to explain why someone would want you when you have that funny nose or big belly or whatever?

Out of fear, you become controlling, hoping to manipulate others' responses toward you. Thus, for all of your alleged "help," you do not connect with other people. You probably go around saying that you should be a psychiatrist because you're so involved in other people's problems. But in truth, my friend, you'd make a bad psychiatrist. You don't know how to listen to people. You only know how to impress them—or rather, how to convince yourself that you're impressing them.

If someone doesn't follow your advice or doesn't even think it's interesting, you get short-tempered with them. You get even more snippy if someone dares to suggest that you displeased them. You'll interrupt people and twist things around so that any responsibility is lifted from your shoulders. Better people should think it's a matter of their own neurosis than to think that you could've done anything wrong.

Once you've turned someone off to wanting to get intimate with you, you probably try to "make it up to them" by giving them more unasked-for favors. When this doesn't work, you throw up your hands and declare that person "hopeless." But on some other level, you know the truth is not that simple.

POSITIVE ASPECTS OF THE PAL
Reliable, helpful, energetic, the host with the most.

CHALLENGES TO BE OVERCOME
Low self-image, dishonest intentions, inability to express needs positively, poor listening skills.

HOW TO CHANGE
First, give yourself a pat on the back for being willing to get involved in other people's lives, when in today's world there is so much indifference. But now it's time to get involved in your own life . . .

Go on a "help fast." You have helped enough people. If you never try to help someone again, you will still have paid well more than your fair share of karmic debt for one lifetime. Morbid though the thought may be, if you were no longer here among us on earth, the world would keep turning. So let other people be. Screen your calls so that people who are used to asking for favors stop doing it. If someone corners you for help, take a deep, long breath and remember your new mantra: "No." Remember, all the favors you do for others come with all kinds of strings attached, so in the long run you're doing both yourself and the other people a great big favor by leaving things alone. You should especially avoid loaning people money. As you well know, *that* can get really .nessy.

This doesn't mean you should not engage in nurturing relationships. If you have a partner, by all means get involved in his life. But do things *with* him, instead of *for* him. If you're a father, of course you have to do things for your kids. But think more about all they give back to you, instead of all the "sacrifices" you're always making for them. If you must do something to help people, do it in ways in which no one will applaud you. For example, make an anonymous donation to a charity. If you're ever going to be any real good to yourself or other people, you have to stop controlling people by helping them.

No comment. When people ask you for advice, don't give any. Say nothing at all. Or if you do say something, keep it limited to "Uh-huh," "That's interesting," "Thanks for sharing," or "Gee, I never thought of that before." If push comes to shove, tell them you have to run along and do something else—which is perfectly true. You have to stop trying to earn people's affection. You don't have to be mean—just don't get into it with them. If people really like you, they won't expect you to solve all their problems. You might lose a lot of false friends once you stop trying to help them. But you'll learn who your real friends are. 'Tis better to have one genuine friend than a dozen phony ones.

In fact, you can try a little experiment: call *nobody* for one whole month. At the end of the month, see who's picked up the phone to call you. Out of those people, see who called to ask you a favor, versus simply wondering how you were doing. The lattermost group of people are your real friends. If no one fits in that category, then I'm afraid you have no real friends. That hurts, of course, but it's better to know the truth. You can start from there to build honest friendships with other people, and not make the same mistakes all over again.

A star is born. Become the star in the movie of your life. Emote in close-up, rather than off-camera, so to speak. Use the time you normally spend focusing on other people to focus on yourself. Cliché though it may be, it's true that until you love yourself, you can't love anyone else. Get in touch with what keeps you from feeling good about yourself. Read books, see a therapist—do whatever it takes to stop being so maniacally obsessed with everyone else. Physician, heal thyself.

As you learn to love yourself, make your needs known to others. By "needs" I don't mean demands. I'm not saying you should go up to people and say, "Love me, damnit." *That's* controlling. But if you're getting to know someone (particularly intimately), present yourself as a flesh-and-blood human being with likes and dislikes. Let people get to know *you,* as opposed to who you think you're supposed to be. Share some of your own bedroom fantasies, rather than just trying to fulfill his. What qualities are important for you in a partner? What are some things you'd find unacceptable? If you have no idea, try making a list of five points for each category.

Love means having to say you're sorry. Everyone's a jerk sometimes. Everyone messes up with other people. What separate the grownups from the kids is that grown-ups take responsibility for their actions. If you've flown off the handle at someone or placed unrealistic demands on them, apologize. But say "I'm sorry" instead of "Please forgive me." Asking to be forgiven is controlling; simply saying you're sorry isn't. Then, if the other person doesn't accept your apology, he's the one who's being the jerk. It's especially important to be able to apologize when someone comes to you with a complaint about your actions. Rather than flying off the handle, consider the possibility that maybe, just maybe, you aren't perfect, and you did say or do something that truly wasn't appreciated. Nobody likes someone who can't admit to making a mistake.

Listen to the silence. Once a week for a ninety-day period, spend an entire day alone. That's right—no phone calls, no fund-raisers, no gossip, no nuthin'. Just you. Go hiking in the park or read a book.

Take up yoga or meditation or even knitting. But learn to appreciate your own company. When you're no longer scared of being alone, when the thought of a day spent by yourself doesn't seem unbearable but maybe even enjoyable, you'll stop living to impress other people and start finding intimacy for the first time.

FINAL THOUGHTS

Though you act like an expert on everyone else's problems, inside you is a hurt and frightened man who both wants and fears love. What makes someone worthy of love? First and foremost, it is the act of asking for it. Not demanding it, and not confusing false respect for love. But by admitting to your human frailties and needs, you can start to build something genuine for the first time. Letting people know the real you is going to be much more rewarding than letting them know who you think you should be.

THE PARTY BOY

. . .

It's been said that life is a cabaret, and no one believes this more than you. Most gay men like to cut loose now and then, but if you more or less *live* to party, then you're a true Party Boy type. You associate having a social life with having a party life. Party Boys such as you are, of course, likely to be found in big cities, where you can keep up with all the circuit events. But even if you're (supposedly) the only gay man in Turkey Creek, Nebraska, your presence guarantees that a social gathering will be the biggest thing since Farmer Bob celebrated Bessie the Hog's triplets.

At gay bars, some men lurk in the shadows, but not you. You're talking and laughing up a storm, with your inevitable drink in hand. Probably you know a lot of people to hang with, but if you don't, you'll meet some. If nothing else, there's always the bartender, whom you're likely to address by name.

You like to keep people entertained, though your wit might not be as sharp as you think; you probably laugh the loudest at your jokes. In any event, you enjoy feeling sophisticated by drinking and saying brittle things. You want people to think you are completely comfortable with yourself. If the gay press is covering an event, you're eager to pose with your arm around another guy to show how sociable you are. If you're young, you probably still have the energy to work out, and you like to take your shirt off on the dance floor, so that everyone can ogle your buff body. (Or if you like the ol' beer and potato chips a bit too much, you might feel it's your duty to get dressed up like Divine.) In any case, you're vulnerable to alcohol and substance abuse and probably exercise less over time.

When you get drunk or high, you're likely to say and do things that are thoughtless or even intentionally cruel. But you see it as all part of the game. If a guy can't stand the heat, he should stay out of the kitchen. You hardly feel it's your fault if someone got his feelings hurt when you snubbed or insulted him.

If you have a partner who doesn't like to party, the difference in your lifestyles will erode your relationship over time. If your partner *does* like to party, you both want to be the center of attention, so conflicts will emerge. Either or both of you might even pick a fight, so that each of you can create his own circle of devotees for the evening.

Over time, life in the fast lane will take its toll on your energy level, and your professional life may suffer. You then might switch to a low-pressure (and lower-paying job) because you need to slow down for "health reasons." But you keep on partying.

Regardless of whether you do drag, there's something of the drag-queen, Auntie Mame spirit about you. Life requires huge body gestures. But sometimes, you're more like Auntie Mame on a bad day. You're so determined to be "outrageous" that you sacrifice connecting with people. As others tire of your shenanigans (or grow afraid of being hurt), they move on, and you find new people to party with. Yet what you never quite succeed in doing is convincing people—starting with yourself—that you aren't in pain. There's obviously something in your past—be it your childhood, a past lover, or both—that you keep trying to party out of your life. But you never quite succeed. In fact, as you weaken yourself physically and mentally, your wounds hurt all the more.

BEDROOM BEHAVIOR

For all of your carousing, you may not be as sexually driven as people assume. Since you first and foremost want to be perceived as socially confident, you might be content to go home alone, once you've proven your main point. If you do score, at least part of your pleasure is demonstrating to onlookers that you are indeed skillful at interacting with others.

Partying tends to diminish one's inhibitions, so you're pretty much an anything-goes kind of guy in the bedroom. This can, of course, be a lot of fun, but you have to be extra-careful to avoid anything unsafe. When you engage in a six-way harness (or whatnot), you're at least as concerned with showing off what a good sport you are as with actually enjoying what's going on.

Sometimes, you frankly will be too inebriated to do much of anything besides get yourself to the nearest bed to pass out. But assuming you're sober enough to engage in sex, you'll regard it as another chance to show off. A night with you is to be remembered as decadent beyond all decadence. Even if you're too tired to do much of anything besides lie there and jerk off, you will do it with a spirit of wickedness that is meant to be seen as an extension of your party spirit. Even behind closed doors, you seem to be saying, *the party isn't over.* The dance-club tracks you've been hearing all night is your idea of music that puts you in a "romantic" mood. In fact, you might be so conditioned to associate this music with sex, you have difficulty performing without it.

If you're genuinely attracted to another man, he probably won't know what to do with your sudden modesty or vulnerability and may interpret it as lack of interest on your part. Also, if your personality has switched from the false bravado to the rather shy and uncertain man you really are, your sex partner might be turned off by your apparent dishonesty.

INTIMACY BLOCKERS

Probably at some point in your life you've joked about how unshy you are—how you haven't got a shy bone in your body, or some such. It's as if to be considered shy is a fate worse than death. But the truth of the matter is that you *are* shy, painfully so. Back where you came from, you probably felt like a social outcast or wallflower and are hell-bent never to be that person again. Much of the time, you're unhappy, which is why you relentlessly drive home how happy, gregarious, and carefree you are. Me thinks thou dost protest too much.

Because you're presenting a front to the world, you aren't really connecting with people. People tire of you (even when you supply them with booze or drugs) because over time they want more of a connection than what you give them.

Partying was a big part of your coming out. It's as if you wouldn't know how to be a gay man without music in the background, a drink in your hand, and a snappy one-liner emitting from your lips. In a way, you *haven't* ever come out, because you haven't ever revealed much about yourself in a sober, everyday context. Though you might give thousands of dollars a year to gay causes, you still have a great deal of internalized homophobia to work through. You try to party away the aspect of yourself that's uncomfortable with being gay, and it never works.

You confuse standing out in a crowd with being liked. Yet when the craziness dies down for a minute or two, you are reminded of how lonely you are. You'd like something more than what you have, but you have no idea how to go about it, because you take for granted that how you live is what it means to be gay.

POSITIVE ASPECTS OF THE PARTY BOY
Spirited, fun-loving, community-builder, active supporter of gay businesses and events.

CHALLENGES TO BE OVERCOME
Overreliance on stimulation, overconcern with others' opinions, lack of confidence, shame-based gay identity.

HOW TO CHANGE
First, reflect on all the good times you've had. You certainly know a lot about not letting life's woes cramp your style. You've been able to boogie away much of your misery. But now learn to boogie to a different beat . . .

Sober up. Even if you aren't an alcoholic or drug addict, you could benefit by learning to enjoy yourself without partaking of an opiate. You tend to believe that sober equals boring, while drinking equals fun, and life should not be so black-and-white as that. Normal people—and I hope you're sitting down—actually enjoy themselves for days at a time without some form of artificial stimulus. Flipping the coin over, normal people find endlessly drinking (or whatever) to be boring. It's easy to be outrageous or daringly out of the closet when you're drunk; now let's see if you can do it without drinking.

Merely being sober hardly guarantees good communication with others. But if you spend quite a lot of time getting loaded, your perspective on who you are and what other people are for has been warped. You need to get grounded for at least a little while, if you're ever going to get genuinely close to people. If going without a drink or drug is harder than you thought it would be, you should see a doctor. But even if you can handle moderate social drinking, see what the world is like *without* a drink. You might just learn something.

Engage in a secret pastime. No, I don't mean the obvious. But for thirty days, take up some sort of hobby. It could be reading a particular book(s), collecting something, or learning a craft. Whatever it is, spend your evenings for one month by yourself, doing this hobby—*and do not tell anyone else about it.* (If you live with someone, obviously your partner should know about it, but do not discuss it in detail.) You need to develop a sense of having things that are yours and only yours, and that everything you do doesn't have to win approval from other people. After a month, it's okay to start telling people about it here and there. But see how it feels to keep your own self company.

Explore your roots. To come back down to earth, you need a sense of continuity in your life. You need to stop feeling like Dorothy, swept away in a tornado to some nonsensical, anything-goes place. Even Dorothy, after all, longed to go back home. For a long time, you've desperately been trying to stop being the person you used to be. You know whom I mean—that quiet guy who felt out of place around other people, and who worried that nobody liked him. The thing is, he's still a part of who you are, because you still feel the same way much of the time, as much as you don't like to admit it. So let that unpopular guy back into your consciousness.

Make a list of five qualities you had before becoming a Party Boy that you would admire in another person. Then ask yourself if these qualities are still a part of who you are today. If they are lying dormant, start embracing them and letting them back in. Also, list any pastimes you used to enjoy that got left behind. Start doing some of these things again, to get reacquainted with your whole self.

If something extremely painful or traumatic happened to you, do whatever you need to do to come to terms with it. See a therapist. Confront this individual(s), if possible. But stop letting it control your life, while all the while bemoaning that no one likes you. It's next to impossible to get close to someone who isn't being himself.

Be gay and proud. As you calm down, find less flamboyant ways of bonding with the gay community. It's true that gay parties are often fund-raisers for worthwhile causes, and attending these events is exactly what certain types of gay men need to do more of. But in your case, other ways of contributing are what's called for. Join a reading club or outdoor club—or become politically active. Find ways of expressing your gay identity that do not revolve solely around partying. Learn to be gay within a context that embraces the full spectrum of who you are, and all you can be.

Discover the Zen of boredom. At Zen retreat centers, each task that is performed—the raking of leaves, the baking of bread—is considered an extension of one's meditation. Everything is connected to the whole. No one feels completely centered all the time, but you'd benefit by learning to feel that way at least *some* of the time. If you do not take up a spiritual practice, you can still learn about this feeling by approaching daily tasks with a different attitude. Rather than ignoring daily responsibilities—or getting them over with as quickly as possible—try focusing in on something basic, such as making your breakfast or folding the laundry. Be present while you do it. Concentrate on what you're doing, not where you're going to be tonight. Consider the profundity of being alive, even if you're not doing something supercharged. If you feel vital and alive in simple ways, you can build intimate relationships, because you'll no longer be using other people for thrills and applause.

FINAL THOUGHTS

The ability to make merry is an important part of life. But it's far from the only thing that matters. It's the icing on the cake, and too much icing does not make for a balanced diet. Too much partying and not enough sleep makes for a distorted worldview. It's next to impossible to feel close to someone when you aren't fully present. To be a well-rounded person, you have to embrace the more mundane parts of yourself as well, then let others take a look. You may find that you're not as "boring" as you fear, and that people like this "less interesting" man better. More important, so will you.

THE PERENNIAL CLOSET CASE

■ ■ ■

PERSONALITY

You're the man who never gets around to coming out. Whatever your occupation, hobby, or physical appearance, your most salient characteristic is that you don't want the world to know you're gay. Your fear of coming out dominates your relationships with men—it's what they remember when they think of you.

Perhaps you're the married man who lives a double life. You figure that it will hurt your wife and/or kids to come out. Or maybe you're one of those "bachelors" who rationalizes that your personal life is nobody else's business. You might even be one of those men who's had a "roommate" for many years, and you say that people probably already know, so it isn't necessary to spell it out.

This lattermost scenario is especially tricky business. One would guess that living with a man would compel you to come out, but ironically, it can keep you in the closet. Since you are, after all, a gay man, you can put quite a lot of energy into making your relationship work. Your partner doesn't want to force you to do anything you're not ready to do (plus he may be a Perennial Closet Case himself), and the next thing you know, ten or twenty years goes by and your family still thinks you have a "roommate." Your relationship might be kinda sorta happy—except for the millions of ways in which guilt, shame, and fear continue to dominate it, and the millions of lost moments when you refused to risk dancing together, touching each other, or even sitting next to each other.

Obviously, there's a lot of homophobia out there, so it's understandable why you'd find it hard to come out. It's also worth noting that to some extent most all of us are still in the closet. As the old saying goes, coming out is a lifelong process. Even if we hold hands in public on Castro Street or in the Village, five minutes later we're in some other part of town and might decide to keep our hands in our pockets. After all, who knows what sort of homophobe might be lurking in the bushes, ready to attack?

Also, some men really do risk professional ruin or visitation rights by coming out. While it's easy to theorize that they should come out anyway (and indeed they probably should), the risks involved might surpass those that many an out gay man has taken.

Having said all this, the truth is that some gay men use this so-called commonsense reasoning as an *excuse* for not coming out. If you're a Perennial Closet Case, there are many situations in which you *could* safely come out, but you don't. Not because "it's nobody's business." Not because Grandpa has a weak heart or because anyone's going to beat you up. You stay in the closet simply because you're ashamed and embarrassed that you're gay.

Thus, you are not letting people know the real you. You worry that you'll lose the people you care about if they know you are gay. What you fail to realize is that you've already lost them. You're already not giving them who you are.

You can rationalize all you want: "My sexuality is only a small part of who I am," "I live in a small town," "I have kids to think about," and so on. But in today's world, the resources are out there to help *everyone* in your life—including your children—make a successful adjustment. A discussion of these resources is better suited to a different book. What I'm here to say is much simpler: until you come out, you'll never know intimacy. If it's more important not to upset anyone than to be a fully integrated adult, the choice is yours. But as long as you're being dishonest with everyone you come in contact with, intimacy shall not be yours.

That's right—even if you live with a man for a lifetime, your relationship will be tangled up with secrecy and shame. As you grow accustomed to hiding the truth, it becomes second nature. No one in your life—not your boss, your kids, your wife, parents, or whoever—is given the chance to see what's really going on with you. Even the man you date or live with will get to know only a fraction of all you are, because your true nature is such a secret.

BEDROOM BEHAVIOR

Whatever form your closeness takes, you take your shame with you to the bedroom. Even if you secretly live with a man, there are things about your sexuality that aren't being realized. Perhaps there's a fetish that you long to explore. Maybe you did it once or twice, but felt embarrassed afterward. Even if you get into kinky stuff, there's something you're leaving out—something you want to do, but aren't giving yourself permission to do.

Beyond the issue of specific sexual acts, a great deal of pretending goes on when you get into bed with a man. You pretend to be relaxed. You pretend you don't feel guilty about what you're doing. You might even pretend that this is some sort of honest expression of love. Yet your "love" for this man is not as strong as your fear of upsetting lesser people in your life. So how much "love" is that?

Thus, your bedroom behavior (whether wild or conservative) leaves something to be desired. Emotionally, it isn't as mutually satisfying as it should be—which can of course serve to further justify your being in the closet. After all, since it wasn't *that* good, maybe you're not really gay. As long as your sexuality isn't quite "real" to you, neither will your sexual encounters be real. You give your sexuality a future orientation. For example: "Tomorrow I'll meet my dream man, and that will give me the confidence to come out." That way, what you're doing today will not be experienced as real.

INTIMACY BLOCKERS

Where to begin? Well, for one thing, all of your rationalizations about why you shouldn't come out are just that. You aren't even telling the truth to yourself. You try to convince yourself that everything's okay the way it is—after all, what people don't know won't hurt them, and so on. Some Closet Cases even insist that their families or friends wouldn't mind, it's just that it's none of their business. But the truth is that you're extremely frightened about losing people. You have little confidence that others will accept you for who you are. Some of the people you're trying to please might well be extremely homophobic—perhaps they said mean things to you as a child, and you're still terrified over how they might respond.

Also, you're carrying a lot of guilt and shame about something that you yourself *are*. How can you expect to have honest relationships with other people—let alone that one special guy—when you aren't even accepting this basic truth about yourself?

If there's a man in your life in some shape or form, in effect you're saying that you're ashamed of him, of what you share together, and what your affection for each other means to you. Does that sound like an intimacy-builder to you?

The reality of your life can be quite pathetic. I once heard of a couple who lived together for ten years, with neither man ever coming out to his family. Even when the one man died, the other remained silent and meekly sat in the back of the room during the memorial service. After all, he wasn't a member of the family. When someone is so willing to be dishonest, when *nothing* seems to move him to tell the truth, why should anyone trust anything he says?

POSITIVE ASPECTS OF THE PERENNIAL CLOSET CASE

I am reluctant to say there are any. To a small extent, it could be said that you are sensitive to the needs of others, are good at concealing the truth (which in some instances might come in handy), have known the humility of feeling like an outsider (which in other contexts could be put to good use), and since you do not live to fulfill your deepest desires, no one can accuse you of excessive selfishness. (Or could they?)

CHALLENGES TO BE OVERCOME

Lack of self-acceptance of gay sexuality, inability to put own happiness above opinions of others, denial of self-loathing, overly accustomed to lying.

HOW TO CHANGE

First, be kind to yourself and take a moment to smile over some of the crazy situations you've found yourself in as a Closet Case. But you've put yourself through enough unhappiness around your sexuality, and now it's time to truly smile at yourself in a whole new way . . .

Get cultured. If you live in a small town or are shy about coming out, a good first step toward coming out is to expose yourself to gay cultural artifacts. There are hundreds of gay novels, for example, and reading about gay characters by an out author can help you feel more connected to the gay experience. The same can be said for gay magazines, and gay-oriented films. (For that matter, there are now a number of gay characters on TV shows.) Come up with at least three role models for yourself—whether they are real-life gay celebrities or fictional characters. Make a list of the qualities you admire about these men, and think about ways you can be more like them—how you can incorporate being out into your daily life.

Make human contacts. Having a support network of gay friends will help you to feel good about yourself. Even if you live hours from the nearest big city or gay bar, you can get in your car (or a bus or whatever) and go there once a week—or even just once a month. If you're not a "bar person," then there are other kinds of activities you can pursue. But friends make a big difference. The gay men you bond with have been through many of the same problems. They can offer emotional support, friendly suggestions, and be role models.

Reevaluate your situation. Are you *sure* you can't come out? Are you *sure* your father will get a heart attack if you tell him, that your boss will fire you, that your kids will never speak to you again? Or is it really just your own fear that's stopping you? In today's world, all kinds of people have come out to all kinds of people, and the results have not always been what they've predicted. Someone who expects his mother to be more supportive than his father finds the reverse to be true; someone's kid tells him that he or she already knew.

You need to stop confusing your own fears and denial with knowing how other people will react. You aren't psychic, after all. Make a list of ten things about being gay that make you afraid. I don't mean specific people, but things like "Everyone will look at me funny" or "I'm ashamed of how some gay men act." These are the real issues you need to work on. Share these fears with at least one person whom you trust. Take care of your own homophobia, and stop worrying about your boss's or mother's.

Put it in writing. If it's hard for you to tell people face-to-face that you're gay, write to them. A letter (or E-mail) gives the other person a chance to think about how to respond. Hasty remarks can be avoided. Also, it means that once you send the message off, there it will be. Don't agonize about making every word perfect. As you yourself sometimes speculate, many people might already have an idea. But once you do it, it's done.

If you have a partner, ask him to help. If he's still in the closet, too, you can help each other. Maybe you're afraid to write to your family about being gay, but your partner can do it for you—and vice versa.

Don't worry, be gay. The best way to stop agonizing over whether people think you're gay is to come out to them. If everyone knows, it never has to come up. If you say that you don't want your sex-uality to be a big deal, then come out. Once that's over and done with, people will get to know you as a full and whole person. If you're dating someone, go ahead and mention him to others. You don't have to give all the gory details. But stop living in secrecy. Honesty really is the best policy. It's simpler to be honest. Over time, you (and everyone else) will dwell less on your sexuality if you're honest about it in the first place.

FINAL THOUGHTS

For all the problems gay people have in our society, there is reason for optimism. Every day, there's a little more acceptance of gays than the day before. There are more gay characters on TV from one season to the next, and opinion polls show increasingly higher percentages of the population favoring same-sex marriage. Over 1 million children are being raised by same-sex couples. There is an increasing shared sense that people are born gay, and that one's sexual orientation cannot be changed. It becomes increasingly unacceptable to make antigay remarks in public or to discriminate against someone for being gay. In many ways, you are lucky to be alive now as a gay person, as opposed to fifty, twenty, or even ten years ago. Even in the smallest towns in the Midwest or South, rainbow flags are proudly flapping in the breeze. Other people have gotten past their fears, and so can you.

THE SEXPOT

. . .

PERSONALITY

What would the gay world be without you? How would we have the courage to come out without you there to remind us of the tantalizing reward that awaits us? If we never know you up close and personal, we admire you from afar and learn from your example how to express gay sexuality with boldness and beauty.

However, I am reasonably certain you get compliments galore, so let's get past all of that, okay? Your problem is that you sexualize all your encounters with men. You believe that the only way to relate to men is through sex. To call you a sex addict misses the point, because you don't crave sex so much as attention. You care less about getting off yourself than about making other men go gaga over you.

Sex goddesses such as Marilyn Monroe or Sharon Stone are your inspiration. You want to turn *all* men on. When men in your life—straight or gay—express interest in some other person, on some level you can't believe it. How could he find this other person preferable to you? When reality hits home—when he moves in with this person or kisses him/her in your presence—your feelings are deeply hurt. Apparently, you aren't universally desired, after all. That is to say, you have no worth as a human being. Of course, this isn't true—but sadly, you believe it is, even if intellectually you know better.

A "good" night at the bars is when more than one man notices you. If only one man does, it's better than nothing, but a truly "bad" experience is when no one comes on to you. Since you tend not to make the first move, that means you'll go home alone. When that happens, you're extremely depressed. You decide that the men were a bunch of losers intimidated by your good looks. It's *so* unfair when men can't see past your physical assets. But wait a minute— only a second ago, that was exactly what you wanted them to notice, wasn't it?

When you come on to other men, you are extremely skillful at turning on the charm. You enjoy it when a man seems like so much putty in your hands. When several men come on to you in a single night, you get full of yourself, and you may even get a charge out of being purposefully cruel to someone. You'll lead a man along for an hour or so, only to tell him you're not interested.

To turn this many heads, nature must have been kind to you. Even if you're not likely to appear on the cover of *Men* magazine, you act as if you are, and there's something magnetic about you. Whatever you look like, you strive to look better. You might dye your hair or subtly wear makeup. Yet no matter how many times men express admiration for your appearance, you don't quite believe them. Compliments fall into a bottomless pit of insecurity, but the slightest snub confirms your worst fear that you're unattractive.

If you have a partner, you are probably much more vivacious than he is. You want to make sure that everyone notices *you* when the two of you walk down the street. He'll be mystified that he's been able to snag someone of your caliber and will be like a loyal subject worshiping at your feet. Over time, the novelty of being with you wears off, and it wounds you deeply when he seems uninterested or even turned off by you. Emotionally, you can give him—or any other man—your attention only for short periods, and he wants much more than that. Essentially, he loses interest as you do, but when you do it, you feel empowered, while when he does it, you feel diminished.

BEDROOM BEHAVIOR

You see yourself as a kind of favored harem dancer, expert at pleasing a man as he's never been pleased before. It's not enough for the man to moan with passion (although that's a step in the right direction). You like being told things like "This is beyond anything I've ever experienced" or "You're like my dream fantasy come true." Since on occasion men have said things like this to you, it disappoints you when they don't say it every time.

There are always jokes between gay men about acting like a whore, but in a real sense you conduct yourself like a high-priced call boy. You're often choosy about your "clientele," but first and foremost you are there to keep the customer satisfied. Name the fantasy, and you know how it's done. If not, hum a few bars and you'll fake it. If you don't literally get paid for what you do, you certainly don't mind if the man wants to take you to an expensive restaurant. Not that you necessarily accept. The mere act of conquest is its own reward, and you might be scornful toward men who try to "buy" you—even as you're a little insulted when they don't.

If the man seems less then hypnotized by your spell, you react with boredom, indifference, even scorn. This doesn't mean you tell him to leave—probably even when the sex is going badly, you feel you ought to finish what you've started. Sex, after all, is what you've been put on this earth to do. So during lackluster sex, your mind goes elsewhere, and in a passive-aggressive way you hope he understands how cold he's making you feel.

Yet whether you're hot or cold in bed, it's all part of your performance—the latest adventure in the ongoing saga of your sexploits. You play your role so well that men either feel they can never keep up with you or else want you so desperately that it turns you off. What they want isn't connected to who you really are, so their attention leaves you with a hollow feeling.

INTIMACY BLOCKERS

You're better at the fifty-yard dash than the long-distance run, so to speak. Once it's been established that, yes, you are easy on the eyes, and, yes, this man is interested, there isn't much of anyplace for things to go. Since his attraction for you is based on the superficial, he may not like or understand you as a person—or even be interested in exploring you that way. Thus, for all the hearts you've broken, yours has been known to crack in several different places, too. When a man dumps you because you're not the one-dimensional sex object he thought you were, it confirms what you suspected all along: that sex is your only possible outlet for connecting to guys.

Somewhere in your past, you learned to fear men. Perhaps your father or older brother made fun of you for not being butch enough. You probably felt nerdy in high school. That suddenly people—in particular, *men*—find you so desirable is almost surreal. You can't quite believe a man really wants you. You want to get back at your childhood tormentors—perhaps also some early gay crush that broke your heart. (Of course, it is also possible that you were sexually abused as a child.)

Whatever the specifics, you are engaged in an ongoing battle in which you indeed sleep with the enemy. You want to feel loved by another man, but your performance as a Sexpot is both what attracts men to you and keeps them at arm's length. Even as one part of you is calling out for warmth and affection, some other part of you is using men to settle an age-old grudge. You're at cross-purposes with yourself and end up feeling more lonely than men with lower expectations.

POSITIVE ASPECTS OF THE SEXPOT
Sensual, accommodating, in touch with gay male sexual power, keeps the home fires burning.

CHALLENGES TO BE OVERCOME
Low self-image, dishonest intentions, inability to express needs positively, poor listening skills.

HOW TO CHANGE

First, acknowledge that in a world of oppression and shame, you have managed to pursue your attraction for other men freely. If you have not always been happy, you've certainly had your share of memorable experiences. But now it's time to create new types of memories . . .

Switch roles. The men who have pined for you from afar might be surprised to learn that you've done your fair share of pining. For you, there also are men who seem "too good" for you, and forever out of reach. If you go out to a bar, introduce yourself and strike up a conversation with at least one of these men. Whether he accepts or rejects you (and of course either can happen), explore how it feels to be in the position you normally reserve for the other man. If he says, "Thanks but no thanks," observe that the universe does not come to an end. The minor wound to your pride will have this funny way of healing. In other words, it really is possible to be a bit vulnerable, exposed, and unsuccessful, and keep on living. Everything does not hinge upon being complimented and admired. You do not have to limit who you are as a gay man.

Relax the dress code. Try being a bit more casual about readying yourself for a night on the town. Make a list of all the things you do to make yourself gorgeous, and cut it in half; then cut it in half again. I'm not saying you should look like a total slob, but try looking more like everyone else. Go out without wearing your "special shirt." Relax—don't have a nervous breakdown if two hairs are sticking out funny. If you have a zit on your nose, don't cover it up. No one notices these things; you already look good. See what it feels like to blend in with the crowd.

Read any good books lately? Lord knows there's nothing wrong with sex. But in your case, sex becomes a way of *not* letting men get close to the real you. So you need to develop other interests that you can share with men. Maybe you already have such a hobby, but you're shy about sharing it. In any case, start sharing it. Make sure it's something unrelated to sex. (Don't let it be massage therapy, for example.) But if you like to read, hike, or go to museums, share it with another gay man. Avoid letting sex creep into the moment; save the sex for later. In fact, don't even talk about sex, romance, or any of the rest of it. Talk about the book you're reading. Ask him where he likes to go hiking or who his favorite painter is. See how it feels to relate to man without being sexual. This leads to the next point . . .

Make nonsexual male friends. To do this, you may need to select a man you'd never want to be sexual with—that is, someone you'd *never* think was cute—but who still has good qualities to offer. Do *not* turn on your sexual energy. Dress plainly. Wear glasses. Don't flirt. Share with him about your love life, and let him share about his. Play matchmaker for him. Talk on the phone. See what it's like to bond with a man without having sex with him. If he starts having sexual feelings toward you, make friends with someone else.

Trade in your role models. Stop identifying with tragic Sexpots of the past. Stop seeing Marilyn when you look in the mirror—or James Dean or whomever. Whether it be through your daily encounters, biographies, or even through fictional characters, find people who aren't sex gods or goddesses whom you can admire and want to emulate. Hypothetically, if you couldn't connect with men through sex, how might you do it? Make a list of three such qualities you'd like to have for getting close to people, then find three different role models who fit the bill. Study these people; if you know them, ask them questions. Learn to model your behavior on people who understand they are more than their sexual energy.

FINAL THOUGHTS

When sex becomes the only way you can relate to other men, you're not going to find the intimacy you're seeking. Unless you are extremely fortunate (or there are a lot of younger guys seeking daddy figures), eventually you'll start to lose your magic touch, and then where will you be? Getting drunk as you tell some stranger about your wild youth? Please—you're worth much more than that. Learn to explore other aspects of yourself—and most of all, learn to share these parts of yourself with another man. When you can combine your great technique with emotional presence, you'll start enjoying sex—and other aspects of relating to a man—in ways you've never dreamed.

THE SHY SNOB

. . .

PERSONALITY

You're shy, in that you have little confidence in your ability to connect with others. From childhood on, you've spent a great deal of time alone. For one reason or another, you've suffered an exceptional amount of pain trying to get close to people, and somewhere along the way you said to yourself, "Okay, so who needs other people anyway?" You're so used to being by yourself that it can be a major challenge to call someone up or say hello to an acquaintance on the street. You might well be very out as a gay man, but this doesn't mean you get close to people, not even—or perhaps especially not—other gay men.

Occasionally, you have a spurt of sociability. Perhaps you move or start a new job and make a gallant effort to connect more with other people. But before long, either you don't like them or they don't like you—or so it seems—and you feel that you'd rather just be alone, after all.

People are likely to interpret your shyness as snobbery—and with good reason. Your inherent good taste makes you acutely attuned to the subtle nuances of human interaction. Things that other people never even notice deeply violate your aesthetic sense. And since you spend so much time on the outside looking in, you've had plenty of opportunity to observe, classify, and pass judgment on other people. You maintain your high standards at the cost of getting close to other people. Feeling disconnected is not a happy feeling, but you can't bring yourself to get past the glaring defects in the people you meet. Even if you wanted to take an emotional risk, the snob part of your personality makes it unlikely that you will.

A Shy Snob of my acquaintance once complained to me about a traumatic first date. The other man had my friend over for dinner and had the audacity to serve a cold pasta salad during the middle of winter. From that moment on, my friend could have nothing to do with this other man. How could my friend possibly get serious over someone so glaringly ignorant, so insensitive to the ebb and flow of life, so totally opposite of what one would want in a partner?

If a guy in a bar thinks you're cute, he'd better approach you first, because there's no way you'll be making the first move. That would be taking a risk: What if he rejects you? What if he knows a lot of other guys in the bar and tells them you're a loser? When you leave to go home alone, you do it with your head held high.

If another guy comes on to you, you'll reject him right away if he seems unsure of himself. Human weakness brings out an almost violent hatred in you. You feel you're being fair in rejecting him, because you would not tolerate such behavior in yourself. If he survives the first crucial moments, you may let him tag along to impress the other men in the bar. Unlike *those* losers, you got picked up. If you've been especially lonely, you may even give the poor guy the temporary impression that you like him more than you do. When he figures out you aren't interested, his feelings will be deeply hurt.

If you're in a relationship, you have a laundry list of things you can't stand about your boyfriend. But you share your feelings sporadically at best, because you have a terrible fear of being misunderstood. He sees that you're a million miles away, and it makes him unhappy that he can't reach you. If you go out together, you cling to him because you dread having to meet new people—that is to say, more people who'll end up rejecting you. Either that or you ignore him, having decided he's "unworthy" of you. Perhaps you even do both on a single occasion.

BEDROOM BEHAVIOR

Your deep awareness makes you extremely proficient in bed. You know how to make a kiss, hug, caress, nibble, lick, bite, or insertion feel just right. If a man complains that you're doing something that doesn't feel good, you apologize at once and do everything you can sexually to make it up to him.

At the same time, your sense of decorum makes you reluctant to speak up if the other man is not pleasing you in return. You'll struggle for some indirect way of letting him know, such as guiding his body elsewhere. If need be, you'll politely say you aren't interested. After all, if he were a lover worth pursuing, he would never have hurt you with his elbow (or whatever) in the first place. So you might as well let go of him here and now.

You know what intimacy should mean. But you have trouble maintaining it for long. If you're feeling exceptionally alone, you may cling to the man you're in bed with, as if clinging for life. But over time (maybe even five minutes later), you are uncomfortable with exposing so much of your soul to another man. If he doesn't pick up on your lack of interest, you might be sarcastic with him just to make him go away—or even let him think you're a total weirdo. Since you don't care what he thinks, you'll do what it takes to get rid of him—hopefully without being too direct about it, since that could involve real feelings. However, if need be, you just tell him to leave—and hate him all the more for making you get so *emotional*.

Casual tricks do not engage you on deeper levels, and you tend to get bored with the sex even before it's finished. The other man suffers confusion over mixed signals. Even though you are technically impressive as a lover, something tells him to stay away from you. Ironically, if he does decide to give things another chance, he earns your scorn for not being smart enough to stay away from you.

INTIMACY BLOCKERS

Because you keep other people at a distance, they don't want to get close to you, so when you see them again, you decide they don't like you—and you then decide to stay away from them, perhaps never even see them again. And this of course serves to confirm that nobody ever likes you, that there's nobody in this world you can really talk to. And you bring this negativity into your next round of encounters.

In your childhood, socializing with others became a major issue. Teachers or parents pressured you to make more friends and to "be like the other children." No matter how out you are as a gay man, it's extremely difficult for you to connect with other people. You come up with excuses to get out of social engagements. If you live with another man, you find reasons to be apart from him whenever possible.

Though you have high standards for others, your standards for yourself are even more severe. You'd rather spend every day alone for the rest of your life than have someone think you were needy or vulnerable—let alone risk being rejected. You have a sensitivity that telegraphs to others that you're gay, yet you're very much like the prototypical straight man in your unwillingness to risk injuring your pride.

You're a good example of how closely related feelings of inferiority and superiority can be. Since other people seem to know something about socializing that you don't, you feel profoundly inadequate when you have to mingle with others. Yet once you force yourself to be in a social setting, you become hypercritical of everyone else and think that men are lucky if you so much as let them touch your garment.

You have a lot to offer and are mystified when others don't appreciate you. What you fail to grasp is that you impose social distance by the things you say and do. You make it clear to other people that for some reason you don't want to get too close to them, and they pick up on this. To be popular—let alone deeply committed to another man—takes much more concentration than you seem willing to put out.

POSITIVE ASPECTS OF THE SHY SNOB
Taste, discernment, awareness, sensitivity.

CHALLENGES TO BE OVERCOME

Feelings of inferiority, feelings of superiority, lack of awareness of how self is coming across, inability to take risks.

HOW TO CHANGE

First, acknowledge that you have some good reasons for keeping to yourself. After all, there are a lot of jerks out there, and you have the good sense to know that life is too short to waste time on them. But speaking of life being short, do you really want to spend all of it alone? . . .

Learn to bond one-on-one. Once a week for a month, spend at least one uninterrupted hour sharing with another person face-to-face. (It should be on a personal level—shrinks don't count.) Be friends with whomever you like, but this exercise should be performed with another gay man—doing so will help you to stop feeling somehow "above it all" when it comes to exploring intimacy. Don't talk to him about work or the movie you just saw, but about what's going on in your life. And listen, in turn, to what's going on with him. Try not to be judgmental or to correct him. Just let him be. If you have a boyfriend, connect with someone else. You need to engage in simple friendship with another gay man. If you aren't friendly with any gay men, go to a social event or run an ad in a newspaper saying that you want to make friends.

Stage fright is normal. If you're getting an attack of stage fright in the presence of one or more people, a good way to combat it is to admit to it. Everyone feels this way sometimes; it's nothing to be ashamed of. It simply proves that you're a human being just like everyone else. But don't say it in a way that turns other people off. Don't say, "You're making me nervous." Say something like "For some reason, I'm feeling very shy." You have a lot of charm, and you could use it to your advantage when you get these shyness attacks. Shyness can be charming; neurotic paranoia isn't. Keep it on a simple, engaging level, and your audience of one or one hundred will be eating out of the palm of your hand.

Welcome to the gray area. You are neither better nor worse than other people. The things that make you happy or get you down affect other people the same way. Just because they don't seem to show it, don't jump to conclusions. After all, how much do *you* show to the outside world? Make a list of ten things about yourself you like, and on the same sheet of paper, list ten things about yourself you don't like. Carry the list in your wallet, to remind yourself that like everyone else you have good and bad qualities. The next time you're feeling worthless, remind yourself of the good qualities you have. The next time you feel superior to everyone, remind yourself of the things you still need to work on.

Accept people for who they are. You don't have to like everyone, but you need to like at least a few people. Even if you're in a relationship, it won't be a healthy pairing if your partner is essentially your one social contact. The people you encounter may not always be as bright as you are, but this doesn't mean that they have nothing to offer. They might surprise you at times with their wisdom. Moreover, they can impress you in other ways, such as with their loyalty, humor, and willingness to get close to you. You, my shy yet snobbish friend, can be hard to get to know in your own way, and other people might be looking past some of *your* character defects, as well.

Change your life. You're probably thinking, "Well, *duh.*" But what I mean is that it could be you're selling yourself short on all kinds of levels. If the people you're meeting don't engage you much, maybe you need to make major changes in your career, hobbies, or geographic location. People who *would* challenge and excite you are out there someplace, but you've held yourself back from finding them. Reevaluate your goals in the areas of career, place of residence, and leisure activities. Then make a list under each heading as to what you can do to meet these new goals. Remember, in the final analysis no one's accountable for what you make of yourself but you. If other people bore you, it's not their fault. You're the one who has to make changes.

FINAL THOUGHTS

When you live as an observer more than a participant, you acquire a great deal of insight into human nature. Now is the time to start sharing what you have to offer with others. Valuable lessons can be learned by standing off to the side, but you've learned these lessons many times over. You've been there and done that. Learn new lessons that come from bonding with other people. When you feel secure enough within yourself to make safe and meaningful social contacts with others, the special intimacy you crave with another man will come your way. Your interactions with him will be within a normal frame of reference. You won't be acting as if you're better or worse than he is—as indeed you are neither, but just another gay man looking for love.

THE THERAPY JUNKIE

■ ■ ■

PERSONALITY

Being gay in a homophobic society isn't exactly a picnic, so it's no wonder that you've often felt disoriented. Like that of many gay men, your childhood had its share of horror stories: parents who were either oblivious of or repulsed by your inherent gayness, playground bullies, and so on. Certainly there's nothing wrong with wanting to come to terms with bad memories. As gay men, we all need to redefine ourselves—to get past the shame and stereotypes drilled into us and build confident, self-informed, and emotionally sound new identities. Obviously, many gay men benefit from therapeutic settings, as well as things like self-help books. Heck, I've even written one, as you can see for yourself.

But if you're a Therapy Junkie, you take it all too far. You can't say or do *anything* without referring to your traumatic past. Let's say that, through a personal ad, you're talking to a man on the phone for the first time. He says something like, "Hello, Bob? This is Mike. You answered my ad. How's it going?" And you, Bob, say something like, "Pretty well, I guess. I had a big breakthrough in therapy today. I figured out my parents never loved me. My family was totally dysfunctional. My mother was an alcoholic drug addict, and my father was a rage-aholic, emotionally unavailable sex addict. They're both in denial. It's impossible to maintain healthy boundaries around them, so I have nothing to do with them."

When Mike relates that his hobby is collecting Ethel Merman memorabilia, it seems rather anticlimactic. If you do somehow make a date with Mike, the slightest problem compels you to fall back on your therapy jargon. If he suggests a movie that doesn't interest you, you tell him that he doesn't "feel safe." Should the sex between you be something less than electric, it's because he's "pushing your buttons." (In point of fact, he might be pushing something else.)

The difference between being a Therapy Junkie and someone who simply sees a therapist is that Junkie types dissect *everything* that happens. In intimacy, this means that other people get dissected, too. It's as if the men you meet are but background props for your relentless psychobabble.

You're a kind of mental hypochondriac. When you hear about a new kind of addiction or mental symptom, you can't *wait* to have it apply to you. Though allegedly you want to get better, on another level you're disappointed if it turns out you're not bipolar or suffering from multiple personalities. It's true that some people suppress painful childhood memories such as incest. But in your case there's always the possibility that you *want* to have suffered incest and blocked it out. So you're never sure if you're making up your "suppressed" memories or not.

When you "need" to say something, you assume it's healthy to say it. After all, you're not supposed to "stuff" your feelings. It mystifies you that the other man is hurt when you say that being in bed with him reminds you of when your father caught you smoking and made you smoke his cigars until you puked. You were being "honest" in sharing this. What could the problem be?

Whether you're single or have a partner, you tend to feel alone. That's because you are. You aren't connecting with anyone in the present moment. You have it in your head that the way you talk to your shrink is how you should talk to everyone, and you can't understand why it doesn't work.

BEDROOM BEHAVIOR

Your sexual prowess is a mixed bag of insatiable cravings and things that you absolutely refuse to do. For example, you might have a thing for having your armpits licked, but under no circumstance can someone touch your nipples. *That* either hurts or tickles—which to you is pretty much the same thing.

Whatever your likes and dislikes are, you have an extremely exotic fantasy life that you seldom explore. There're all sorts of kinky things—or at least things you think of as kinky—that could bring you deep pleasure. But part of you is convinced that "intimacy" has to fit some sort of textbook definition, and that your secret desires will be conquered once you are completely mentally sound. Ironically, you're a little like those tragic men who join "ex-gay" movements: if only you can get enough therapy, this desire to do whatever it is will go away.

Yet paradoxically, your shame about these fantasies is such that you might never talk about them in therapy. For all the time and money you spend on "self-wellness," you don't discuss the sex issues that are weighing you down. You keep *meaning* to, once you get enough courage. In the meantime, you work hard to suppress your fantasies, then wonder why the men you have sex with don't seem satisfied.

You take many ghosts, so to speak, into the bedroom with you. You do not have sex so much as try to prove a point. To whom are you trying to prove it? Usually, people from your past who you feel were mean to you. And so you aren't really present—your mind and emotions are elsewhere. You obsess on unpleasant memories and wonder why you aren't happy.

At the most basic level, you want to prove to whomever that it's okay to be lying in bed with another man. You aren't connecting to him so much as making a kind of psychopolitical statement. Then there's your shame about your body, the "old tapes" that tell you you aren't worthy of being loved, and who knows? Maybe you *were* a victim of incest as a child, only you just don't remember, since you certainly seem to have a lot of the symptoms . . . My point is not to make you feel bad for being less than a fully realized person, but to give you a sense of just how difficult you make things for yourself. Would *you* want to be in bed with a man who was about 99 percent absent as you kissed him or looked into his eyes?

INTIMACY BLOCKERS

The reason for your rather erratic behavior in the bedroom and elsewhere is simple. When someone is extremely self-absorbed, he doesn't really let in any information from other people. Probably even your therapist makes little headway; he or she makes suggestions that you instantly reject, as if never even hearing them. For the suggestions he, she, or anyone else makes do not fit into your narrow, stilted image of yourself. So what other people say does not compute. For all of your attempts at being honest, you at best give people a partial picture of who you are.

You don't really connect with anyone. You just kind of show off or narcissistically use people as a sounding board. You have a hard time asking other people how *they* are. If you do, you have a way of bringing the topic back to yourself and your own issues. For someone to be your friend—let alone lover—he needs to feel that you regard his world as important, too.

You share extremely intimate details about yourself as easily as other people comment on the weather. You think that talking about what your parents did to you when you were five years old is the way to get close to people. You're forgetting that closeness also involves letting in some genuine feelings and expressing them. It's about being courteous and attentive to the other person's needs. In the final analysis, all of your talk is aimed at keeping people away, not at letting them in.

You're trying to prove to yourself that you're worthy of being loved as a gay man—and you are. But you deny yourself the opportunity to find this love by refusing to relax and enjoy yourself. *Fun,* believe it or not, is a component of intimacy. It's not always about being serious and talking about complex abstractions. If you can't have fun with another man, you'll never be intimate with him.

POSITIVE ASPECTS OF THE THERAPY JUNKIE

Introspection, truth-seeking, willingness to face childhood traumas, willingness to explore self-improvement.

CHALLENGES TO BE OVERCOME

Emotional stuntedness, inability to have fun, overdefensiveness, inability to let go of the past.

HOW TO CHANGE

First, acknowledge all the hard work you've done to improve yourself and come to terms with your past. Many people are afraid to delve as deeply as you have into painful memories. But it's time to let go of the past and create a different kind of future . . .

Go on a past fast. Limit your discussions of past hurts to your shrink. That's what he/she is there for. And make that time real—focus on the things that really did happen; if you're not sure something happened, figure it out once and for all and follow your therapist's program. But keep your conversations with others—especially potential love interests—focused on the present. Otherwise, he'll either decide you're a total basket case, that you need much more emotional attention than he can give, or—possibly worst of all—that he's willing to be your caretaker. And caretaking relationships have a way of being extremely unstable, with highly painful breakups. For once in your life, talk about things like the weather, that funny movie you saw, and so forth. Let him think you're a cute little airhead. Learn to enjoy living in the now.

Go on a jargon diet. Similarly, stop talking about all of your experiences in psychological terms. Instead of saying "This is a toxic relationship," try saying "I don't like you." Instead of saying "You're pushing my buttons," try saying "You're pissing me off." Instead of saying "I'm a compulsive overeater," try saying "I love food." Let people get to know you in a nonclinical, everyday kind of way. Also, see what happens to your worldview when you start talking more like a regular human being. Make a list of your top ten jargon sayings about your life, then describe these people or situations in everyday, down-to-earth language. See what it feels like. To find the intimacy you seek, you need to act like a human, not a patient.

Have fun. Read the Sunday funnies. Go to an amusement park. See a dumb movie. Send someone a silly greeting card. Spend an entire day doing nothing "serious." If you find yourself dwelling on your "issues," do something to tune them out. Call up a friend. Spend the day at the mall. Be superficial. No one—you included—wants a relationship that turns into some relentless encounter group. There's a time and a place for serious communication, but if you can't just be silly with another man, you'll never be happy with him. If you can't just have fun with him, you're holding something back—you aren't really connecting.

Fantasy shall set you free. Let loose with all your kinky fantasies. Enacting them will empower you. You'll be expressing the full range of who you are, and getting familiar with aspects of yourself that you've been hiding from others—including yourself. If you don't know anyone who's into these things, run ads in newspapers, magazines, and on the Internet. Look up sex clubs in your vicinity. Go for it. (But remember to keep it safe.)

Let go of preconceptions. Some gay men are dangerously naive or careless, but you have the opposite problem. You have such set ideas about what is and isn't acceptable that you censor your life before a possibility has a chance to develop. It's normal to feel a little bent out of shape now and then—it doesn't automatically mean the other guy is "toxic" or "emotionally unsafe." Now, if you're feeling crummy all the time, your relationship has serious problems. But give things a chance to develop before rushing to judgment. Don't assume that you know exactly what's "normal" or "healthy," or that you know what's good or bad for you. Someone a bit off the beaten path might just be what you need to grow into the kind of gay man you want to be.

FINAL THOUGHTS

To explore oneself is an admirable pursuit. It also is important to be open to new information. But it also is important to remember to *live,* and to enjoy being who you are at present. If you can't enjoy or appreciate who you are as of this moment, no one else will, either. Obsessing over things that happened long ago can be a way of avoiding the present—that is to say, of avoiding the possibility for intimacy with another man.

PART TWO

. . .

MALE
MATCHMAKING

WHICHEVER OWTA TYPE YOU ARE, you'll find more intimacy in your life if you can get past its limitations. By striving to change yourself, you *will* change, but the change may not be absolute. Most of us carry through life an essential nature that can improve over time, but which stays fundamentally recognizable. A Creature of Habit (for example) will probably always tend to compartmentalize his life, but he can become *more* flexible and learn to make time for intimacy.

Moreover, the people we encounter in our lives can influence how we grow and change. Some people seem to inspire and challenge us to improve. Others seem to influence us very little. Still other people we encounter bring out the worst in us. Ultimately, who each of us is, is our own responsibility; if you want to get past the Intimacy Blockers of your OWTA type, it's up to you. Still, some types of men can help you to accomplish this more than others. Intimacy is never easy, but sometimes you meet a man who makes it seem easier. By contrast, other men tend to reinforce business as usual. Somehow, when the two of you get together, you bring out the worst habits in each other when it comes to avoiding intimacy.

However you feel about your OWTA type, you're probably wondering what other OWTAs you are and are not compatible with. So I've paired up each OWTA with all twelve of the OWTA types. Some combinations are more likely than others to inspire intimacy and improvement of one's character. However, working on the premise that no relationship is without its problems, and that no relationship is without its good points (yeah, right), I've included the following information in each description:

- *What's Good:* The strengths of the relationship—the fun stuff. What happens when you and the other guy are manifesting the positive qualities of your OWTAs and are working on overcoming your Intimacy Blockers (as through the exercises outlined above).
- *What Needs Work:* The challenges posed by the partnership—the not-such-fun stuff. The type of relationship you have when you and your partner are emphasizing your Intimacy Blockers, and the two of you are not doing your homework to overcome them.

So that you can see at a glance how good a match each relationship is, I've devised a four-star rating system, just like for movies:

★★★★

PICK OUT THE CHINA PATTERN. A GREAT MATCH! ALL YOUR FRIENDS WILL HATE YOU WHEN THEY SEE HOW TERRIFIC YOUR RELATIONSHIP IS. BUT WHAT WILL YOU CARE?

★★★

IT BEATS PLAYING SOLITAIRE. IT'S NOT THE ROMANCE YOU ENVISIONED, BUT YOU'RE MORE HAPPY THAN UNHAPPY (AS YOU SOMETIMES REMIND YOURSELF).

★★

THE JURY'S OUT. WITH WORK, YOU CAN MAKE IT HAPPEN—PROVIDED THAT HE'S WILLING, TOO. BUT DON'T SAY I DIDN'T WARN YOU.

★

DON'T EVEN GO THERE. WHAT ARE YOU THINKING? DIDN'T YOUR MOTHER TEACH YOU ANYTHING? GO TO YOUR ROOM. NO TV FOR A WEEK.

All OWTAs have three four-star relationships, three three-star relationships, and so on. (Even if you're blond, you should be able to figure out that four times three equals twelve.) The one exception is the Perennial Closet Case. Such men simply don't have four-star relationships. However, sometimes they have two- or even three-star relationships. This is bad news as much as good news, because a fairly comfortable relationship can keep these men in the closet that much longer.

Of course, all of these combinations assume that there's a *mutual* attraction. Don't assume that just because you and some other guy *could* have a four-star relationship, you automatically *will*. He may not be interested in you in That Way. And even four-star relationships require a lot of work.

Also, if you and your partner seem to have a measly, pathetic, depressingly tragic one-star relationship, don't give up hope. Remember, if you're both working hard on overcoming your OWTAs, anything's possible. So go ahead and prove me wrong, and if you succeed, all the more power to you.

Here they are—all the different combinations. Happy hunting!

BLUE COLLAR GUY AND BLUE COLLAR GUY
★★★★

What's Good: Not all OWTAs pair up wonderfully with their same type, but two Blue Collar Guys definitely do. You share the same values. You both expect to be married—you see it as something people simply do. You'll both go into the relationship expecting it to be for keeps. At the same time, you're both down-to-earth in your expectations. Blue Collar Guys expect squabbles and struggles. Since you both wear your emotions plainly, neither of you will freak out if one of you raises his voice.

Both of you believe in hard work and saving money. Simple pleasures like TV, bowling, and camping out are what you expect out of life, so neither of you will get antsy when you can't afford to summer at Cannes.

Moreover, each of you will validate the other's need to be identified with the masculine. You'll provide each other with a guy type of affection. Neither of you will mind if the other puts on a few pounds or starts to lose his hair. In fact, so much the better—it will seem more "manly."

You both know about staying off a guy's case, and if something around the house isn't getting tended to the way it should, you both can live with it. You speak the same shorthand, and if a question is responded to with a shrug or an "I don't know," it's good enough; neither of you will be complaining that your partner doesn't communicate enough.

If one of you starts to take on too much of a homemaker role, it will make both of you uneasy—it will seem "too gay." So the house might tend to get messy, but neither of you will mind. If you straighten up the house, it will probably be together, and with a kind of "industrial" approach. You'll use no-frills tools and products and think of it as plastering or fixing the plumbing, even if you're vacuuming and washing the dishes.

Sexually, you both understand (without having to explain it) that once again it is important to validate each other's masculinity. You'll find ways of making the bottom or passive role seem butch in its own way. And you both are comfortable with clearly defined sex roles. Even if you switch back and forth, it will be important to have a sense of top versus bottom, and what the different roles symbolize when it comes to gender. If either or both of you get into taking on "feminine" imagery in bed, it's still done very much as men. There's nothing campy or swishy about it, but a kind of kinkiness aimed at heightening the contrast between being a man and being a woman.

Sex will be an important outlet for both of you to express your needs, and you'll gladly fall asleep lying close to each other, even if someone's arm is a little uncomfortable.

What Needs Work: Since neither of you is particularly articulate, when serious problems arise, you'll have a hard time getting them talked about. Unresolved feelings can fester, and one or both of you might start drinking or eating too much, or doing something else that signifies misdirected energy—such as being unfaithful. This doesn't just mean having outside sex; some Blue Collar couples enjoy open relationships. But it's done with a sense that the spouse is the spouse, and these other flings are just for fun. If one of you is being secretive about getting it on the sly, you'll know your relationship is in serious trouble. But fixing it will not be easy, since you do not gravitate toward therapy or couple's counseling.

Also, your need to be validated as masculine can keep you from truly bonding. To some extent, it's inescapably who you are, but it can force you to make stupid choices at times (just as it can with straight men). If you lose your job or have to do something you consider feminine, you're likely to lose your temper and say or do something you'll regret. Your shared fear of the feminine will at times be an obstacle to intimacy, because on a certain level neither of you ever fully lets down his guard.

But on balance, you can have a great time together. Just keep working on your intimacy issues, be willing to change, and be open to new information.

BLUE COLLAR GUY AND CREATURE OF HABIT
★★★

What's Good: While not a perfect match, the two of you will still have a lot in common. You both like to get the job done—whatever it is—and resent interruptions. Especially when they're coming from a partner nagging you to pay more attention to him. You respect each other for having clear priorities and share a strong work ethic.

You both believe in keeping busy. Blue Collar sees this as a "guy thing," while Creature of Habit just sees it as who he is. But you'd both feel lost without something to do and are not comfortable being alone with your feelings. So even if Creature of Habit's obsessive hobby is collecting Barbie dolls, Blue Collar will empathize. To show his love, he'll build the dolls a display case. If recreational plans have to be altered because of someone's work schedule, neither of you is likely to pull a "you don't love me" scene. (Though whichever one of you doesn't have to work might experience anxiety for having unexpected time on your hands.)

Creature of Habit is not easy to pin down, so Blue Collar will have to take the initiative if he wants a relationship. If Creature of Habit is still quite young, he might be too oblivious to take Blue Collar seriously. But as Creature of Habit ages, he'll appreciate the straightforward, emotionally uncluttered way Blue Collar makes his affections known. Creature of Habit has more complex needs than Blue Collar, but he'll appreciate Blue Collar's respect for daily routines. He'll also like that Blue Collar doesn't play a lot of mind games. If Blue Collar says he'll be there at six, he's there at six.

If you guys end up living together, Creature of Habit will take his daily agenda more seriously and will get more upset when little things go wrong. Blue Collar will seem a mountain of strength and patience by contrast. However, when it comes to major emotional problems or conflicts, Blue Collar will let fly his anger or tears, while Creature of Habit likes to keep things "civilized" and humming along. Some might say this makes you incompatible, but another way of looking at it is that you balance each other out.

What Needs Work: The most crucial problem presented by this coupling is what happens under the sheets—or rather, what doesn't happen. Blue Collar wants a great deal of emotional reassurance from making love. Creature of Habit is good at this sort of thing only sporadically. He gets too distracted to be intensely affectionate all the time. He isn't always happy when he's alone, but when he lives with someone, he looks forward to being by himself to an extent that Blue Collar may not understand. Despite Creature of Habit's fondness for routine, having the same partner day after day may start to feel too intimate, and Blue Collar will take Creature of Habit's coolness as a sign of rejection.

If both parties work on maximizing their positive energy, a compromise will be reached that both parties can live with. Creature of Habit will find unemotional actions he can take to prove his love (such as being a good cook or helping Blue Collar with his taxes), and Blue Collar can regard the frequent lack of passion as an inevitable part of being married. Also, if the two of you share some goal or purpose beyond yourselves, your practical natures will find a productive outlet. For example, your combined energies make you good candidates for fatherhood.

BLUE COLLAR GUY AND DISCRIMINATING SHOPPER
★★

What's Good: For this combination to get off the ground, Blue Collar must survive the veritable trial by fire that Discriminating Shopper will put him through. Given his old-fashioned values, Blue Collar will rise to the challenge better than a lot of other types of guys. Just like in the movies, he expects a certain amount of courtship or playing hard to get. The first time Discriminating Shopper says he's busy this week, a lot of guys will assume that means no. But Blue Collar will give it another shot. This doesn't mean he'll turn into a stalker, but since he assumes everyone wants to get a partner as much as he does, it may take a second or third no for him to move on.

If Blue Collar happens to be what Discriminating Shopper is looking for, things just might take off. If he's not, Discriminating Shopper might still appreciate Blue Collar's sincere efforts to impress him. Even if Discriminating Shopper ends up rejecting Blue Collar, he'll give him an A for effort. Additionally, Blue Collar doesn't take a lot of superficial details seriously, so if Discriminating Shopper wants him to change his hair or shirt, Blue Collar will probably be obliging—at first, anyway.

You Discriminating Shoppers can have all kinds of criteria for your potential partner, but there's a pretty good chance that a masculine appearance is on your list. Blue Collar passes that test with flying colors. In return, Discriminating Shopper can expose Blue Collar to a whole new universe of excellence. He can improve Blue Collar's tastes, wardrobe—perhaps even his salary or career—by encouraging Blue Collar to strive for more. At the same time, Blue Collar can teach Discriminating Shopper to have more patience, and to be less of a hypercritical perfectionist. He can teach Discriminating Shopper that reality can be nicer than a fantasy ideal.

What Needs Work: As with the Creature of Habit, the Discriminating Shopper is not up to the emotional challenge of satisfying Blue Collar in bed. The difference is that Discriminating Shopper will have less patience to tough things out than Creature does. What will make matters worse, Discriminating Shopper will at first be far more demonstrative and affectionate than Creature, so Blue Collar will be that much more hurt when Discriminating Shopper starts to withdraw emotionally. Discriminating Shopper gravitates less toward constancy than Creature does, so he'll be more inclined to call it quits when things aren't working exactly right.

Also, it will be an ongoing challenge for Discriminating Shopper to look past the ways in which Blue Collar doesn't fit his ideal. He wants to make love to a total man, and if Blue Collar only partially fits the bill, he's likely to think of making love as mere sex and lose interest. Blue Collar might start to feel that Discriminating Shopper is always nagging him to change. He can feel intimidated by Discriminating Shopper's perfectionism. Blue Collar just doesn't care about the same things that Discriminating Shopper does and has trouble remembering all the "rules" that Discriminating Shopper is teaching him.

While your profiles do not guarantee a good match, you'll probably both feel enriched for having given things a try. If you can remember the lessons you can teach each other, your problems can be minimized over time.

BLUE COLLAR GUY AND HYPER-ROMANTIC
★★★

What's Good: Both you guys want to settle down in a big way. Blue Collar doesn't expect perfection, and Hyper-Romantic thinks he can be compatible with anyone, so it shouldn't be difficult for the two of you to start dating.

If you get together in a big way, you should be able to get along well day to day. Hyper-Romantic will not be very critical of Blue Collar when he makes a mess around the house. After all, Hyper-Romantic is happy just to have a man. In fact, he'll romanticize Blue Collar's character defects and think these qualities make Blue Collar that much more manly. At the end of a workday, Hyper-Romantic will be more than happy to give Blue Collar a full body massage or draw him a hot bath. Blue Collar will be flattered by Hyper-Romantic's willingness to please him. The sex will be extremely demonstrative. You both crave a lot of affection.

Blue Collar is nothing if not down-to-earth, and through his influence Hyper-Romantic might start living a little less in the clouds. The everyday issues that Blue Collar emphasizes—mowing the lawn, fixing the pipes—can teach Hyper-Romantic more about what a relationship really is and isn't about.

Hyper-Romantic can remind Blue Collar about keeping the romance alive. Unless you're raising twelve kids and you're both out of work, your relationship is not quite as grim as Blue Collar sometimes depicts it to be. Life is about more than paying the electric bill. There *is* time for a little candlelight and lush music. It doesn't have to be all about work. And so Blue Collar might feel free to explore his softer side with Hyper-Romantic.

Unless the romantic bubble has burst, Hyper-Romantic will be drawn to Blue Collar's strong commitment to the relationship. As a couple, you have the potential to withstand whatever rough weather fate may bring you. This is important, since you'll probably take more than a few chances together. Hyper-Romantic's dewy-eyed belief in his lover inspires Blue Collar to be daring, and you're likely to build your own house or sailboat or do *something* together that represents a major investment of time and money.

What Needs Work: Though agreeing to date shouldn't be a problem, there can be obstacles toward accepting each other. In this pairing, Blue Collar tends to call the shots during courtship. If Hyper-

Romantic is on the fey side, Blue Collar might not find him butch enough. Blue Collar can relate to a man acting a fem role on a fantasy level, but he expects his partner to be at least fairly comfortable in the world of guy stuff. Even if his partner does drag and loves to cook, he will still be expected to enjoy watching the Indy 500. If Hyper-Romantic is faking an interest in Blue Collar's world, Blue Collar will sense something phony and not trust in it.

Also, as much as Blue Collar wants to find a husband, he may feel that his partner is crowding him. Because he takes his commitments seriously, Blue Collar takes his time in sorting through his feelings. But Hyper-Romantic wants marriage in the first five minutes. Though you both seek validation through making love, the difference will be that Blue Collar is being sincere, while Hyper-Romantic is exaggerating his responses. Instinctively, Blue Collar senses that Hyper-Romantic isn't being genuine and wonders if Hyper-Romantic really loves him as much as he says he does.

Also, as much as Blue Collar wants companionship, he likes having his own space. On weekends, he might want to relax by fiddling around with an old radio or working in the garage. Hyper-Romantic will tend to interrupt him for attention, and Blue Collar will start to withdraw emotionally.

Though Blue Collar's heart is in the right place, he may not always say or do the most romantic things. He may forget his partner's birthday or not have the words to say something deeply felt. Anger is often easier to express than more vulnerable feelings. Hyper-Romantic might feel taken for granted or unloved. (Though Blue Collar will probably apologize for his thoughtlessness.)

Perhaps most important, neither of you is inclined to take decisive action if your relationship isn't working. Blue Collar will tolerate a lot before calling it quits, and Hyper-Romantic can't stand the thought of being single again. However, if your mutual desire to make things work is strong enough, you can challenge your respective shortcomings and build something that lasts.

BLUE COLLAR GUY AND MISFIT
★★★★

What's Good: More than likely, a lot of what a Misfit doesn't like about the gay world has to do with "masculinity." Glittery discos and show tunes aren't "male" enough for him. So he's likely to find a Blue Collar guy refreshingly masculine. Misfit tends to make things much more intellectually and emotionally challenging than Blue Collar. He sees his needs as much more complex than simply preferring butch to fem. But the mere fact that Misfit is bonding with another man will help him to feel better about being gay. Blue Collar will respond to Misfit's nonstereotypic tastes and sensibilities and take them as a sign of butchness.

Past a certain point, Blue Collar may not care about (or understand) some of the issues that Misfit gets all hot and bothered about. But he senses that Misfit is sincere, and that's the most important thing. Blue Collar respects fancy ideas as long as they seem rooted in honesty. He'll do his best to learn from what Misfit has to say.

Blue Collar will be a calming influence in Misfit's life. Misfit has gotten extremely wound up in the idiosyncratic notions of his mind, and being with Blue Collar will help ground him in reality. The affection that Blue Collar is willing to share will help make up for Misfit's lack of popularity with others. And if Misfit can tough things out, he may emerge a more personable individual for being with Blue Collar. So making friends with other gay guys might become easier.

Both Blue Collar and Misfit view lovemaking as a total experience. For Blue Collar this happens simply and intuitively, while for Misfit it is arrived at through detailed introspection. But this difference can be experienced as complimentary. Misfit is so starved for validation from another man that it will be quite a while before the novelty of Blue Collar's affection wears off. And Misfit responds in kind by wanting to do what he can to please Blue Collar. You two might sexually experiment more with each other than with other any other type of man.

Blue Collar senses that there are parts of Misfit he isn't reaching, but somehow they seem reachable, because Misfit isn't shutting down so much as being himself. Unlike some types of gay men, both of you expect life to be painful sometimes, and in the bedroom you instinctively try to heal each other's wounds.

What Needs Work: The main obstacle to happiness is that Blue Collar strives to learn to keep life simple while Misfit strives to keep it complicated. At times, Blue Collar wishes that Misfit could just shut up and live. Misfit, in turn, feels frustrated when Blue Collar doesn't seem interested in the point he's trying to make. Much more than Blue Collar, Misfit will want to talk about a problem.

Misfit can talk circles around Blue Collar and can be most adept at putting Blue Collar down, should the two of you argue. But Blue Collar is not always the world's best loser, and he can far outdistance Misfit when it comes to expressing anger. Both of you have to be careful not to cause permanent damage to your relationship when you disagree. Misfit has to learn to keep things on a practical level. Blue Collar is action-oriented; tell him what he needs to do, not how he needs to think. At the same time, Blue Collar should be open-minded about receiving a new insight from Misfit and understand that it's an opportunity to learn.

Additionally, your relationship will suffer over time if you don't keep challenging yourselves to get past your respective hang-ups over butch/fem. You both need to view being a gay male as a multifaceted experience. Otherwise, you'll both limit your emotional and behavioral responses to situations in which you're afraid to say or do something that's "too gay."

If both of you can keep working on these issues, if Misfit can accept and learn from Blue Collar's easier way of living and if Blue Collar can see himself as capable of entering Misfit's larger world, your relationship can be the best kind of keeper.

BLUE COLLAR GUY AND NICE BOY
★★

What's Good: This somewhat unlikely combination can start happening if Nice Boy is very, very much Blue Collar's physical type. By this I mean, if Blue Collar is into (for example) five-foot-ten redheads with brown eyes and a goatee, and that's exactly what the Nice Boy looks like, it will spark an interest. Otherwise, Blue Collar is likely to find Nice Boy something of a turnoff. Blue Collar doesn't trust Nice Boy's "friendliness"—even if he gets involved with him. Nice Boy is likely to find Blue Collar a bit rough around the edges, but if Blue Collar is on his most gentlemanly behavior, Nice Boy might think he has potential.

If there's an initial spark, it's possible to develop something that benefits both parties. Blue Collar can help Nice Boy get off his high moral horse and learn the joy of stepping in messes. Nice Boy can teach Blue Collar more about how being a man can mean many things, and that it's possible to respond to certain situations in gentler ways.

Since Nice Boy tends to let down his guard in bed, sexual sparks can fly. Nice Boy usually isn't the most macho type of gay man, but if he knows just how to please Blue Collar, Blue Collar might start eroticizing Nice Boy's more androgynous qualities. If nothing else, Blue Collar shouldn't have too much trouble feeling like the more masculine partner.

You're the sort of couple that other people have difficulty understanding—but then, other people are not privy to the intimate details of your love life. Inventiveness will not be your forte, but you'll both be attentive. In any event, the sex will probably be the least troubled part of your relationship. (In fact, if the sex isn't instantly great, it's unlikely that either of you will pursue things any further.)

What Needs Work: Both parties need to work on their Intimacy Blockers to become more open-minded to their differences. Otherwise, the relationship will not last—or even worse, it will. Blue

Collar and Nice Boy are at risk for becoming one of those awful couples who drink too much and put each other down in front of an audience, which they assume is entertained by their bitterness. (Perhaps such a relationship can even become abusive.)

In the ongoing contest of wills, Blue Collar tries to get a rise out of Nice Boy, who responds with emotionally distant, superficially polite nastiness. Blue Collar doesn't like to think of divorce, and Nice Boy doesn't want to hurt Blue Collar's feelings (or risk being exposed to his temper), so things can drag on indefinitely unless someone starts changing.

If you aren't both working on improving yourselves, Nice Boy will be frightened by the intensity of Blue Collar's feelings, and emotionally—yet smilingly—withdraw. This will piss off Blue Collar, who will come to regard Nice Boy as being emotionally frigid. Passive-aggressive put-downs or squabbles over trivial things that aren't the issue will start to dominate the relationship. Under the sheets you can kiss and make up—but the process is wearying over time.

You don't naturally help each other get past your limitations. Blue Collar will interpret Nice Boy's combative style as feminine, and Nice Boy will be more convinced than ever that it doesn't pay to let your emotions loose. If you find each other, staying together will be less of a problem than finding a way to stay happily together. If you can, you might have something pretty special, since you probably already click in bed.

BLUE COLLAR GUY AND PAL
★★★★

What's Good: You two stand a good chance of meeting up. It doesn't even have to be at a gay social event. Maybe Pal offers to trim his sister's hedges, and Blue Collar is visiting for a family barbecue. However you meet, you'll both enjoy the way your relationship seems enmeshed with the full spectrum of your lives and does not revolve exclusively around the gay scene. You both express your affection for others through your actions. Since neither of you is especially introspective, you're unlikely to accuse each other of keeping busy to avoid intimacy.

Blue Collar (more than many other types of men) will be in sympathy with Pal's desire to help others. While Blue Collar wants to settle down, he doesn't expect married life to be some endless sea cruise through the Bahamas. He'll be understanding when Pal hasn't time for fluff because he has to drive Aunt Cecile to the hospital. Such errands will make Blue Collar feel that his is a "real" marriage, in which work and responsibility come first.

Pal will find much to nurture in Blue Collar. He'll enjoy doing things to make Blue Collar feel happy and secure and will probably even get physically aroused by waiting on him. Pal will find Blue Collar to be poignantly sincere and is relatively unlikely to tire of Blue Collar's straightforward declarations of love.

This is a good combination for parenthood, as both of you have a lot of energy to burn when it comes to giving to others. Yours is not a relationship destined to have much quiet time for just the two of you, but if you can share in a mutual activity such as parenting, you'll get quite a lot of satisfaction from your fleeting moments of togetherness.

Temperamentally, you can help each other become more fully integrated people. Blue Collar is very much his own boss in life. Through his example, Pal can learn more about becoming the star of his own destiny and to not always put other people first. By observing Pal and accompanying him on his errands of goodwill, Blue Collar might start exploring the less demanding and more giving parts of his own nature. He might get more of a sense that being a man can mean many things.

What Needs Work: Despite all the positive ways you mesh, there are also ways in which you reinforce your respective bad habits. Pal needs to get focused within himself and learn to enjoy his own company. These sorts of issues are likely to be out of Blue Collar's depth. Blue Collar needs to stop fearing his softer, "feminine" side, and Pal is likely to encourage just the opposite by hogging the nurturing role for himself.

Moreover, Blue Collar will feel jealous and unloved over time if Pal doesn't remember to give his man lots of TLC. Pal is more sociable and outgoing than Blue Collar, and he'll sometimes feel trapped by having to revolve so much of his life around one person, when there are so many other favors he could be doing for other people.

Since neither of you are particularly fond of looking inside yourselves, when problems arise, there will be a tendency to ignore them by keeping busy. Perhaps you'll even get into the habit of drinking a bit too much to keep your anxieties at bay, so that you can continue with your many different projects. Sooner or later, something will erupt, and it won't be a pleasant sight. Blue Collar has an easy time venting his temper, and Pal, when pushed to the limits, can be just as nasty.

But if both of you are working on the issues holding you back from intimacy, this can be a good match. Blue Collar's steadfastness can be a calming influence on Pal, and through Pal's example Blue Collar can learn new ways of expressing himself as a man.

BLUE COLLAR GUY AND PARTY BOY
★★

What's Good: As with Nice Boy, Blue Collar will have to find Party Boy to be very much his physical type to take an interest. Otherwise, Party Boy will seem too lightweight for Blue Collar's tastes. Party Boy might initially regard Blue Collar as an amusing trophy for his collection ("Darling, you'll never believe the hunky truck driver I brought home last night. *Too* divine!"). But once under the sheets, Party Boy might just get into one of those sincere moods of his and start to feel something for Blue Collar. After all, Blue Collar seems the type of man who used to torment Party Boy back in his nerd phase, and Party Boy might experience an important catharsis from being with Blue Collar.

If all these circumstances are in alignment, it's possible for you two to make a go of it. It's unlikely that it will be a lasting partnership, unless both of you are extremely willing to change. But if both of you truly want to make things work, good things can happen. Party Boy can jazz up Blue Collar's life and teach him to be less of a homebody, and Blue Collar can help Party Boy to slow down, drop his pretentiousness, and stop fearing his maleness. He can teach Party Boy something about the beauty of plainness.

You'll need to have a sense of humor about each other. Blue Collar must see Party Boy as a kind of amusingly ditsy butterfly, and Party Boy will have to regard Blue Collar with a stand-up comedian's patience toward his impossible, couch-potato spouse. If you can keep things light, you can teach each other important lessons.

Whatever your intimate problems are, on the surface of things you can seem a generous and sociable couple. Neither of you gravitate toward highly complex pleasures, and guests to your home come to expect generous portions of food and limitless barrels of wine.

You will probably entertain quite a lot, since it's a way of avoiding being alone together. Blue Collar will think Party Boy likes company too much, while Party Boy will think Blue Collar doesn't like company enough. But unless you both get quite inebriated, you'll set aside your differences for the sake of appearance. Some of your closest moments together will be spent with other people.

What Needs Work: The differences in your lifestyles will inevitably cause friction, and since neither of you wants to talk things out, the friction is likely to lead to a breakup. Blue Collar can have a bad temper, and Party Boy has been known to enjoy his share of opiates, so the arguments between the two of you can be pretty gruesome.

You're at odds with each other because Blue Collar essentially wants to settle down, while Party Boy (despite whatever he may say) acts as if he never wants to settle down. However, it is important to remember that these personality traits are something of a fabrication (especially for Party Boy) and not who each of you necessarily is on the inside.

Even if you never explicitly talk about it, a major strain in your relationship will concern Blue Collar's appreciation of traditional male values, versus Party Boy's fear of them. Time and again, you will disappoint each other, as Blue Collar does something "too manly" and Party Boy does something "too fem." Conflicts over differing tastes in movies or what sorts of people are worth knowing as friends will seem symbolic of the important ways in which you differ as people.

Underneath it all, there's something important that each of you can embrace in the other. Party Boy is in many ways the type of gay man that Blue Collar thinks gives gay men a bad name. He sees Party Boy as flighty, irresponsible, superficial, and fey. If he can learn to appreciate Party Boy on deeper levels, it will help Blue Collar feel better about himself as a gay man. Blue Collar is the kind of man that Party Boy fears. If he can accept that Blue Collar Guys are also part of the gay experience, he might stop having such a stereotypical view of what it means to be gay—and stop trying to be nothing more than a gay stereotype himself.

To accomplish all this, though, will take a great deal of work and commitment. Continually, you'll both need to remember that what you're reacting against is not who each of you really is on the inside.

BLUE COLLAR GUY AND PERENNIAL CLOSET CASE
★

What's Good: On the surface of things, this may seem like a fairly decent match: Blue Collar likes to feel butch, and Closet Case has a lot of hang-ups about people knowing he's gay. So it might seem as if you can have a lot of fun together, hanging out in working-class bars and whatnot. And for about five minutes or so, you might (which is about all that's good about this partnership).

Superficially, you might also seem to have a lot of values in common. Blue Collar is pretty well enmeshed in the everyday world, so every other word out of his mouth is not *gay*. And since Closet Case isn't comfortable with being gay, he, too, may talk a lot about things unrelated to the gay experience.

But before long, a deeply troubling conflict will emerge between you, and about the best that can be said about it is that you'll hopefully both know enough to walk away from each other.

What Needs Work: Closet Case needs to come out for this relationship to work at all—ironically, he needs to come out even more so than when partnered with other types of men. Blue Collar morally disapproves of men who are married to women and are leading double lives. Even if Blue Collar is willing to fool around a little with a married man, over time he will not take the arrangement seriously, and his underlying morals will win out. But even when Closet Case is willing to live with him as a closeted couple, Blue Collar will not be a happy camper.

Blue Collar essentially wants what he was taught to have: marriage and close family ties. He wants to send lovey-dovey holiday cards of himself and his partner, go to family barbecues, help his niece learn to ride her bike—maybe even become a father. He expects his gay relationship to be a marriage just like any other. Blue Collar *will* come out to his family; if they're not supportive, he'll be devastated, but he doesn't believe in keeping something so important from them.

So when Closet Case has problems with all this—problems with living together or with people knowing that he lives with a man—Blue Collar becomes profoundly unhappy. If they get to the live-in stage, even if Blue Collar is out to *his* family, the preoccupying shame and secretiveness of Closet Case will fester over time.

Blue Collar will say or do things indicative of intimacy, and Closet Case will be repulsed—repulsed, really, with his own inability to accept himself as a gay man. He'll be moody and distant, or else snappish. Blue Collar will ask what's bothering him, and Closet Case will insist that it's nothing.

Yours will be a deeply troubled relationship in which one man is committed to his partner while the other is committed to the impression he's making on others. Sadly, you may never understand that the closetness of the one is at the root of so much that's troubling your partnership. You may think it has to do with something totally unrelated. Depression, volatile tempers, and extreme tension will characterize this relationship. Only if Closet Case starts to come out can this couple begin to have honest sharing and real commitment.

BLUE COLLAR GUY AND SEXPOT
★★★

What's Good: The attraction between you will be immediate. Sexpot is accustomed to receiving compliments, but Blue Collar knows how to make those flattering remarks that make Sexpot feel validated: "Where have you been all my life?" or "I think I just met my one true love" or words to that effect. Blue Collar belies the stereotype that gay men are all witty and clever, but what Sexpot wants to hear are well-worn phrases and clichés, and Blue Collar knows them all.

Blue Collar doesn't consider good looks a requirement in a partner, but they certainly do no harm, and he'll be proud as can be to show off Sexpot to his family and friends. Sexpot will bask in the security that Blue Collar offers, not to mention the initial shower of gifts he lays at Sexpot's feet. Blue Collar might even offer to financially support Sexpot. In other words, Blue Collar is eager to do what Sexpot on one level wants all men to do: dedicate his life to Sexpot's allure.

In the bedroom, Blue Collar will feel ravenously turned on by Sexpot's prowess and willingness to please. The essence of your relationship is Sexpot sexily dancing around the room while Blue Collar watches. Sexpot gets to be the total object of desire, and Blue Collar gets off on Sexpot's beauty. Blue Collar, after all, has not the most refined touch in bed, and he appreciates Sexpot's good looks more than his superb technique—which he probably doesn't notice that much. He'll keep wanting to *look* at Sexpot during lovemaking. In fact, he'll probably want to look at Sexpot all the time.

Sexpot will enjoy seeing this seemingly tough guy turn into so much Jell-O in his hands. He'll feel safe knowing that he can control this man whose masculinity makes him symbolic of *all* men. Sexpot may start to miss having more of a social life, but as long as Blue Collar keeps the relationship alive with compliments, Sexpot will appreciate the depth of his affections.

On a different level, Sexpot loathes men who see him only as a beautiful body. So he'll be genuinely moved by how all-encompassing Blue Collar's affections seem to be. Even if Blue Collar only does love Sexpot for his looks, it will *seem* as if it's about much more than that. Blue Collar will take delight in having such a hot-looking lover and will make it his manly duty to show his appreciation in as many ways as he can. Sexpot can meet men who are more imaginative, but he'll be genuinely touched by the breadth of Blue Collar's passion.

From Blue Collar, Sexpot can learn that love can be simple and moving. Perhaps he can start to reevaluate the tangled web of allure he has so often woven in the past. Sexpot can teach Blue Collar to aim higher in life, that he doesn't always have to settle for the run-of-the-mill.

What Needs Work: Blue Collar is big on compliments—at first. But over time, he becomes less romantic, and the sweet nothings and boxes of candy become fewer and farther between. Sexpot gets nervous being a homebody and will start to feel like some sort of housewife drudge or (if Blue Collar makes good money) kept woman. Blue Collar makes no apologies for being jealous and possessive, and he may declare outright that he doesn't want Sexpot going to lots of bars and parties.

Because Blue Collar doesn't express himself much, Sexpot will eventually wonder if Blue Collar really does care as much as he claims, or does he actually only love Sexpot for his looks? Over time, Sexpot can grow bored and disillusioned with Blue Collar, and Blue Collar can start to feel unloved.

More important are the ways in which you don't challenge each other as people. Blue Collar will reinforce Sexpot's self-image of being good for one thing only. Sexpot will let Blue Collar continue to feel like the powerful male head of the household. For if the two of you clash in the butch department, Blue Collar will win out— or else the relationship will dissolve.

Even if Sexpot "passes for straight," with Blue Collar he becomes the less powerful partner. If Sexpot thinks he has Blue Collar wound around his little finger, he may just need to think twice. Sexpot is somewhat afraid of Blue Collar's masculinity, and over time he might feel that Blue Collar is bullying him and trying to take total control of his life.

If Blue Collar can keep things lively and engaging and can learn to love Sexpot's looks as but the icing on the cake, and if Sexpot can learn that he really does have value as a person beyond his looks, this can be a good match. The challenges presented by it can provide valuable lessons to both of you.

BLUE COLLAR GUY AND SHY SNOB
★

What's Good: Not a whole heck of a lot. About the best that can be said is that it's pretty unlikely that the two of you will get past first base. Blue Collar doesn't trust people who don't seem to be laying their cards on the table, and Shy Snob's complicated secrets will turn Blue Collar right off. Blue Collar isn't beyond trying to impress a guy whom he has little in common with, but to do so he has to feel there's something he can latch onto or identify with, and Shy Snob gives him virtually nothing to work with.

There might be an initial spark of something, in that Blue Collar will appreciate how Shy Snob kind of keeps to himself. He might see Shy Snob as a challenge. And since Shy Snob often is hungry for attention, he might appreciate—for a little while—Blue Collar's keen, puppy-dog-like interest. There might be a tender moment or two in bed, before Shy Snob's pride makes him feel foolish for having reached out for Blue Collar's comforting touch. Blue Collar might even think for a minute or so that he can help this man in his arms to heal from whatever it is that's troubling him—that all Shy Snob needs is some tenderness.

But before long, Shy Snob starts dissecting all that will be wrong with the relationship and will preempt it before it goes too far (which might well be fortunate for all concerned). Blue Collar is unlikely to be hurt for long, because the whole thing will seem too weird to dwell on.

What Needs Work: Just about everything. If both of you are feeling especially lonely or desperate, you might decide to hook up. Shy Snob might be in an exceptionally humble mood, and if Blue Collar is feeling especially needy (maybe he just ended a relationship), Shy Snob's rather limited capacity for giving to another person might seem more than what it is.

Shy Snob alternately feels he's better or worse than other people. But in either case, he keeps his elation or depression to himself. He will feel deeply invaded by Blue Collar's affections, as if Blue Collar is performing a kind of emotional rape. In fact, when the relationship ends—and it will—Shy Snob might well look back on it and wonder if Blue Collar did rape him, since it must have been apparent that Shy Snob wasn't in the mood on any number of occasions. But what is more likely to be true is that Shy Snob, in his passive-aggressive way, won out over Blue Collar and found ways to avoid nightly intimacy.

Blue Collar seeks a very *present* type of relationship. In his everyday way, he expects his partner to be concentrating on him and not be off in the clouds. He'll be annoyed and frustrated with Shy Snob's complex and changeable moods, and the way he seems to need Blue Collar's strength, yet is repulsed by him at the same time.

In the end, Blue Collar will feel emotionally damaged for having committed himself to so unloving an arrangement, and Shy Snob will feel emotionally *and* psychologically damaged for having given himself to someone who never understood a single thing about him.

BLUE COLLAR GUY AND THERAPY JUNKIE
★

What's Good: The best that can be said here is that it's highly unlikely that the two of you will get together for any length of time. Therapy Junkie only has to open his mouth for Blue Collar to see that he's way out of his depth with all this psychological mumbo jumbo. Therapy Junkie thinks that anyone who isn't dissecting all his childhood issues is in denial, and he'll think Blue Collar is one of those "toxic" people he'd best avoid. And there is a certain ironic truth in this.

For a short duration, Therapy Junkie might appreciate Blue Collar's solidity, and Blue Collar might think Therapy Junkie is an interesting person. But know when to say good-bye. Therapy Junkie needs to stop living in his head, but Blue Collar is unlikely to be the man to teach him this lesson, since he doesn't understand him. Blue Collar could benefit from exploring his past more critically, but he needs to do so with a partner who doesn't force him to reduce everything to unfamiliar and intimidating psychological jargon.

What Needs Work: To begin with, Blue Collar sees little purpose in "working" on himself. He lacks the introspection to view himself as a kind of separate object and is baffled when Junkie describes himself or his "issues" as if describing a third person. Blue Collar is extremely action-oriented, and if Therapy Junkie wants (for example) to stop being afraid of his boss, Blue Collar doesn't see why he can't just be a man and *do* it.

Furthermore, even if Blue Collar complains about his family, he is uncomfortable with considering that he had an unhappy childhood. To his way of thinking, parents are to be treated with respect, and the family should stick together no matter what. When Therapy

Junkie says things like "I haven't spoken to my parents in five years," Blue Collar is offended—even if he pretends to be sympathetic. Also, this signals to Blue Collar a kind of emotional instability on the part of Therapy Junkie, making him less than husband material.

Therapy Junkie lives to become psychologically improved and is dumbfounded by the number of issues that Blue Collar has never even thought of. Blue Collar strikes him as an overgrown child, acting out whatever mood strikes him at the moment. Even worse, Blue Collar will start to remind him of his family, and he'll start to fear and loathe Blue Collar the way he already fears and loathes his primary caregivers. When he fails to change Blue Collar—when he's unable to get him to look at life as he does—it will rekindle his sense of failure with his own family, and the heartbreak he experienced when they failed to understand or take an interest in the things that mattered to him. He'll feel completely defeated, as if life inevitably turns into the ugliness he's worked so hard to leave behind.

Early on, when you both get the sense that things won't work, it's wise to heed what your instincts are telling you.

CREATURE OF HABIT AND CREATURE OF HABIT
★★★

What's Good: Obviously, you'll have a lot in common. You both might even share the same obsessive hobby and meet at a tulip growers' festival or at an auction for Mama Cass memorabilia or some such. But even if your hobbies are different, you'll respect each other's need to have an activity that takes up lots of time.

If your daily life habits are in sync—if you're both day people or night people or neatness freaks or slobs—you'll be able to function under the same roof without getting in each other's way or getting on each other's nerves. And for Creatures of Habit, it is extremely important to get through one's routines without physical or emotional interruptions.

Even if your habits are different, there can still be ways you complement each other. A day person can appreciate having a night-person partner because it can give him more space to himself—provided that night person does not force him to conform to his schedule or vice versa. Since Creatures of Habit feel they have to stay busy, a neatness freak can enjoy having a slob to pick up after, because it will give him something to do. Even if the neatness freak complains, on another level he relishes attacking a mound of mess.

In the bedroom, you're lucky if you happen to have the exact same practices or fetishes in common, because you'll be able to do these things to your heart's content. Probably even then you won't stay up all night indulging. There are checkbooks to be balanced, so many lists of things to do. If your sexual tastes are different, it shouldn't matter too much, since neither of you is especially passionate. Sex will only be a problem if it involves profound disruptions of someone's routine or rigid belief system.

In other words, yours will not be the grand passion of the century, but since neither of you realistically craves anything along those lines, you'll bring out the practical side in each other and can have a fairly happy go of it.

What Needs Work: You also tend to bring out the mediocre in each other. You both have fallen into the trap of putting activity over intimacy, routine over humanity, and when you get together, you hardly challenge each other to break these blasé patterns. Instead, you'll decide that having a relationship is one more thing you've knocked out of the way—like an item on your things-to-do list—and relieved, you can now go back to doing things as you've done them before. You both need to work at getting past the false security of routine in order to genuinely connect—with yourselves and with each other.

Sooner or later, life will present you with a crisis of some sort that will threaten the humdrum stability of your relationship. Unless you've been working on expanding your horizons, you'll both be ill-equipped to deal with it. You'll go about your daily chores, acting as if nothing were wrong . . . until something explodes. Since neither of you like to squabble, your first disagreement might literally be your last. You'll break up rather than face anything so nasty again.

Ho-hum sex can be tolerated, as it technically provides company while not challenging you to become more emotionally vulnerable. But this is true only to a point. After a while, you both might feel that you would be happier alone, rather than having to deal with all this intimacy nonsense. You can convince each other that intimacy is destined to be short-lived and unsatisfying, not realizing that intimacy was seldom what you gave each other.

Still, day to day, you can do much worse than to find a fellow Creature of Habit. If you do both challenge yourselves—and each other—you can be more than a mere habit to each other and become a genuine source of happiness and strength in each other's life.

CREATURE OF HABIT AND DISCRIMINATING SHOPPER ★★

What's Good: You're likely to be the sort of twosome that seems to hit it off fine on the first date, promises to be in touch, and then never sees each other again. Creature of Habit will go obliviously about his business while Discriminating Shopper tries to make up his mind. Even if you spent your first date mutually bemoaning the state of your love lives, in the proverbial light of day you both may feel you have better things to do than see each other again.

For things to click, Discriminating Shopper has to believe that Creature of Habit is just what he's been looking for. If such is the case, and if Creature of Habit doesn't think Discriminating Shopper will upset his routine, the two of you might give it a whirl.

Discriminating Shopper will give Creature of Habit quite a lot of leeway—at first, anyway—to do things as he's always done them. Since Discriminating Shopper has unrealistic standards, when a guy does happen to seem "perfect," he'll be forgiven a lot. If Creature of Habit doesn't want to go to the movies after all because he has an early-morning errand or he wants to mess around with his aphid

collection, the normally rather uppity Discriminating Shopper experiences the humbling lesson of letting someone else's will dominate his own. This can help Discriminating Shopper come down a
few notches and start to have a more realistic sense of what relationships are about. Discriminating Shopper's passionate tastes can,
in turn, help Creature of Habit to set his horizons higher and not
be content with business as usual.

Under the sheets, you can be compatible, unless—or until—
Discriminating Shopper becomes disillusioned. If Creature of Habit
disappoints him in bed, he's likely to start withdrawing emotionally—and physically. However, if neither of you snore or hog the
blankets, Creature of Habit might not seem to notice that anything's
wrong. Discriminating Shopper will start to look elsewhere, though
he may keep Creature of Habit around as he marks time.

You're both opinionated and unyielding personalities, and you
respect this in each other. If your opinions are largely in agreement,
the potential is there to forge a useful partnership. For however long
things last, you can be the kind of couple who save a lot of money
or do all sorts of interesting things—provided, of course, that you
can mesh in the first place.

What Needs Work: There's a tendency for you to reinforce patterns
of nonintimacy in each other. When you get together, Creature of
Habit can pretty much do things as he's always done them. Discriminating Shopper can pretend that he's met his fantasy ideal, since
Creature of Habit tends toward a monolithic way of life. When the
bubble bursts, there will have been little communication. Creature
of Habit doesn't like to reveal much about himself, so Discriminating Shopper may decide that Creature of Habit wasn't his ideal,
after all, but that the ideal still exists out there someplace.

Discriminating Shopper feels he's all but conferred royalty on
Creature of Habit by deeming him worthy of pursuit. But Creature
of Habit will have little sense of just what an emotional risk Discriminating Shopper is making, how seldom he even attempts to
commit himself to another man. Discriminating Shopper works
much harder at the relationship. He starts to feel disempowered, as

indeed he is, because in this combination Creature of Habit does little yet still calls all the shots. He hasn't the same emotional investment that Discriminating Shopper has, so it's easier for him to take or leave whatever's happening.

If Discriminating Shopper keeps insisting that Creature of Habit is his dream man, even when all the evidence indicates that theory is flawed, and if Creature of Habit finds Discriminating Shopper's presence in his life makes his routine run even more smoothly, you may be reluctant to break up. However, if Discriminating Shopper finds flaws in Creature of Habit, or if he seems to be nagging Creature of Habit to change, that will pretty much be it.

The breakup will be relatively painless, as breakups go. Discriminating Shopper will be hurt by how indifferent Creature of Habit seems, and Creature of Habit will be perplexed that Discriminating Shopper doesn't want to remain friends. But you'll forget each other quickly enough and move on. After all, you probably never really fully penetrated each other's life in the first place.

CREATURE OF HABIT AND HYPER-ROMANTIC
★

What's Good: If one had to be generous, one could say that Hyper-Romantic certainly will be patient with Creature of Habit and give him lots of second chances to be something other than the self-absorbed man that he is. There might even be an initial moment of fun when the two of you meet, since Hyper-Romantic is willing to sell himself as something he's not, and Creature of Habit likes to be superficially pleasant.

Briefly, Creature of Habit might appreciate the convenience of having Hyper-Romantic around. Hyper-Romantic will call and come over and give Creature of Habit a ride and do whatever it takes, so Creature of Habit can still have plenty of time to do what he needs to do.

Hyper-Romantic is so determined to please in the bedroom, he might manage to awaken something in Creature of Habit for a while. And since Hyper-Romantic will want to keep the door open, so to speak, he probably won't share much of the pain he's feeling with Creature of Habit, making for a relatively bloodless breakup. But this simply isn't a good match.

What Needs Work: Hyper-Romantic seeks end-all, be-all love, and he's highly unlikely to find it with Creature of Habit—who will find Hyper-Romantic to be a clingy, over-emotional nuisance. Before long, Creature of Habit will resent having his routine disrupted, especially since Hyper-Romantic seems to be taking up space in his life for no good reason. Clearly, Hyper-Romantic is unrealistic, and from Creature of Habit's point of view, what's the good in *that?*

This is not a case of difference being good, because the differences between the two of you are unlikely to be a springboard for positive change. Creature of Habit will regard Hyper-Romantic's emotional shenanigans as proof that one is better off remaining unattached— if he thinks about him at all. However, Hyper-Romantic can misinterpret bad chemistry for Tragic Love and feel deeply wounded when things don't work out. He'll be that much more determined to find his next boyfriend, so as to heal from the pain caused by Creature of Habit.

Creature of Habit can use help in getting out of his self-imposed rut, but it's doubtful that Hyper-Romantic will be of much assistance. From Creature of Habit's point of view, Hyper-Romantic wants too much too soon. The connection doesn't seem real, so Creature of Habit has few second thoughts about nipping things in the bud. If nothing else, Hyper-Romantic is too intense for Creature of Habit, whom he scares away. Creature of Habit might even think that Hyper-Romantic is "stalking" him or in any case is highly unbalanced.

Hyper-Romantic needs to develop patience, discernment, and a sense of himself. But Creature of Habit is far too enmeshed in his own world to have the patience to teach him this. Hyper-Romantic will simply fail to understand why Creature of Habit is so unwilling to give things a try—and with so little explanation for his reasons herein. He'll remember Creature of Habit as cold and heartless—even a hypocrite if Creature of Habit promotes himself to be a humanitarian. For how could such a great "humanitarian" be so mean?

It's difficult to envision your relationship as anything other than short-lived. Creature of Habit simply has no patience for Hyper-Romantic. Moreover, he finds it easy to tell Hyper-Romantic as much, since he doesn't think Hyper-Romantic is worth taking seriously.

The best bet for both of you is to walk away. You might make okay friends, but when it comes to romance, you're unlikely to click.

CREATURE OF HABIT AND MISFIT
★★★

What's Good: Both of you tend to be solitary figures, albeit in contrasting ways. Creature of Habit likes to feel in control. Misfit has intellectual, cultural, or moral objections to the gay community and often feels as if he fits in with neither the gay nor the straight world. Still, you both understand about feeling a step removed from the crowd. If you two become a couple, it won't be a match made in heaven, but you can build something together that works.

Some of Creature's habits might involve the gay community—perhaps he always attends certain fund-raisers or sees certain friends—but since he views these as things that *he* does, it won't be a big deal if Misfit declines to join him. As long as Misfit isn't closeted so much as discontent, Creature won't mind his partner's lack of gay identity, because it will enable him to have more breathing room. Ideally, he might want a lover who was more into being gay, but if things are good in other ways, Creature of Habit might decide that such concerns are none of his business.

Misfit might respond to the lack of pressure to conform to anything but Creature of Habit's often-eccentric routines and develop a sense of humor about the gay world for the first time. Since Misfit asks a lot of questions about life, Creature of Habit might start to question some of his assumptions about how to live.

In any case, something about Creature of Habit's obsessions strikes Misfit as being out of the ordinary gay groove. Creature of Habit seems somehow more solid or "manly" than some of the more fluttery types of gay men, and this appeals to Misfit. This is especially true when Creature of Habit has interests that seem either unusual (such as collecting recordings of Gregorian chants) or else stereotypically male (such as woodworking). Creature of Habit can help Misfit feel better about being a gay man because there's something substantial about him for Misfit to latch onto.

In the bedroom, Creature of Habit's particular brand of emotional distance is based on his mental energy being elsewhere. While this is not Misfit's ideal arrangement, he can respect the way that Creature of Habit's universe does not revolve exclusively around gay stuff. You're a twosome who might be able to successfully incorporate conversations unrelated to sex into your lovemaking. As long as you don't disagree on anything major, and as long as Misfit is willing to engage in whatever Creature of Habit's steady sexual diet is, you should have a relatively hassle-free time in bed.

Though yours will not be a total, end-all, be-all type of connection, your particular ways of distancing yourselves from the full range of your gayness should mesh together comfortably, because you're unlikely to make unrealistic demands on each other.

What Needs Work: Despite all that might work in your favor, you do not function from quite the same standpoint. Misfit is far more open to new information and change than is Creature of Habit. And Misfit questions, critiques, and dissects in ways that Creature of Habit does not. Over time, Creature of Habit might grow tired of Misfit's endless objections to this or that. At the same time, Misfit might become impatient with Creature of Habit's stubborn business-as-usual manner of living.

While you can help each other to grow in important ways, it can be at the cost of everyday contentment. Misfit discusses things much more than Creature of Habit does, so neither one of you will be happy with how the other handles disagreements. What you like about each other is something that neither one of you quite understands or can articulate, so at times you'll feel as if your relationship is a kind of addiction, or ball and chain—something that you wish would go away. Neither one of you enjoys ambiguity, but to keep your relationship going you'll have to learn to live with it.

Yours is a relationship that might seem more positive in retrospect, after you've broken up and gone your separate ways. You'll think of the ways you gained and grew for having known each other and will tend to forget a lot of the everyday annoyances. If you both decide to stick around for the long haul, you'll want to keep working at the things that hold you back. Creature of Habit has to continually try to be open to new experiences, and Misfit has to let certain realities about the gay experience just *be*, without always wishing they were something else.

CREATURE OF HABIT AND NICE BOY
★★★★

What's Good: Creature of Habit's desire for sameness can mesh quite well with Nice Boy's desire to keep everything humming along happily. Creature of Habit will be drawn to Nice Boy's seemingly uncomplicated manner, and Nice Boy will respond to Creature of Habit's constancy. When there's mutual attraction, you should have a relatively untroubled courtship.

Cynical onlookers at a gay bar might make disparaging remarks about what a goody-two-shoes type of pair you make, and the straight people in your lives might regard you as a stereotypical gay couple. Indeed your conjoined chemistry brings out something that seems a bit fussy and fringy to outsiders. However you actually live as a couple—even if Creature of Habit is into welding or pro wrestling—together you give off an aura of feather-dusted antiques and French poodles. Some might even mistake your relationship for asexual—which it certainly is not. But stereotypes to the contrary, you give each other a great deal of strength, love, and support. You probably couldn't care less about what other people think of your relationship. (And there's nothing wrong with antiques or French poodles.)

Nice Boy will not feel neglected as he stays out of Creature of Habit's way. Instead, he'll feel as if he's part of the picture—it's his role to give his man some space. Because he lives to please others, Nice Boy will be well attuned to Creature of Habit's moods, and he'll know when to bring him a nice, unobtrusive lemonade.

Creature of Habit will enjoy having a partner who stays out of his way and so will come to trust Nice Boy when he suggests that they try something a little different for a change. Creature of Habit might even go so far as to relent on some of his control over daily routines and let Nice Boy call the shots. In giving Creature of Habit space, Nice Boy will learn that detachment can be a way of helping people, and that he need not control other people's moods to be a positive influence in their lives.

In bed, the two of you can explore passion safely, knowing that when it's over, it will not intrude on the smooth fabric of your lives. You're like a happily married Victorian couple who let all sorts of stuff go on behind closed doors, only to act utterly "civilized" at the breakfast table, as though nothing happened the night before. Neither one of you likes to dwell on contradictions, so if your sex life seems incongruous with other aspects of your lives—if it's much kinkier or more aggressive—neither of you will wonder why this is.

You both avoid emotional messes, so you're disinclined to go to sleep angry. You don't exactly talk things out, but Nice Boy will say he's sorry, Creature of Habit will give Nice Boy a kiss, and that will pretty much be that. You have a kind of shorthand together, so outsiders don't understand all that's being communicated between you with just a few words.

What Needs Work: The good times will sometimes be hard to distinguish from the bad, since everything almost always appears to be calm and content—even when it's not. Though you manage to take care of each other quite well considering how little you talk through things, at times *some* unpleasantness will need to be addressed. Nice Boy will have difficulty admitting that he's hurt, angry, or frightened and will insist that he wants only to help Creature of Habit. But Creature of Habit will resist, because this time he does feel crowded; he feels that Nice Boy is trying to manipulate him to avoid the truth, and he's right. Nice Boy needs more reassurance than an occasional shrug, and Creature of Habit will have to learn how to give it. Concurrently, Nice Boy must learn to accept that love and commitment can be present even when his partner is a bit out of sorts.

Also, Creature of Habit often takes for granted the amusing activities a partner brings into his life, and he might find Nice Boy a bit too unexciting. If this happens, Creature of Habit will need to remember that he's probably not contributing toward the creation of an exciting environment that brings out the best in people. After all, is it really fair to criticize your boyfriend for being dull if all you do is invite him over for an evening of cribbage and TV?

At the same time, if there isn't a crisis to shake things up, you both run the risk of falling into the traps of your respective OWTAs. Creature of Habit needs to get out of his rut, and Nice Boy needs to develop a few rough edges, and unless you're both working on improving yourselves, this may not happen. You may end up staying together, but not being nearly as close as you could be. But if in your alert, optimistic ways you are trying to be attentive to your respective needs, strengths, and shortcomings, yours is a match that can go far.

CREATURE OF HABIT AND PAL
★★★★

What's Good: You both like to keep busy. In fact, you're likely to notice each other in an active type of setting other than a bar. Pal will come across much more positively when he's doing something more dynamic than playing campy Cupid. So it's better if Creature of Habit meets Pal when he's running the show at the recycling center or gay hot line. The two of you will sense something simpatico in each other, and the sparks will ignite from there.

Creature of Habit will be happy to have Pal busy himself with other people, because Creature of Habit will want a lot of time to himself. If Pal can learn not to "crowd" Creature of Habit with too many "helpful" suggestions, you should be able to have a harmonious time together.

Pal's quest to keep busy will attract the curiosity of Creature of Habit, who might start giving more of himself to others through Pal's example. He'll still be a Creature of Habit, but in a more altruistic, less isolated way. Under the surface, Pal is extremely shy or insecure about being worthy of intimacy. Creature of Habit's low-key, matter-of-fact approach can help ease him into things. Pal need not feel that too much vulnerability is expected of him all at once.

Neither of you has much staying power when it comes to making love, so neither of you will be deeply hurt if one of you cuts things short to do something else. And by not feeling pressure to prolong bedroom activities, you both might learn to relax and ironically *stop* coming up with excuses for avoiding intimacy. Pal will be happy to oblige Creature of Habit's preferred menu. And if Pal is working on expressing his own needs, he can draw on his instincts for dealing with others to introduce some of his own preferences into Creature of Habit's routine.

This is an especially good combination for parenting. Creature of Habit will gravitate toward a more "masculine" role of bringing home the bacon and fixing things, while Pal will tend to be the motherlike nurturer. (If you live in a progressive, pro-gay community, Pal might take pleasure in chairing the PTA and organizing bake sales.) But whether you raise children or not, you can be a positive and loving influence in each other's life. As a couple you feel as if you're accomplishing something, rather than just taking up space.

What Needs Work: Sitting down to share what's really going on inside is always an issue for Creature of Habit, and Pal is not necessarily the best kind of guy to get him to do so. Pal, after all, also tends to avoid sharing his feelings. Pal might think it's his duty to get Creature of Habit to open up. But Creature of Habit is smart enough to know a one-way street when he sees one and will resent that Pal is asking him to share in ways that Pal is not willing to do himself. You both need to keep working on getting past your Intimacy Blockers to keep your relationship at a four-star level.

Also, Pal had better learn to let Creature of Habit have space to himself, and to offer assistance only when asked for. Otherwise, Creature of Habit will become irritable. He likes to do things himself, and Pal has to avoid the temptation of making Creature of Habit's life his own life. Creature of Habit had best remember to give Pal some periodic assurance that he cares about him—even, yes, loves him—or else Pal will go into his frenzy mode, never slowing down for a second as he flees the insecurity he's feeling.

You also both need to remember that as much as you admire each other for keeping busy, at least some of this busyness stems from an avoidance of other people. Pal may seem much more outgoing, but he isn't. When he's busy with other people, it is but variations on the same theme that Creature of Habit partakes of. Keep this in mind when you're tempted to negatively compare each other by how "sociable" you are or are not.

If you both can remember to take time to appreciate each other, to consider your own needs and the needs of the other, you ought to have a good time together.

CREATURE OF HABIT AND PARTY BOY
★

What's Good: You're the type of gay men who probably barely even notice each other's existence. You might be introduced at a party and nod hello before going off in your respective directions. Creature of Habit will find someone he knows or seems "safe" before looking at his watch to make his excuses and leave, while Party Boy will blather on and on, as if holding court—probably with his back to Creature of Habit. If Creature of Habit gets involved with someone Party Boy knows—or vice versa—you still won't hit it off as friends.

Not getting to know each other is about the best that can be said for the two of you. You have little in common, other than—hopefully—the good sense to stay away from each other.

However, it is of course possible that you'll get together. It's unlikely that Party Boy will live forever in a town without much gay life. But if such is the case—and if Party Boy has already tried out every other guy in town—the two of you might decide that getting involved with each other will be better than nothing. This will be a mistake, but sometimes we learn from our mistakes. (I'm scrounging around for something good to say here, in case you couldn't tell.)

What Needs Work: Essentially, you are each a kind of nightmare reflection of the other. You represent each other's worst fears about what it means to be a gay man. Party Boy lives in dread fear of being like Creature of Habit—the sort of gay man who goes home *alone* to his houseplants, goldfish, or whatever. Creature of Habit cannot begin to comprehend how Party Boy could live the way he does year in and year out. It makes him tired just to think about it. While Creature of Habit doesn't regard himself as the happiest kid on the block, at least he *does things,* whereas Party Boy seems to do nothing but waste time showing off. He is exactly what Creature of Habit avoids trying to be.

If you end up in bed together, it ill be one of those nonsexy sexual interludes that leave you both feeling more hungry for sex than before you bedded up. Whichever one of you played host might even feel the need to shower alone and immediately wash the sheets and towels afterward to dispel any lingering essence of the experience.

Should you decide to become involved, you will clash every step of the way as Party Boy seeks to get out and do things while Creature of Habit seeks the comforts of home. In a social setting, Party Boy will be embarrassed by Creature of Habit's inability to cut loose, while Creature of Habit will be embarrassed by Party Boy's showing off. Home, for Creature of Habit, is where he lives, while for Party Boy it's where he changes his clothes.

You both like to avoid unhappy scenes (though if Party Boy is Under the Influence, he may say things he regrets or doesn't remember). But whether you have a knockdown, drag-out fight or simply stop calling each other, the point will get made that you never want to see each other again. Your failure to hit it off will but reinforce your more extreme habits, since neither one of you wants to be anything like the other.

In group therapy, with professional supervision, it might be worthwhile for you to be forced to talk to each other. But in everyday life, it is highly doubtful that you'll get anything out of being together.

CREATURE OF HABIT AND PERENNIAL CLOSET CASE
★★

What's Good: I've said it before and I'll say it again: I'm reluctant to admit that anything good can come from being or getting involved with a Perennial Closet Case. But sometimes, within the parameters of the relationship per se, some fairly doable combinations exist, and this is one of them. If Creature's habits are not deeply enmeshed in gay activism, and if Perennial Closet Case is willing to quietly pursue a relationship, the two of you might have a fairly good time of it. (Of course, if Perennial Closet Case is some sort of married man seeking a quickie on the sly, Creature of Habit might find it convenient to oblige, whereby there's a whole other way the two of you can hit it off. But such a scenario might be better suited to a porn video. I'm not here to morally judge, but that type of thing is not characteristically what one would mean by *intimacy,* or at least not in a way that's useful for my purposes here. After all, if a quickie's what you want, you don't have to read a book to find it.)

Since Creature of Habit seeks solace, Closet Case's secrecy will not necessarily be a day-to-day problem. Closetness impedes true intimacy, but since Creature of Habit wants to be intimate only here and there, he may not mind the emotional distance in the relationship—in fact, it might seem all too comfortable. Closet Case will feel enabled to stay pretty much in the closet—he won't be constantly hounded or reminded to come out. In the long run, this isn't healthy for him or his relationship, but day by day he can convince himself he has a life.

You both tend to hold back in bed, but if you fall into the routine of being together, you won't mind the lack of passion all that much—or at least you can convince yourselves that such is the case. If the relationship becomes another major routine for Creature of Habit, it may last a long time—and given its longevity, it might even help Closet Case to eventually come out. But what is more likely is that it will fall into a complacent pattern of keeping Closet Case in the closet. If he does eventually come out, it might end the relationship, since Closet Case will symbolically associate Creature of Habit's routines with secrecy and not connecting to others.

As you sort of pleasantly stay out of each other's way, you can both accomplish a great deal in other aspects of your lives. Certainly this is not likely to be a relationship that impedes anyone's professional progress due to its intense emotional turmoil.

What Needs Work: It's always a good idea for Closet Case to come out, so right there is something to be worked on. And if Creature of Habit is working on being more flexible, he can play an active role in helping Closet Case to do so, and the relationship can be stronger, rather than fall apart.

However, once Closet Case comes out, there's no telling *who* he really is, and Creature of Habit might have to be willing to make a lot of adjustments. He might have thought he lived with a Methodist businessman who liked to watch CNN, but suddenly he's living with a Hindu cross-dresser who likes to go hang-gliding. While we're on the subject, Closet Case usually has some sort of sexual kink he doesn't want to face, so once he comes out, Creature of Habit may have to make adjustments in *that* area as well.

In the meantime, Closet Case will experience a fair amount of existential loneliness. Since he isn't really happy with who he is, he'll want more emotional assurance than Creature of Habit is inclined to give him. The kind of blah despair Closet Case feels at times will reinforce his notions about the "inferiority" of same-sex bonding. He might wrongly try to convince himself that his problem is that he's not with a woman. At this point, he might even give being with a woman a try—in which case an innocent party is made part of his web of deceit. Or he might just keep this idea on the back burner and continue to be half-present in his relationship with a man.

This doesn't make Creature of Habit happy, either. He'll retreat even further into his gardening or reading or whatever and pretend that it's all gone away.

Both of you will need to do a lot of reevaluation of yourselves and your relationship, if you are to remain not just together but happily together.

CREATURE OF HABIT AND SEXPOT
★★

What's Good: Like any other red-blooded gay man, Creature of Habit notices Sexpot's obvious charms. But he's likely not to take them seriously. He may be interested in a quick fling with Sexpot, but unless Sexpot shows a more grounded side of himself, it's relatively unlikely that Creature of Habit will be interested in taking things to the next level. Similarly, Sexpot craves a lot of attention, and unless Creature is willing to make Sexpot one of his major pastimes, Sexpot will not be interested, either.

But if these criteria are met, the two of you might try to make things happen. In theory, you can be a positive influence on each other. Sexpot can teach Creature of Habit how to have a little spontaneous fun, and that he has assets beyond the things he usually does. And Creature of Habit can help Sexpot to have more of a "real" life in which everything does not revolve around but one dimension of existence.

But in actual practice, your partnership is likelier to be a partial success at best. It's asking a lot from both of you to meet in the middle when neither of you is inclined to give of yourself in new ways. Nonetheless, you can have your share of pleasurable moments together.

Sexually, Creature of Habit will get his needs more than met by Sexpot. He might even state how nice it is to finally meet a man who knows just how to do whatever it is that Creature likes best. Sexpot will be flattered, of course.

Outside the bedroom, there can probably be at least a few nice moments of exposing each other to your respective worlds. Creature of Habit can give Sexpot a glimpse into a more rigorous way of living. Sexpot can enlighten Creature of Habit on the finer points of cultivating sex appeal. Though it's doubtful that either of you will have a radical effect on the other, you can at least open new windows of opportunity for change.

What Needs Work: In a strange way, you intimidate each other. Creature of Habit is in awe of Sexpot's ability to turn on the allure, and Sexpot is envious of Creature's ability to keep himself company. It's sort of like Katharine Hepburn Meets Marilyn Monroe—or, to use a male example, Woody Allen Meets Fabio. Creature of Habit might well be sexy in his own right, but in comparison with Sexpot he feels decidedly unsexy. Sexpot, in turn, might well be intelligent or diligent in many ways, but next to Creature of Habit he feels dizzy and scattered.

You each represent a kind of "impossible dream" to the other, so you take your failures in your relationship personally. They signal to you that you can't really change, that it was foolish for you to even try. You both need to realize that no Rome to speak of was built in a day. Given the very different viewpoints you function from, it's quite commendable that you're doing as well as you are.

Sexpot is likely to become restless being around Creature of Habit for any length of time. Unless you call time-out and remind yourselves that your differences are similarly about hiding from intimacy, it's likely that major disagreements will erupt. Creature of Habit will emerge more determined than ever to go about his modest routine, and Sexpot will feel more convinced than ever that sex is the only way to get close to a man.

There's a lot of built-in instability in your partnering, but if you both work at it hard, you might be able to get past it all and prove all the skeptics who doubted your relationship wrong. If you can get past your stereotypical view of each other, you'll recognize all you have in *common* as gay men. And from there, you might help each other to realize all your potential, both as individuals and as a couple.

CREATURE OF HABIT AND SHY SNOB
★★★★

What's Good: You two hit it off fast. You recognize in each other an essentially serious approach to life—and this can be especially apparent at a bar or a party, when everyone else is being superficial or frivolous. You don't really share the same sensibility. Shy Snob is much more complicated and changeable. But at first, anyway, you think that you're alike, and you can build something solid from there, even as differences emerge.

Besides, there's a lot you do have in common. Both of you would rather be alone that be in the company of someone who bores you or makes you feel uncomfortable. You'll give each other plenty of room to breathe, because you understand how important it is to have time and space to yourself. And both of you have strong likes and dislikes. One way of getting a conversation going is to commiserate on how flighty or out of control certain people are.

The fundamental difference between you is that Creature of

Habit has resigned himself to never really connecting with people, while Shy Snob intermittently thinks that it's possible. Thus, Shy Snob is both more optimistic and more disappointed. If Creature of Habit can remember to offer a bit of comfort now and then, he can be a calming influence in Shy Snob's life. Shy Snob can learn to have more constancy in his relationships with others from Creature of Habit. He can help Shy Snob realize that he need not constantly change his mind about himself and everyone else just because of minor fluctuations in his encounters.

Shy Snob can help Creature of Habit to set higher standards for himself. Since Shy Snob has a lot of insights to share, Creature of Habit might actually start to question some of his assumptions. And since Shy Snob doesn't pressure him to change, Creature of Habit might actually feel relaxed enough to do so.

If you're lucky, you both have the same strong likes and dislikes in bed. If not, you're both probably willing to look the other way. After all, you feel like a pair of co-conspirators, as if you're in on a secret about life that escapes other people. There's a spirit or attitude to the sex that you both like, anyway. You may or may not resolve your sexual differences down the road, but by then it may not matter much to either of you.

What Needs Work: Creature of Habit may not be the most sociable person in the world, but he probably has some sort of predictable circle of social contacts. Shy Snob, by contrast, is always changing his mind about whom he likes or who likes him. At times he will feel much less socially adept than Creature of Habit. But when he's feeling confident, he can far outshine Creature of Habit socially. Though Shy Snob has trouble making friends, he might be good (for example) at speaking in front of a group.

Thus, he will fluctuate between feeling socially inferior and superior to Creature of Habit. And since so much of Shy Snob's misery revolves around feeling out of place with others, he will feel uncertain about Creature of Habit: Does he envy him or feel sorry for him? Creature of Habit will need to take Shy Snob's attitude shifts with a grain of salt.

Since Creature of Habit is pretty steady, he'll cope with these changes pretty well. But at times he'll feel it's all a big hassle over nothing. Shy Snob will also sometimes be hurt that Creature of Habit values his routines more than he does his lover—especially in those moments when Shy Snob has made a minor mess of his social life.

Also, there's a tendency for the two of you to be a bit too independent. You often have some of your most important experiences alone, and this continues to be the case after you get together as a couple. You need to remember to share with each other what's going on—not just the troubling moments, but the intensely beautiful ones, as well.

If you both can remember that you don't know everything, if Creature of Habit can remember that change is possible, and if Shy Snob can remember that sometimes he's wrong about people, you ought to be able to have a solid and mutually satisfying relationship.

CREATURE OF HABIT AND THERAPY JUNKIE
★

What's Good: Oy, what a mismatch. About the only good thing about it is that it will probably be a mercifully short interlude. Therapy Junkie will be going on and on about his childhood this or that as Creature of Habit sweeps or fixes or whatever he does, and the shared understanding between them will be less than zero. As with the Blue Collar Guy, Therapy Junkie finds that Creature of Habit reminds him of his family in the worst possible way. The communication just isn't going to be there.

Creature of Habit intimidates Therapy Junkie for his steady focus on things that Therapy Junkie finds trivial. So when the breakup comes, Therapy Junkie will probably lack the courage to say all he wants to to Creature of Habit, and the parting of ways will not be as painful or ugly as it could be (which is maybe another relatively good thing about this pairing).

The only way you'll get together in the first place is if Therapy Junkie somehow mistakes Creature of Habit for one of his own kind. Perhaps Creature of Habit thinks Therapy Junkie is cute and pretends to be interested at first when Therapy Junkie goes on about himself. But the truth will soon enough be revealed: you just can't talk to each other. In any event, another kind of "good" thing about this pairing is that there might be a few nice minutes at first, before you both realize how wrong you are about each other.

What Needs Work: The sex will be a disaster because Therapy Junkie will feel as if he's committing incest—and unlike sex with Blue Collar Guy, there isn't even the pretense of deeper intimacy. So to make matters worse, it will seem like *crummy* incest. Creature of Habit, for his part, will know only that something isn't clicking. He often excuses himself early from sexual interludes, but this time it won't be just because he's missing his favorite TV show. It will be because he has to regain his sense of self and control of the situation.

Creature of Habit is uncomfortable dwelling on the type of information that Therapy Junkie lives and breathes for. He won't say the "right things" after Therapy Junkie shares one of his anecdotes; instead he might say something like "It sounds to me like you have it all wrong" or "That reminds me—I have to feed the parakeet." Needless to say, Therapy Junkie will not be impressed, nor will he feel that this is someone safe to be confiding in. To him, Creature of Habit is all he strives not to be: a mindless automaton like his parents. Creature of Habit thinks that Therapy Junkie is immature and narcissistic.

You'll be the opposite of a good influence on each other, because your unpleasant experiences together will make both of you self-righteous about your respective ways of life. Creature of Habit will become that much more a Creature of Habit, and Therapy Junkie will make his shrink wealthy by taking up entire sessions bad-mouthing Creature. You'll convince each other that your respective ruts are better than risking change.

DISCRIMINATING SHOPPER
AND DISCRIMINATING SHOPPER
★★★★

What's Good: Even if you have mismatched standards of perfection in a partner, the capacity is there for the two of you to get something happening big time. Of course, if your standards happen to be compatible, so much the better. The one of you will finally meet that five-ten, black-haired man with a beard who likes Mozart, and the other of you will meet the six-four, punk-rock blond of your dreams. If nothing else, the two of you will for once actually become involved with someone, and this is a big deal in itself.

But even if you don't complement each other appearance-wise (usually a key issue for Discriminating Shoppers), or whatever way else is a must, you'll know a kindred spirit when you see one. Keep a sense of humor about your fantasy ideals, talk about them openly, become close friends, and the capacity is there for The Real Thing. Your lofty ideals are, after all, really just a way of keeping you from getting close to people, and as you get to know each other, you start to realize this. You've both been called the same kind of names by other men and can sympathize with each other's dilemma. You relax for having met someone whom you consider to be your equal—which doesn't happen often. Though you may eventually become more friends than lovers, you'll feel as if you share a secret language no one else understands.

Sexually, you're both able to cut loose. Even if either or both of you are not performing at peak capacity, there will be something deliciously sensual about your pairing. Splitting a glass of ice water, you'll feel as if you were drinking some exotic wine from ancient Greece. You'll let yourselves experiment and be playful. Afterward, you'll feel comfortable and secure about getting dressed and going about your business. You won't worry that you should've lingered longer in bed or that you shouldn't have risked being quite so vulnerable. Something in your pairing indicates that whatever happened, it was fundamentally okay.

You bring out the upscale in each other. How you dress, how

you appoint your home, where you eat or vacation, will become featured aspects of your relationship—not so much out of snobbery, but as an extension of your feelings for each other. You both feel you both deserve the best.

If your existing friendship networks don't fit together well, you'll probably develop your own network together. Yet even if you frequently socialize with others, there's something formal about it, as if you're doing your regal duty to smile and be sociable. You each remain private individuals, but you create another kind of privacy together as a couple. Even your "friends" probably know little about your relationship and sense that it is best not to ask.

What Needs Work: If you got together because you thought you found your perfect match, you will of course have to face the rude awakening of just how superficial your standards were. There's a flesh-and-blood human being behind that tall blond or medium-height brunet, and he may not be easy to live with day to day. Who takes out the garbage and paying the monthly bills become issues in *all* relationships, and the shock of these realities—though they will help you both to grow up—can be challenging.

If you got together despite not matching each other's fantasy, your impossible ideals will continue to haunt you. You'll both have to work at accepting all that's good in what you have, rather than thinking there's some better imaginary ideal out there.

In either case, while the capacity is there to help each other grow as human beings, you both must also remain mindful of your similar shortcomings. You need to reflect on how unrealistic expectations often keep you from being happy—as individuals and as a couple. Remember that your standards don't really reflect what people are like—you only *think* that they do.

Also, since your relationship tends to somewhat distance you from friends, if there are problems in your marriage—or if it comes to an end—you may feel you have no one to turn to. Try to remember that other people are still an important part of your lives. You need to resist the temptation to put other people down behind their back. It's great that the two of you have such a close bond, but don't use it to put yourselves on a pedestal. You need to foster kindness and understanding in each other for your relationship to work, and if you encourage each other to be snooty, it will come back to haunt you.

DISCRIMINATING SHOPPER AND HYPER-ROMANTIC
★

What's Good: Unless there's some desperate situation—say, you're the only two gay men left in the world—it's doubtful that you're going to hook up for long. The only way anything will happen at all is if Hyper-Romantic has the mixed fortune of being Discriminating Shopper's type.

For a while, Discriminating Shopper might put out all kinds of signals to Hyper-Romantic that he's the great love of his life, and Hyper-Romantic will eat it up like so much ambrosia. There might even be a highly impassioned sexual interlude or two. And if it's true that time heals everything, perhaps eventually you can both look back on this philosophically. You can both say to yourselves, "Gee, for two seconds in there, so-and-so said he loved me, and that's a nice little memory."

You both need to wake up to reality, and perhaps you can help each other to do so. Discriminating Shopper needs to learn that his standards are unrealistic and shallow, while Hyper-Romantic must learn about *having* standards, and not just throwing himself at any man who comes along. But you're more likely to cause each other depression and disillusionment, and when that happens, try to heal from it as best you can.

What Needs Work: Though time may well heal everything, in the meanwhile you're likely to put each other through a great deal of pain. Hyper-Romantic will be more convinced than ever that he's somehow unlovable, that even when someone says "You're for me," it turns out not to be true. Because he is so naive, Hyper-Romantic can think being told "I love your red hair" is the same thing as being told "I love you." He doesn't realize it won't be enough to build a relationship on, and neither, of course, does Discriminating Shopper.

If Discriminating Shopper is very young, he may not even be cognizant of how much he's hurt Hyper-Romantic, but if he's been through this kind of thing a few times, he probably feels quite guilty about setting someone up only to have to shoot him down. Hopefully, Hyper-Romantic can lick his wounds and go on to his next instant crush, but it's possible for this to be one of those intense types of relationships in which Hyper-Romantic has trouble letting go.

If you do actually become a couple for any length of time, you will do little to help each other with your respective problems with intimacy. Your fantasies will prove false as you get to know each other as people, but there won't be any sort of communication foundation in place to work past your disillusionment. You haven't a clue as to who each other is as a person. So keeping things together—let alone happily—is going to be a major undertaking.

Of course, it's also possible that Hyper-Romantic will not be Discriminating Shopper's type in the first place, so nothing will develop besides a typical Hyper-Romantic short-term infatuation. In many ways, this will actually be more good than bad.

DISCRIMINATING SHOPPER AND MISFIT
★★★

What's Good: You both have your reasons for keeping people at a distance, and you both understand about principles being more important than momentary pleasure. Discriminating Shopper's issues have to do with specific individuals, while Misfit's are about the gay community in general, and this difference will make for some tensions in your relationship. Nonetheless, it's possible for the two of you to have a pretty good go of it.

Initially, Misfit will need to impress Discriminating Shopper with his unusual worldview. Discriminating Shopper will be intrigued by how much Misfit has to offer. This is a type of man that Discriminating Shopper never thought about before, and Misfit's original ideas just might get Discriminating Shopper to challenge his set ways of thinking. Even if Misfit isn't his type physically, Discriminating Shopper might just decide to give things a try—especially if the two of you know each other as friends first. (However, Misfit should be prepared to have Discriminating Shopper try to change certain things about his appearance.)

Hooking up with Misfit can help Discriminating Shopper to broaden his ideas about gay men and romance and commitment and all that type of stuff. At the same time, Misfit can potentially start to feel more comfortable with the gay world by experiencing it with someone else who can be critical of it, yet—unlike Misfit—is willing to be a part of it.

Socially, it will be like people from two different religions trying to be sporting about meeting people from a different tradition. You may not see eye to eye, but there's a lot of respect there. Your respective friends will probably become pleasant acquaintances at best for your partner, but that can be a lot nicer than bitter enemies.

In bed, the two of you will be at ease—more or less. There will be a slight tendency to talk more than make love. Yours is the type of union that improves with time—as Misfit becomes more comfortable with himself and as Discriminating Shopper learns that imperfection can be pretty good, after all. You work together especially well if Misfit has some large-scale goal for his life. In such a scenario, Discriminating Shopper will excuse Misfit's somewhat erratic personality in admiration for his "genius" and will use his taste and judgment to help Misfit get ahead.

What Needs Work: Especially at first, Discriminating Shopper will need to be patient about partnering with someone who is much more complex than any fantasy ideal. It will be good for Discriminating Shopper to experience this, as it will help him get past his superficial stereotypes. But for this to happen, he has to hang in there.

Additionally, Misfit must be willing to set aside some of his own tastes and habits, because Discriminating Shopper (though he will be a supportive mate) is nobody's drudge, and he has no intention of completely buying into Misfit's world. If you both approach your relationship as something that will enrich you as individuals, you ought to be able to keep the big picture in mind.

At first, Discriminating Shopper will seem to have the upper hand, since he's more reluctant to make a commitment. But over time, the balance will shift over to Misfit. Once Discriminating Shopper commits, he's idealistic and will be the supportive one as Misfit elaborates his worldview. Discriminating Shopper will act as if he's married to a genius and will subordinate his own needs so that Misfit can have his way.

Thus, Discriminating Shopper will have to make sure that petty resentments don't fester into major ones. When Misfit gets on his nerves, he needs to say so, but in a way that encourages open communication. Rather than simply being critical, Discriminating Shopper should emphasize the special world the two of you share, and how much more special it will be if you can work together on changing some things about it.

Also, Misfit needs to continually work on accepting himself as a gay man. Discriminating Shopper is not particularly imaginative, and his perfectionist standards are usually gay male norms taken to an extreme (i.e., a man who's butch enough, well-dressed enough, or what have you). Therefore, at times Misfit's essential bad feeling about the gay world will clash with Discriminating Shopper's essentially good feeling about it. At such moments, you'll need to meet somewhere in the middle and realize that both of you are being extreme in your thinking.

DISCRIMINATING SHOPPER AND NICE BOY
★★

What's Good: If on the surface Nice Boy is very much Discriminating Shopper's type, and if Nice Boy doesn't find Discriminating
Shopper a bit too emotionally distant, the two of you might start
something up. Your arrangement will come as a surprise to your
friends, because you don't seem temperamentally well-matched.
Even if you hang out in the same circles, Discriminating Shopper
is somehow too restless and distracted to be an easy match for Nice
Boy—who everyone always felt would end up with someone . . .
well, *nicer*. It's not that Discriminating Shopper is mean, but he can
be impatient and self-directed, and even if his manners are impec-
cable, his perfectionism makes him seem much more embattled than
Nice Boy.

This said, it's possible for the two of you to maintain something
together, provided that Nice Boy is working on being less super-
nice and lets loose with a few acerbic thoughts once in a while.
Otherwise, Discriminating Shopper is likely to get bored. Similarly,
Discriminating Shopper needs to be working on acceptance of other
people's flaws in order to remember that Nice Boy's responses often
stem from insecurity or fear.

When you feel like you're communicating, the sex between you
can get pretty hot. Nice Boy will let fly with his horniness, and
Discriminating Shopper will stay interested. But there's a strong possibility you'll eventually do better as friends. Even if he's physical
perfection for Discriminating Shopper, Nice Boy may not have
enough edges for Discriminating Shopper to sink his teeth into (I
am speaking purely metaphorically, of course). But even then it's
possible to look back on your time together as a pleasant interlude.

If you end up living together, things run the risk of getting a bit
humdrum. Discriminating Shopper will be antsy for a new adventure, and Nice Boy will go about dusting and ironing as though
nothing were wrong. But at least it's unlikely for anything truly *ugly*
to happen.

What Needs Work: Nice Boy has an ambivalent attitude toward Discriminating Shopper. Part of him senses he should stay away, that there are things going on inside this other man that are out of his range. But since Nice Boy likes to think that being nice can solve everything (plus it's a way of camouflaging his fear), another part of him sees Discriminating Shopper as a challenge.

Therefore, Discriminating Shopper tends to bring out the same old Intimacy Blockers in Nice Boy—he inspires him to hide behind his nice-nice mask. Simultaneously, Nice Boy can earn the perfectionist scorn of Discriminating Shopper when he seems relatively monolithic over time. When Nice Boy no longer engages him, Discriminating Shopper will abruptly start to look elsewhere and repeat his usual patterns.

Even though he's often more polite about it as he matures, Discriminating Shopper will ultimately speak up when he's not interested in taking things further, and Nice Boy will not know how to respond, other than to act as if everything were perfectly okay. It isn't, of course, and Discriminating Shopper sees through Nice Boy's act.

Since he doesn't like to think that there are things more important than his pursuit of Mr. Perfect, Discriminating Shopper will not want to dwell on having hurt Nice Boy's feelings. He'll resent Nice Boy's mere presence if it reminds him of having done so. Nice Boy will need to back off for at least a while when Discriminating Shopper is distancing himself emotionally—for his own good as much as for the continuation of some sort of friendship.

Your combined chemistry does not easily inspire strong emotional affinity, nor does it lend itself to deep communication. Being on different wavelengths can be interesting and useful in a relationship, but the two of you will have to work hard on yourselves to make it happen.

DISCRIMINATING SHOPPER AND PAL
★

What's Good: As with certain other combinations, the two of you are unlikely to be in sync, unless Discriminating Shopper somehow feels that Pal is his type. Even as such, the attraction is likely to be short-lived—at least on the part of Discriminating Shopper. Pal might well have a major torch for Discriminating Shopper, but he's unlikely to express it in a way that Discriminating Shopper finds appealing. Pal's energies are focused on too many people, and he shies away from romance for himself. So Discriminating Shopper is likely to move on—whereupon Pal is likely to drown his sorrows in helping other people.

However, the lack of chemistry between the two of you will be experienced in a fairly nonlethal way. Discriminating Shopper is well accustomed to discovering that a man isn't right for him, and Pal never really believed that someone as loftily sure of himself as Discriminating Shopper could ever have taken him seriously as a love interest. So he'll be saddened but not surprised when things don't work out.

The two of you might be able to make good friends. Pal can help Discriminating Shopper to shop around, which of course is not really good for either one of you, but it can give you something in common. In fact, even if you become intimate, there may well be an element of this going on. It's as if Pal takes it for granted that Discriminating Shopper will eventually look elsewhere, and so he'll do him the favor of pointing out this or that cute guy to get it over with, and to make it seem as if he were a good sport.

In sum, what's good ain't all that good. But technically, it won't kill either of you to give it a try.

What Needs Work: For the two of you to tough it out for the long haul, something needs to happen that makes it unlikely for you to split up—or more to the point, for Discriminating Shopper to leave Pal. Perhaps Pal has serious health problems, or Discriminating Shopper is out of work. Or maybe Discriminating Shopper was recently taught a lesson in humility, and so he says things to Pal about love and commitment he doesn't really mean—and then he doesn't know how to take them back.

However it happens that the two of you become committed to each other, you both need to work hard on the issues that keep you from having intimacy. Discriminating Shopper will need to radically reprogram his thinking about an ideal mate, and Pal will need to work especially hard at seeing himself as a gay man entitled to love and sexiness and the whole enchilada.

Sexually, you connect out of neediness, but not in a way that encourages closeness. Discriminating Shopper's mind will be elsewhere, and he'll fluctuate between resenting Pal's presence in his life and feeling guilty that he feels that way. Pal will be hurt and confused by the mixed signals and will ask Discriminating Shopper if something's bothering him, because if so, Pal is all ears and wants to help. You both keep feeling worse and worse. The more you talk, the more you feel yourselves slipping into something unhealthy, until finally the whole thing comes to an end—maybe by forging a new type of relationship together, but probably by splitting up.

DISCRIMINATING SHOPPER AND PARTY BOY
★★★★

What's Good: The two of you can provide each other with the right kind of love and support to get beyond your hang-ups with intimacy. Discriminating Shopper will provide Party Boy with a deeper, healthily cynical sense of what's transpiring beyond the drinking and dancing and noise. This helps Party Boy start to feel grounded in reality, and to stop being quite so awed by escapism. In a lighthearted way, Party Boy can participate in Discriminating Shopper's ongoing evaluation of other men, whereby Discriminating Shopper might start to take some of his rigid standards less seriously and see the good—and the fun—in all kinds of different people.

Even if there's not an immediate spark, you can be like one of those couples in the movies that start out as friends, commiserate on the lack of good men, and end up realizing that what you wanted was right there in your own backyard, so to speak. You can be on similar wavelengths, something that you both often avoid having with another person, but which can be a most welcome surprise when it doesn't feel threatening. It will probably take a little time for things to really start to gel between you—and patience is not the strongest suit for either of you. But with humor and a relaxed attitude about the whole thing, the two of you can make it together in a big way.

The surprise of finding each other can awaken you both sexually, and you'll be at your most daring and playful together. Even if either or both of you are feeling tired or distracted, there's something breezy and sexy about your being together. You'll want to be mindful, though, of not doing anything too risky in bed, as the potential is there to let out all stops. Hopefully, you're having a sobering influence on each other and will be able to intelligently talk these issues out.

You both have good social skills when you feel like it, and being with each other will tend to make that happen. Party Boy will keep Discriminating Shopper from withdrawing too far into himself, and Discriminating Shopper's high standards will keep Party Boy from lapsing over into rudeness. Of course, at times you'll be a *bad* influence on each other and get a bit full of yourselves, showing off or putting other people down. But if you can keep yourselves grounded in reality most of the time, you'll be much more good for each other than bad.

What Needs Work: Discriminating Shopper so seldom gives another guy a chance that he'll be hurt when the rather casual Party Boy doesn't seem to realize what a big deal it was to have been let into his life. In fact, Party Boy will tend to hold the upper hand over time, even thought it may at first seem the other way around. Discriminating Shopper will be more concerned about breaking up, because it was so unusual of him to come even this far, while Party

Boy can fairly easily fall back into his old habits of trying to drown his pain.

This is not to say that Discriminating Shopper is otherwise totally content. Since he's socializing more than ever by hanging with Party Boy, he'll see that many more men—and male couples—to stir his feelings of restlessness. He'll want some apple on a farther branch of the tree and think his relationship pales besides someone else's.

Discriminating Shopper might occasionally be offended by Party Boy's over-the-top behavior. In a way, this is good for Discriminating Shopper, as it can help to get him off his high horse. But he's unlikely to think so in the spur of the moment. Party Boy will also need to resist the temptation to make fun of Discriminating Shopper—particularly in the presence of other people. *That* will most definitely not be well received.

You need to be extremely honest with each other about your lifelong habits as gay men avoiding intimacy—that Discriminating Shopper dissects everything away so that he doesn't have to commit to it, and that Party Boy tries to hide from his feelings and essential aloneness through overstimulation. If you can keep these issues in mind, you should be able to have a fun and meaningful time together.

DISCRIMINATING SHOPPER
AND PERENNIAL CLOSET CASE
★

What's Good: Not much. Discriminating Shopper wants what he wants, and a man who's afraid to come out is not likely to rank high on his list. If Closet Case is very, very much his type otherwise, Discriminating Shopper might take a chance. There's even the possibility of some extremely hot sex at first, since Discriminating Shopper tends to run hot and cold in the bedroom (and this time he's hot), and Closet Case often puts a lot of passion into his lovemaking (even if he still holds back).

Also, since Discriminating Shopper tends to move on fast and Closet Case keeps doing whatever it is that he does, you're likely to get over each other quickly, like dogs shaking themselves dry. And before you get to that point, there might be some pleasant moments of the two of you trying to bond, to maximize that spark of attraction and get past all that is preventing you from getting close.

What Needs Work: When he makes a commitment, Discriminating Shopper takes it seriously. He wants to believe he chose well, and that all the comparison shopping he did was well worth the wait. Moreover, he wants to show off his catch to others. Even if at first he tries to rationalize and say, "Oh, well, I'm not always out to everybody, either," over time, Closet Case's inability to own up to who he is will depress Discriminating Shopper, who will come to feel trapped and unhappy. He'll learn that just because a man has curly black hair, it doesn't mean he's right for him—but not in a constructive, introspective kind of way, because Closet Case's inability to get close will be much too annoying.

Since Discriminating Shopper tends to base his choices on superficial qualities, he isn't prepared for the lack of closeness he'll feel with Closet Case. And Closet Case will not be encouraged to come out, because Discriminating Shopper appears willing to forgive him his closetness since he wears a brown crew cut. In other words, you do little to help each other get past the issues keeping you from finding intimacy.

The initial sexual chemistry will dissipate rather quickly. Probably Closet Case will be the one who tries to keep things happening, and he won't understand why Discriminating Shopper is withdrawing—becoming less present in bed, and even being in the mood for sex less and less often. Closet Case relates to the gay experience largely through sex, and so he'll feel that much more cut off from his gay identity when he feels his lover is rejecting him.

DISCRIMINATING SHOPPER AND SEXPOT
★★★

What's Good: Obviously, if Sexpot is Discriminating Shopper's type, he will be his type and then some. Sexpot really knows how to turn on the charm, and Discriminating Shopper will be as proud as can be to show off his catch. Discriminating Shopper doesn't fall for just anybody, so his enthusiasm will make Sexpot feel especially flattered.

If Sexpot isn't Discriminating Shopper's exact type, he still has plenty of natural assets. Discriminating Shopper might find himself thinking that while he usually doesn't go for redheads or shorter men (or whatever Sexpot looks like), this time he finds himself strangely attracted. Of course, Discriminating Shopper will fail to grasp that so does most everyone else—that he isn't being nearly as profound as he thinks he is. Still, since both of you live largely for looks, it shouldn't be too difficult to form an alliance.

Discriminating Shopper has a lot of pent-up need to give, and Sexpot will be an eager recipient. Sexpot's mere presence in his life will do much to convince Discriminating Shopper that he really does deserve the best.

In so many words, yours becomes the sort of gay relationship that others often criticize for being shallow. You'll buy this and travel to there and be impressive to look at, but people might wonder what the two of you talk about when no one's watching. Of course there's more to your relationship than meets the eye, but your combined energies make for a coupling based excessively on style. Still, you could both do much worse.

Sexually, things will be hot and heavy, if not especially emotional. It will be more like a first-rate porn movie than a romance. Sexpot is always eager to please in bed, and Discriminating Shopper will feel rather like a pampered sugar daddy as his most exotic fantasies are fulfilled. Discriminating Shopper will not get to give of himself as much as he secretly longs to do, but he'll manage to have a pretty good time, anyway.

Over time, you'll probably develop a kind of sexy semi-estrangement. You'll be together and apart, and back together again, with numerous interludes with other men along the way. Somehow, all the fluctuations are carried out with spirit and mutual respect, as if you're at your closest and sexiest as a couple when you're furthest apart from each other. It's not the kind of arrangement that works for everyone, but the two of you can have fun with it.

What Needs Work: Discriminating Shopper needs to grow beyond his fickleness, and Sexpot needs to learn he has more to offer than looks and/or sex. You will not tend to help each other in the ways you need to grow. If anything, Sexpot will confirm Discriminating Shopper's callow values, and Discriminating Shopper will reinforce Sexpot's limited notions regarding the way to a man's heart. You both need to look beyond the surface and find qualities in yourself—and each other—to forge a deeper union.

You gravitate toward upscale activities, and though some of these events might benefit worthy causes, you tend to get a bit full of yourselves and lose empathy for those less fortunate. You'll tend to attract other upscale gay men—especially couples—and though you have an active social circle, they tend to be fair-weather friends. When problems arise, you may feel that you have no one to turn to.

In fact, a major crisis might well prove to be the turning point of your relationship. Since you haven't based much of your interactions on inner qualities, a big disaster might well signal the parting of ways. Yet it's also possible that such an experience can be the starting point for a new kind of closeness beyond the surface niceties of life. If you feel that you need each other much more than you realized, you can grow closer than ever before. By working on your intimacy issues, you can each discover the "real" man that you're involved with and maybe even decide—surprise of surprises—that you like who he is for himself.

But it's also possible that you'll simply get bored with each other. Sexpot often has a short attention span with men, and Discriminating Shopper might realize that great looks aren't always all they're cracked up to be. If things don't last forever, the parting of ways will probably be relatively quick and painless, because underneath it all you understand each other. You both are energized by a certain type of scorn toward other men. You won't have much reason to remain friendly, but over time you'll remember each other in a sensual way.

DISCRIMINATING SHOPPER AND SHY SNOB
★★★★

What's Good: Even if Shy Snob is not Discriminating Shopper's perfect physical type, the possibilities are there for a strong long-term match that enables each of you to grow as people. You might need to become friends first, but that shouldn't be too difficult. You're the type of twosome who start talking at a bar and in about five minutes feel as if you've known each other all your lives. Shy Snob is much more introspective than Discriminating Shopper, but you both have experienced a lot of hot/cold relationships with men, and this forms a bond between you. If you're both immature, you might simply become jaded best friends. But if time has improved your characters, you'll see the wisdom of pairing up with someone who understands your peculiar type of aloneness.

You probably won't have much of a social life together. Your combined energies tend to keep other people at arm's length, as if there's a special language that only the two of you know. But you can keep each other well entertained, so it probably won't matter that much. What is more important is that you both have a kind of strength that serves the other well. To be accepted by Discriminating Shopper is all but the equivalent of being knighted, and so Shy Snob will feel more confident and likable. His tendency to feel either better or worse than other people can get a bit more anchored in the middle, between the two extremes. And Shy Snob can get inside Discriminating Shopper's drive for perfection in a partner and help him to unravel the Intimacy Blockers standing in his way.

Not that your being together will be a twenty-four-hour-a-day encounter group. You'll make each other laugh—at other people, but also at yourselves. You can appreciate the "finer" (that is, expensive) things in life, yet you also permit each other to let down your respective facades and admit to some of life's more mundane pleasures. You're like a pair of rich kids from an old movie who have the greatest time in the world tripping in the mud.

Sexually, you can both be on fire, but if one or both of you is in an icy mood, that can be okay, too. With trust and good communication, you can develop patience for each other's moments of emotional distance—which for both of you also signals physical distance. And with a little imagination, you can engage in some interesting domination fantasies during those times that neither one of you feels like being mushy.

When it comes to emotions and commitment, Shy Snob will feel more insecure. But he'll tend to run the show when it comes to sharing ideas and information. He may even serve as a kind of mentor to Discriminating Shopper, helping him to refine his intellect and to direct his inherent good taste into a more creative and productive outlet.

What Needs Work: Discriminating Shopper will not be accustomed to living on quite so complex a level as Shy Snob and will at times wish that life could be simpler. Also, of course, Discriminating Shopper must work at getting beyond his unrealistic standards of perfection. Shy Snob will sense when Discriminating Shopper isn't fully present. At the same time, Shy Snob often retreats into himself in his own way. There will be moments of silence that tend to make both of you uncomfortable.

This goes for sex, too. Neither of you is inclined to speak up if something is happening that *isn't* making it happen for you. Discriminating Shopper is accustomed to making his excuses and leaving at such moments, but if he wants to remain in a committed relationship, he'll have to do better than that. Shy Snob will need to stop "nobly" enduring such instances and learn how to assert his needs to another man.

Socially, you'll need to be careful that you don't shut out too many people. Even when you have old friends over, there will be something stilted about it—no one will be at ease, and there is often a feeling of "Thank God I survived that" at the end of the evening. If your friends are not meshing well with your coupledom, make a point of seeing your friends individually.

But if both of you are working on the issues that stand in the way of intimacy, any problems you suffer ought to be quite workable.

DISCRIMINATING SHOPPER AND THERAPY JUNKIE
★★★

What's Good: The two of you ought to be able to hit it off—though like other types of men, Therapy Junkie may have to win Discriminating Shopper's friendship first if he isn't his exact type. Over time, Discriminating Shopper can look past the surface and see that Therapy Junkie has a lot to teach him about exploring himself and looking less to other people to make him happy. Therapy Junkie will be flattered that a man with such obvious high standards chose him, and he may just start to mellow out and learn to live more spontaneously.

Since you both have strong likes and dislikes in the bedroom, you ought to be able to respect each other's tastes. And since you both also have a desire to go hog wild with the right partner, you can make all kinds of fun stuff happen. Unless Discriminating Shopper is completely turned off by what turns on Therapy Junkie, he could well be the man who finally enables Therapy Junkie to cut loose in bed and explore his suppressed fantasies.

Discriminating Shopper can encourage Therapy Junkie to start actualizing his goals in life and stop putting them off until some lofty point in the future when he's "ready" for them. Therapy Junkie can imbue Discriminating Shopper's daily routine with more depth and insight, and more understanding of other people. In contrasting ways, you can help each other to get ahead in life.

Probably you'll both like *some* of your partner's friends and family, but not all of them. Discriminating Shopper will find some of the people in Therapy Junkie's world simply too flaky or weird. In fact, he might well help Therapy Junkie to develop different standards in making friends, and to stop being quite so drawn to people on the basis of how messed up they are. Therapy Junkie will probably think some of Discriminating Shopper's friends are rather vapid, and he can help Discriminating Shopper to bring people into his life that have more depth.

What Needs Work: Therapy Junkie will need to remember that life is to be enjoyed, not dissected, and that people are for getting close to, not analyzed. Otherwise, Discriminating Shopper will tend to get bored with Therapy Junkie's endless commiserations about his past and his "issues" and the like. This can be especially true in the bedroom. Past a certain point, Discriminating Shopper simply wants to get on with it, but Therapy Junkie can get carried away with all sorts of psychological concerns.

Furthermore, Discriminating Shopper needs to remember that many of his standards are unrealistic and come from a fear of what the neighbors (or whomever) will think of him. Though Therapy Junkie gets carried away with his "problems," it must be remembered that he has a sincere desire to be true to *himself,* and not other people. When Discriminating Shopper feels exasperated with Therapy Junkie or simply feels like moving on, he'll need to remember that Therapy Junkie has something to teach him.

The differences in your social worlds can make for some heated disputes. There simply might be people you'll both have to put on hold, if you want the relationship to work. It's one thing to expect each other to make allowances for yourself, but quite another to expect each other to make the same allowances for outsiders. If Discriminating Shopper finds one of Therapy Junkie's friends to be infantile, Therapy Junkie may just need to cool it with said friend as politely as possible. The same can be said for the friend of Discriminating Shopper's that Therapy Junkie deems a total airhead. Usually, I don't advocate dropping friends for the sake of your lover, but in this instance you're both probably right, and you both would be better off meeting new people.

If you both can remember to respect your differences, and to realize you can learn from them, you can have a relationship in which the good very much outweighs the bad.

———

HYPER-ROMANTIC AND HYPER-ROMANTIC
★★★

What's Good: At first, the two of you will be pretty disgusting to be around. It will be like Pepe Le Pew meets Pepe Le Pew. You'll slobber over each other like there's no tomorrow. What is more, you'll both be totally convinced that what the two of you share is unprecedented in human history. You'll get smug and smarmy when you think about all those poor single gay men out there (in particular the ones who rejected both of you) who do not know the ecstasy of having your relationship. What's their problem, anyway? Why don't they want your total, all-encompassing love that takes them to undreamed-of heights?

There will be no such thing as keeping the other party on the phone too long—if indeed you are out of each other's sight long enough to necessitate a phone call. Friends, family, career responsibilities—all pale in comparison with finally having found The Real Thing, and indeed other responsibilities will no longer receive your best effort.

Sexually, you're both ready to let it all hang out and then some. Since you both like to show off in bed, you'll all but engage in a competition over who can give the most pleasure to whom—just as you'll each want to be the one who loves the other the most. Even if what your partner is doing ain't as great as all that, you'll probably act as if it is, to keep the momentum going. You want nothing to get in the way of true love—ironically, not even the man you're supposedly in love with.

You'll want to move in together quickly. As for who pays what bill when, or who likes what TV show, all that can be sorted out later. This is a chance for love, and neither of you is about to throw it away over anything so trivial as real life. You'll give each other every conceivable benefit of the doubt . . . at first, anyway.

What Needs Work: Incredible as it may seem, your rapturous rush of being in a relationship will wear off. You may say in advance, "Oh, well, that won't bother me. I'll always just be so grateful to be married that I'll never complain about my partner." But in reality, it will bother you, because you think that being in a relationship will do things for you that it doesn't do. That's when you have to start getting to know each other as human beings—and, yes, money squabbles or even different tastes in TV shows can take their toll.

If your initial mutual attraction is extremely powerful—and if you've already gone ahead and moved in together—there might be enough basis for continuing the relationship. After all, you've come this far, and as long as no one is being cruel to anyone else, you might be able to work through whatever differences emerge and learn something about yourselves in the bargain.

To hang in there, you'll both have to develop some tough skin PDQ and learn to articulate—and listen to—what you really think of the relationship: "No, I don't really like it when you nibble my ear." "No, I don't really want to learn how to go sailing." "Actually, I think your boss is right and you're wrong." *Ouch!* The truth can hurt, especially when it flies in the face of the romantic fallacy you thought was the truth.

To some extent, you'll both always be the kind of gay men who are eager to settle down, and this is no minor sensibility to have in common. But you need to work diligently on the ways you keep yourselves from finding true intimacy—the ways in which you try to obliterate your real needs, feelings, and personalities for the sup-posedly higher purpose of being married. As you become more centered within yourselves, you might well find a relationship to-gether that features both a strong commitment and honest com-munication. This will actually be a better relationship than the one you *think* you want.

HYPER-ROMANTIC AND MISFIT
★★

What's Good: You both feel you have the right to sing the blues when it comes to the gay world. Of course, it's for different reasons. Hyper-Romantic bemoans that he can't nab a husband, while Misfit bemoans something more sociocultural. But somewhere along the way you both might use the word *superficial* and think you have more in common than you do. Since Hyper-Romantic will initially try to blend into the man he's with, Misfit won't have to try to be "more gay" than he wants to be, and the two of you might decide to make things happen.

How well it works will depend a lot on what Hyper-Romantic is actually like, as opposed to the personality he projects in his quest to get married no matter what. If he's too "gay acting"—or perhaps, even worse, has stereotypical gay tastes—Misfit won't stay in the relationship for long. The exception occurs when Misfit is simply so lonely for a partner that he'll make a go of it despite his reservations (though one could argue that this is not exactly a plus).

Sexually, Hyper-Romantic will have to follow Misfit's lead and tone it down a few notches. Misfit, after all, has to work on getting fully comfortable with his gay identity, and too much intensity too soon can turn him off. Especially when it isn't backed up by something deeper.

If Hyper-Romantic is willing to take on Misfit's social world as his own—and if he can do so convincingly—Misfit will be pleased in an oblivious, rather stereotypically male way. In other words, this is a combination in which Hyper-Romantic must assume a sort of traditional wifely role of following the lead of the Misfit husband. Hyper-Romantic will have to play a shrewd hand of cards—and truly enjoy doing so—for this pairing to last.

What Needs Work: Even if you tough it out, you need to work hard at understanding each other. Hyper-Romantic needs to realize that Misfit has some internalized homophobia to work through.

Underneath Misfit's bravado and often articulate criticisms of the gay world is a man who's insecure in his gay identity, and who also doesn't feel quite at ease in the straight world. He feels it's unfair to be regarded as a social outcast simply because he's being himself. His resentments run deep—more so than Hyper-Romantic might be willing to have patience for.

Hyper-Romantic is insecure, too, though it has more to do with a fear of being left all alone. Misfit needs to understand a level of loneliness he doesn't know much about. Not that Misfit never feels lonely. But he's a deep thinker and he's resourceful within himself in ways that Hyper-Romantic has never explored. The way Misfit might feel on an especially disconfirming day is how Hyper-Romantic feels regularly.

Try though he may to turn into a different person, Hyper-Romantic will find his actual personality peeping out over time, and if he's dying to play his Madonna records, Misfit will have to let him. Though a seemingly small gesture, it is wrought with symbolic meaning for Misfit. It signals that he's letting his partner follow the gay herd—and perhaps by extension, he is giving permission to himself, as well.

Sexually, Misfit should encourage Hyper-Romantic to express himself and let him take the lead once in a while. Otherwise, Hyper-Romantic will feel crushed and defeated over time, and—impossible though it may seem—actually start to withdraw sexually.

Despite having in common a sense of disappointment with the gay experience, you don't really speak the same language. Only if you tap into something honest within yourselves will you build a relationship that not only technically exists, but is mutually fulfilling.

HYPER-ROMANTIC AND NICE BOY
★★★★

What's Good: Though outsiders might find your relationship to be a bit on the vanilla side, inspiring brittle declarations of "How nice" behind your backs, you make a good couple. You do not find each other to be a threat, since you both shy away from edginess and attitude. The two of you not only get along but bring out a quiet strength in each other. As you go through life together, you have the potential to grow and gain and stop fearing the things that hold you back. Since neither of you likes to dwell on life's unpleasantries, you're unlikely to care what other people think of you as a couple.

Besides, there are things about your relationship that nobody else knows. Nice Boy can be something of a Bad Boy when it comes to sex. He can also encourage Hyper-Romantic to relax and be himself. Hyper-Romantic is unlikely to care—or perhaps will not even notice—how Nice Boy's demeanor changes in the bedroom. So Nice Boy is unlikely to end up pissing him off (as can happen with certain other types of men).

Your home life will be orderly. Nice Boy usually likes things to be just so, and Hyper-Romantic will do his best to conform. Unless Hyper-Romantic is a total slob around the house, Nice Boy won't mind having to pick up after him from time to time. When you entertain, there will be coasters under every glass. The conversation will purposefully be on the polite, noncontroversial side—a kind of after-dinner-mint atmosphere will dominate.

Nice Boy is not the type to do whatever it takes to get ahead in life, and Hyper-Romantic doesn't care much about his career, unless it's a chance to meet a husband. So unless one of you comes from a wealthy family, money might be more of a problem than it appears to be on the surface. But you'll make the most of the social opportunities available to you.

Hyper-Romantic needs to learn that happiness starts with himself, and Nice Boy must learn to face the more unseemly side of life—he has to learn that not everything has to be "nice." Your ability to hang in there together will take you both a long way toward accomplishing these goals. As life presents its inevitable challenges, you'll have the potential to rise to the occasion and find ways of being brave that you never knew you had in you.

What Needs Work: Whether you actually *do* rise to the occasion will be up to the both of you. There's always the possibility that Hyper-Romantic's desire to have a boyfriend no matter what and Nice Boy's determination to keep everything under his control will undermine the relationship. Things will start to go wrong, and there will be little to fall back on as you both go about pretending everything's okay.

Even before there's a serious problem, the temptation will be there to avoid confrontations. Minor resentments have a way of festering into major ones if they aren't talked out. There will be a tendency for Nice Boy, in his quiet, passive-aggressive way, to control the tone of the relationship. Hyper-Romantic has to take the energy he puts into selling himself and redirect it toward asserting himself. Because if he's not going to be himself, Hyper-Romantic isn't going to be happy over time. If he can remember to be romantic about it—if he can couch his criticisms with compliments and kisses and maybe even a few small trinkets—Nice Boy will have an easier time accepting the "unpleasantness" at hand.

Also, Hyper-Romantic must be careful not to make himself into whatever Nice Boy wants him to be—and beneath his gentle facade, Nice Boy always has an agenda. Hyper-Romantic tends to be compliant and passive in relationships, but at times he'll need to affect his butchest demeanor to lay down the law with Nice Boy. Again, Hyper-Romantic should do it in a kind, friendly way, but he needs to make it clear that his destiny is his own. Nice Boy, in turn, will have to accept Hyper-Romantic's extreme emotional expressiveness and let down his guard enough to feel flattered by it.

Keep working away at learning to be comfortable within yourselves, and you should have a happy time together—if not always "nice."

HYPER-ROMANTIC AND PAL
★★★★

What's Good: You will probably start out as friends, because Pal is not one to wear his heart on his sleeve. Even if you have sex right away, it might take Hyper-Romantic a while to understand how Pal feels about him. At first, he might interpret Pal's relentless pre-occupation with others as rejection.

Once you've figured out that you both want the same thing, you can be beneficial to each other. Hyper-Romantic will help Pal to realize he's worthy of being loved. Pal might just slow down a bit and start acting like his own man. His good deeds, when enacted moderately and out of self-worth, can help Hyper-Romantic de-velop concern for matters beyond his marital state. You're the kind of couple that can have a *romantic* time volunteering to stuff enve-lopes for a gay rights fund-raiser.

Your combined chemistry makes for a great deal of shyness in bed. For contrasting reasons, you both want to please your partner more than yourself, so you're like a dancing couple in which nobody knows how to lead. But over time, this can prove to be an advan-tage. You'll have to develop from square one a sexual rhythm that's mutually satisfying, beyond all the games and false generosity you think is expected of yourselves.

You energize each other, and as a couple you tend to be on the go. Your house will not always be immaculate, and even if one of you is a gourmet chef, you'll tend to just throw stuff together for dinner. You'll often feel as if you're working on a project together, even if it's just shopping together at the supermarket. Chances are you would make good fathers, if that's something you want to do.

Men in general often have an easier time doing than being, but the two of you together can find a way to imbue your activities with a sense of self and purpose.

What Needs Work: Hyper-Romantic tends to force-fit himself into another man's life. So when he starts imitating Pal's helpfulness, Pal might resent Hyper-Romantic for stealing some of his thunder. At his worst, Pal wants to be acclaimed for his good deeds as much as he wants the problem at hand to be resolved. Pal will need to remember that he has value as a person beyond the things he does for other people. And Hyper-Romantic needs to develop his own life and not just try to glom on to someone else's.

With all due respect for the way the two of you can create something splendid under the sheets, there's always the possibility that either or both of you won't be willing to get beyond your Intimacy Blockers in this regard. If such is the case, your sex life can be a major dud. You both need to ask each other what you enjoy sexually, since neither of you is likely to be self-assertive. If the truthful answer is "I don't know," the other partner should simply start experimenting until something clicks.

When Pal is feeling moody or irritable, Hyper-Romantic will not think he has much of a romance. Hyper-Romantic will need to remember that in real life nothing is romantic all the time. Pal must get in touch with whatever it is that's bugging him and realize that it might have to do with feeling underappreciated—whether by his partner or by somebody else. If Pal can remember to ask for a little TLC at such moments, Hyper-Romantic will probably be happy to oblige, and all the grumpiness will melt away.

You might tend to encourage each other's self-defeating cycles. Hyper-Romantic does not like to directly challenge the object of his affection, and Pal is often preoccupied with other things. But as long as you both keep plugging away at seeking intimacy over cheap fixes, your relationship will benefit you both.

HYPER-ROMANTIC AND PARTY BOY
★

What's Good: As with other ill-fated matches, one of the best things about this one is its relative unlikeliness. Even if Hyper-Romantic decides that Party Boy is the one for him, Party Boy will lack the stamina for Hyper-Romantic's energy and will quickly lose interest.

If he's in a patient mood, Party Boy will break it to Hyper-Romantic gently. But if he's feeling nasty or has a hangover (or for that matter is under the influence), he might be less gentle in his methods. He might simply stand Hyper-Romantic up. If Hyper-Romantic later confronts him, Party Boy might testily remark that he had something better to do, and anyway, all this romance stuff is *so* old-fashioned. Hopefully, Hyper-Romantic will realize that Party Boy's world isn't for him and move on.

If the two of you agree to try something serious, there might be some initial rush of passion. Hyper-Romantic lays it on pretty thick, and Party Boy likes to be dramatic, so it might seem like you're onto something. But it's probably going to fizzle fast. The first time Party Boy ignores Hyper-Romantic at a social event ought to pretty much do it. You'll both see that you're coming from incompatibly different places.

If this doesn't do the trick, and you still keep seeing each other, then maybe someday you'll both manage to go into couple's counseling and get the help you'll so desperately need.

What Needs Work: There's a major clash of wills built into your relationship. Hyper-Romantic is often passive and compliant in matters of the heart, but with Party Boy he gets surprisingly aggressive—albeit not in a way that's likely to pay off. He thinks that all Party Boy needs is his true and simple love, and Party Boy will slow down and end up ministering to a leper colony, or some such. It's as if real life is going to match the plot of an old Joan Crawford–Clark Gable movie.

Party Boy has other ideas. He has a terrible dread of the kind of tenderness Hyper-Romantic could offer. Such displays of affection put Party Boy in touch with the pain he's trying to avoid. Prolonged gentleness reminds him of his human frailty. It will be all he can do to get away from it. He'll get moody or hostile in bed and ignore or put down Hyper-Romantic in social settings.

Hyper-Romantic will be hurt and confused: Why would someone *not* want romance? It will reinforce his fear that no one will ever love him and make him all the more determined to find the all-encompassing love he erroneously thinks is the answer. Party Boy will keep on partying, relieved to be freed from what he feels were Hyper-Romantic's tentacles.

Ironically, if somehow you find yourselves willing to give your relationship a try, all the work you'll need to do on yourselves could be extremely beneficial. But the road to getting to there is destined to be bumpy. Hyper-Romantic might take on Party Boy's ways, so the arguments will be full of adrenaline and quite nasty. Party Boy will party all the more for the pain that Hyper-Romantic's presence seems to bring into his life.

HYPER-ROMANTIC AND PERENNIAL CLOSET CASE
★★

What's Good: A closeted relationship—with no wedding cake or vows or rings—is not Hyper-Romantic's ideal. In fact, you're likely to clash on issues pertaining to being out as a couple. But Hyper-Romantic can romanticize virtually any relationship, so perhaps he can find something sadly noble or wistful in being married to Perennial Closet Case. (Of course, this is assuming that Closet Case is not already married to someone else, i.e., a woman. If he is, Hyper-Romantic is likely to suffer a major broken heart.) Since Closet Case often funnels his gay energy into a relationship, and since Hyper-Romantic wants wedded bliss no matter what, it's possible for the two of you to have some nice moments together.

In bed, Hyper-Romantic will have to be extremely attentive to Closet Case's actual moods and needs and not just simply treat making love as another performance. If Hyper-Romantic is able to earn Closet Case's trust, Closet Case might start to come out to at least one man about the true nature of his sexual urges. If Closet Case tries to truly give of himself to Hyper-Romantic, then Hyper-Romantic will have to be willing to relax in his own way and let another man please him for a change.

Hyper-Romantic will not be a happy camper when he has to

pretend he's Closet Case's "roommate," but looking at the big cosmic picture, it might make for an interesting learning experience. It might discipline Hyper-Romantic into being a bit less hyper about these things. Closet Case will not appreciate Hyper-Romantic's desire to have a relationship that's out in the open, but it's certainly good for Closet Case to have this idea drilled into him. Perhaps over time, if there's enough trust and good stuff there, Closet Case might even start to come out.

What Needs Work: I don't like having to repeat myself, but Closet Case needs to come out. Hyper-Romantic deserves better than having to sleep on the sofa when his in-laws visit. And he might just have the strength and devotion that can help Closet Case come to terms with himself. A loving partner, after all, can make the transition a lot easier.

As long as Closet Case is living up to his name, there will be no social life to speak of. Closet Case won't be comfortable with Hyper-Romantic's more flamboyant friends, and Hyper-Romantic will resent the double life that Closet Case forces him to live when in *his* social circle. So you'll both feel listless and cut off from others, even if you technically socialize with other people fairly often.

It's likely that you'll tend to isolate over time. Hyper-Romantic will continue to misplace his energies by mindlessly devoting himself to another man, and Closet Case will feel little incentive to come out, because with Hyper-Romantic he can have his cake and eat it, too.

Your bedroom enterprises will need a lot of work. If Closet Case is holding back, and if Hyper-Romantic is exaggerating his responses, you'll be reinforcing your respective worst habits in bed. You'll need to take the risk of expressing your genuine needs to each other. But so doing will not come naturally. Closet Case is not predisposed to sharing about himself, and neither is Hyper-Romantic.

It's a relationship that will take a lot of work and diligence. If Hyper-Romantic is willing to compromise much of his hard-won identity as a gay man, it's possible he'll be the ticket for Closet Case's eventually coming out. But there are other men that Hyper-Romantic will hit it off with more easily, and there's certainly no honor lost in refusing to get involved with a closeted man.

HYPER-ROMANTIC AND SEXPOT
★★★★

What's Good: When you meet, there can be such a powerful feeling of attraction that it might be able to sustain whatever problems you'll have down the road. Sexpot will seem like Hyper-Romantic's dream come true: a sexy man who's eager to please. And Sexpot will not exactly mind when Hyper-Romantic all but gives him his life savings in the first five minutes of making his acquaintance. Needless to say, life will bring many complications into your relationship. But Sexpot will make Hyper-Romantic feel that he's worthy of being loved (and by such a hot guy, at that), and if Hyper-Romantic continues to find new and interesting ways to say "I love you," Sexpot will be satisfied in his own way that he truly is loved. From there, you can provide a foundation for each other to grow past the insecurities blocking you from finding intimacy.

Bedroom-wise, Sexpot will outshine Hyper-Romantic—but this will be healthy for Hyper-Romantic. He's hung up on giving a performance in bed to show what a great partner he makes. So when Sexpot's technique blows him out of the water (if you'll pardon the expression), Hyper-Romantic figures that he can't compete and just might relax for once and actually *enjoy* sex (novel idea). Hyper-Romantic will reward Sexpot with the intense validation he craves. In fact, he may do this so much that Sexpot actually reaches the point of "been there, done that" and starts to look for another way to bring meaning into his life.

Hyper-Romantic will feel compelled to shower Sexpot with tokens of esteem, perhaps going so far as to offer to financially support Sexpot. While this has a downside, Hyper-Romantic will nonetheless be inspired to greater material success. While money, one has been told, is not everything, Hyper-Romantic will still be learning how to apply himself to goals other than getting a husband. Sexpot is better off maintaining his own income, but in any case if he learns to be supportive of Hyper-Romantic's aspirations, he will be learning that there are ways of nurturing men besides having sex with them.

As you get to know each other as people, you'll both receive the much needed experience of learning what being with a man is actually like. This will help Hyper-Romantic to become more realistic in his expectations for a relationship and will similarly enable Sexpot to become more realistic about the place that sex occupies in an ongoing commitment—which, though certainly right up there in importance, is not everything.

What Needs Work: At some point in your relationship, reality will come knocking in all its rudeness. Hyper-Romantic will figure out that Sexpot is a human being with a personality, and not just something that appeared in a cloud. Sexpot will discover that Hyper-Romantic does not just exist to validate Sexpot's self-image, but has actual feelings, moods, and desires.

If you want to stay together, you must remember all that was special about your initial attraction, and how much you meant all those things you said. Bear in mind that most relationships suffer a crisis when the first romantic blush starts to fade, and that any two people are going to have disagreements while a couple.

Hyper-Romantic will tend to be possessive of Sexpot, who will have to demonstrate that he can interact with other men without flirting. If Sexpot can pull it off, it will be a good experience for him. He'll learn about other ways of bonding with men. Still, Hyper-Romantic will have to remind himself that the universe does not exist solely to provide him with a love life, and that other people are not his possessions.

Yours is a partnership in which Hyper-Romantic will strive to have the upper hand, because he wants so very much to hold on to Sexpot that he's especially afraid of not being in control. He's hoping that he'll be *so* good to Sexpot that Sexpot will never leave him. This will bring out the I-eat-chocolates-in-bed-all-day-and-file-my-nails aspect of Sexpot's personality. To some extent this is simply who you both are. But it's important that Sexpot learns that a deeper happiness can be found by validating himself, rather than looking to other men for it. And Hyper-Romantic needs to know that he doesn't have to "prove" his worth. Each of you needs to remember that intimacy starts with liking *yourself*.

HYPER-ROMANTIC AND SHY SNOB
★★★

What's Good: Since Hyper-Romantic can romanticize virtually anything, he can see Shy Snob's reserve as a challenge. He'll think that here is a man who wants to connect to him, but for some reason is afraid. Hyper-Romantic will summon up his considerable energy to break through to Shy Snob, and when there's a mutual attraction, Shy Snob will respond in kind. Shy Snob may have some difficulty confronting his feelings come the proverbial light of day (he might feel embarrassed for having shared "too much" of himself), but if Hyper-Romantic can remember to keep things light and breezy at those moments when Shy Snob's attention seems to go bye-bye, the two of you can be a good influence on each other.

Sexually, Shy Snob has a way of switching moods in a flash. Ironically, this can be good for Hyper-Romantic, because he'll experience the reality of staying committed to someone who has needs, thoughts, and desires beyond the schlock of romance. Hyper-Romantic's loyalty can help Shy Snob learn to relax around other people.

Though Shy Snob might not always feel comfortable admitting it, he is pleased to have an ally, and privately—much more than the outside world understands—the two of you develop an us-against-the-world way of being together. Shy Snob might complain at times that he's being "crowded" by Hyper-Romantic—who could indeed stand to back off a little. But overall, Shy Snob will appreciate having Hyper-Romantic around and paradoxically will be the first one to get nervous or upset if things do start to cool between the two of you.

Shy Snob can teach Hyper-Romantic to become more intro-spective, and to care more about the world around him. Though at times Hyper-Romantic will fear that he isn't smart or interesting enough for Shy Snob, overall he will appreciate the opportunity to expand his horizons. Hyper-Romantic can show Shy Snob that it's possible to lead with one's feelings and not always with one's mind, and that bringing happiness to others can be worth the trouble.

What Needs Work: Shy Snob wants to feel somewhat set apart from others, and he'll get upset when Hyper-Romantic "embarrasses" him in front of other people with a lovey-dovey display of affection. Shy Snob likes to keep a certain distance or mystery about himself, and there's something too smug or set about being happily married. Even if at first he cooperates with Hyper-Romantic's displays of affection, over time they will make him uncomfortable. It's not a matter of being closeted; when the mood strikes him, Shy Snob can practically perform an X-rated sex scene in public. But he's more at ease doing something like that with a *stranger*.

If Hyper-Romantic is smart, he'll cultivate his own air of mys-tery; he'll keep things playful and just a little bit aloof. He needs to remember that in the final analysis we never know everything about each other, and it's unrealistic to expect some sort of total naked intensity twenty-four hours a day. If he wants to show off how happily married he is, he might be better off engaging in witty repartee with Shy Snob or doing something silly. Keep the tone comedy instead of high drama, and Shy Snob will be eating out of Hyper-Romantic's hand.

Shy Snob has high standards, and Hyper-Romantic tends to su-perficially adopt them rather than internalize them. Shy Snob will see what Hyper-Romantic is doing and will be partially flattered by it, but also partially angry. When people's intentions are transparent, it tends to tick him off. Hyper-Romantic is better off sticking to his own way of dressing or talking to the boss than he is trying to do everything as Shy Snob would.

At the most basic level, Shy Snob can be rather changeable, and his mixed signals can wear down Hyper-Romantic over time. With good communication, Shy Snob can start to become cognizant of just how dramatic and baffling his shifting moods can be and perhaps start training himself to respond differently. Hyper-Romantic can learn that just because someone doesn't literally say "I love you" every ten seconds, a relationship can still be worthwhile.

HYPER-ROMANTIC AND THERAPY JUNKIE
★★

What's Good: For this relationship to happen, there will need to be some willingness on Hyper-Romantic's part to take the concerns of Therapy Junkie seriously. Pretending to won't cut it; he needs to genuinely believe that Therapy Junkie's approach to life is worth listening to, because he will certainly be hearing about it. Simultaneously, Therapy Junkie must feel that what Hyper-Romantic has to offer is genuine love and companionship, and not mere "co-dependency" or "sex addiction" or a way of acting out some post-oedipal drama.

If such a scenario is in place, Therapy Junkie might actually feel that he's found the "unconditional love" he's been seeking, for certainly Hyper-Romantic is willing to be devoted to him. And Hyper-Romantic can have a husband who needs a lot of healing love energy that he is only too willing to give.

There will be a tendency for Therapy Junkie to complicate the rather simple, straightforward intentions of Hyper-Romantic with all sorts of labels about things such as "denial" or "control issues." It can be useful for Hyper-Romantic to consider that telling a man he loves him might not be what it seems to be. Therapy Junkie can learn to let go and relax a little in Hyper-Romantic's balm of love—to *live* and not just think about living.

If Therapy Junkie responds to Hyper-Romantic's rather insistent technique, things can gel in the bedroom. Therapy Junkie will certainly have a partner willing to explore his hidden sexual fantasies. And if Hyper-Romantic doesn't take it too personally when Therapy Junkie says something like "Don't rub my shoulder—it reminds me of my drunken stepfather," he can learn something about responding to his lover's actual needs, as opposed to what he thinks should be his needs.

What Needs Work: Therapy Junkie lives in a universe in which everyone dissects everything. His idea of a fun evening is to take some sort of personality test or undergo hypnosis to explore suppressed childhood memories. Though it would be useful for him to give all that a rest, Hyper-Romantic may not be the best man to show him the way. Hyper-Romantic is likely to pale in Therapy Junkie's eyes, especially when Therapy Junkie's friends from his encounter group (or whatever) come over to visit. Hyper-Romantic will try to make himself useful serving apple cider and Fig Newtons, but his lack of "issues" will make Therapy Junkie both bored and suspicious.

Hyper-Romantic characteristically is supportive of his partner (albeit for rather insecure reasons), but Therapy Junkie might benefit more from a partner who challenges his assumptions. When Therapy Junkie comes home from work and says, "My boss offered me a raise, but I felt he had a hidden agenda that made me uncomfortable, so I turned it down," Hyper-Romantic is likely to say, "That's nice, honey. Can I get your dinner now?" What Therapy Junkie needs at times like that is someone who can tell him—albeit in a loving way—a few home truths.

Speaking of hidden agendas, both of you will have one. Hyper-Romantic, of course, simply wants to be whatever he needs to be to have a partner, and Therapy Junkie will be convinced that Hyper-Romantic needs to get counseling and read books and so on to upgrade his mental wellness. This type of thing doesn't lend itself to intimacy, because neither of you is experiencing the other for who he actually is.

Your goals for your own lives and for what you want from a relationship are not the same. If you work on being honest with each other, perhaps you'll find that you like who this other man is, after all, and be able to build a life together.

MISFIT AND MISFIT
★★★★

What's Good: You both speak the same language. Both of you wish the gay community were some other way, and you can keep each other up all night sharing your respective laundry lists of complaints about the awful music, clothes, personalities, sexual lifestyles, etc., that dominate the gay world.

Of course, you can also keep yourselves awake doing other things as well. You both want to connect with another man on all sorts of levels, and unless there's some major obstacle to sexual compatibility, you're likely to find each other attractive. The mere fact that you've found another gay man who shares your worldview is going to seem sexy. You might just find yourselves exploring all sorts of uninhibited passions together.

You both tend to feel like fish out of water, not exactly fitting in with either the gay or straight world. However, if you each have even one or two close friends (male or female, gay or straight), you ought to be able to create a small but closely knit social scene for yourselves. You probably both have a lot of interests and can have a good time exploring them as a couple—or with your friends.

As your relationship develops, you may even find that you have more in common with other gay couples than you realized. Or in any event, a long-term commitment to each other ought to make you both feel better about being gay. In fact, your combined energies make for a unique and potentially useful take on the gay experience that could provide beneficial outreach to people who do not usually travel in gay circles.

Now that I've said all of this, you might be wondering just where you can meet a fellow Misfit. It might be easier than you realize. The most important thing to remember is not to make the same mistake you think the gay community often makes—which is to judge a book by its cover. For all you know, the guy standing next to you in the bar thinks much like you do, if you'd give him a chance to talk about himself.

What Needs Work: Helpful though it may be to find a kindred spirit, you run the risk of bringing out a lot of antigay sentiment in each other. This may not seem as if it matters, but it does. Because by putting down gays, you're putting down a part of yourselves, no matter how much you think you're "not like those other gay men." Your tendency to be more critical of the gay world than the straight world prevents you from experiencing full intimacy, because somewhere along the way it speaks to internalized homophobia.

There's a tendency for you to base your relationship on what each other *isn't* as opposed to what each of you *is:* "Wow, finally—another gay man who hates musicals." The problem is that over time this won't be much of a basis for a relationship—or at least not a happy one. Once the novelty of meeting a fellow Misfit wears off, you'll have to dig deeper inside yourselves to discover what you need to make a relationship work over time.

Also, that things *can* work between you might come as such a shock that you won't know what to do with it. You're both so accustomed to not meeting someone you have a lot in common with that the thought of really finding someone you can be happy with might be scary. In particular, you both need to work on being present in the bedroom, because you have the capacity for much more intimacy together than either of you ever realistically thought you could have. When either or both of you start to drift off emotionally, you need to communicate honestly about what you're thinking and feeling, rather than just saying that everything's fine.

In sum, the two of you have the potential to give each other what you've both always complained that you wanted but could never have. Give each other the kind of honesty you both know you're capable of, and you should have a great life together.

MISFIT AND NICE BOY
★

What's Good: In an effort to be nice, Nice Boy might try to befriend that unhappy-looking Misfit standing off by himself and make the dangerous assumption that Misfit is merely shy. If Misfit is in a particularly lonely (indeed, desperate) mood, he might momentarily turn to Nice Boy for tea and sympathy.

But Misfit will probably get bored—if not angry—quickly around Nice Boy, because Nice Boy embodies so much of what Misfit dislikes about so many gay men: that they act so *nice* all the time. Nice Boy simply does not give indication of the depth or adventurousness that Misfit craves in another man. And Misfit's intensity and male energy is likely to frighten Nice Boy. His worst fears will only be confirmed when Misfit verbally slices him into little pieces.

Technically, there is the potential for some wild sex. Nice Boy tends to cut loose in bed, and Misfit can respond with an impassioned horniness. Over time, this might make for a pleasant memory for both of you.

What Needs Work: In the meanwhile, you are likely to despise each other, even if—or especially if—you actually end up becoming a couple. Misfit will say things to Nice Boy aimed at trying to snap him out of his complacency—in other words, he'll get mean. He won't see it as doing anything wrong; he'll feel it's justified, given Nice Boy's annoying denial of all things unpleasant.

Nice Boy will respond with a passive-aggressive pleasantness. He'll try to turn Misfit into someone more manageable—into another Nice Boy, which is something Misfit has no intention of becoming. The tension between the two of you will feel unbearable at times.

In the long run, even something as seemingly positive as hot sex will lead to unhappiness. Nice Boy will be hurt—much more so than he will let on—by how Misfit toys with his emotions. Misfit will resent the way Nice Boy acts so differently in bed, for so doing embodies the kind of contradictions he sees in the gay community. He'll take it personally, as if everything he's saying and doing is being ignored or rejected by Nice Boy. Which of course is exactly the truth.

If you both are working extremely hard at changing yourselves, you could be a good influence on each other, as both of you have qualities the other could benefit from. But there's bound to be some serious misunderstandings and some major hurt feelings along the way.

MISFIT AND PAL
★★

What's Good: As someone who goes around trying to be everyone's friend, Pal is likely to have one foot in and one foot outside of the gay community. If being a Pal means doing traditional "male" things like helping someone build a patio or teaching a kid how to throw a baseball, Misfit might find Pal attractive, and the potential is there for something to happen.

Pal isn't the most adroit person at making his romantic intentions known, but then, neither is Misfit. You should be able to get across what you both mean without saying much about it. However, over time, Misfit will be inclined to communicate much more than Pal. If Pal can listen nondefensively to what Misfit has to say, the relationship might go smoothly.

When it comes to sex, you can probably give each other a great deal of affection. Neither of you is accustomed to letting your emotions all hang out, but in a guy type of way you understand about each other's loneliness and can put a lot into a simple hug. Being around Misfit brings out something guyish in Pal. Even if he's being nurturing to Misfit in bed—offering to give him a massage or whatever—he'll feel very male when he's doing it.

Pal can be helpful to Misfit in ways that Misfit is unaccustomed to. If Misfit's friends are coming over, Pal will make sure good refreshments are provided. He may not understand all the things that Misfit is trying to do with his life, but he'll give as much practical and emotional support as he can.

Misfit's original observations might be more than Pal can handle, but Pal can grow as a person from Misfit's influence and start to think about his life in new kinds of ways. Misfit will not appreciate all the needy souls Pal wants to help, as Misfit will feel that many of them would be better off learning to take care of themselves. Misfit will be suspicious of Pal's motives. Still, this can be a positive influence on Pal, depending on how Misfit communicates his opinion, and how Pal chooses to take it.

What Needs Work: You live your lives for different purposes. Misfit is trying to construct an identity for himself, while Pal likes to believe he already knows who he is. Misfit is much more comfortable with introspection than is Pal. Perhaps most important of all, Misfit can stand being alone (and sometimes prefers it), while Pal has a great deal of difficulty getting through a single day without schmoozing up to at least one person.

Hence, when the times get rough, Misfit is ready to move on, while Pal wants to do more "helpful" things to hold on to what he has. For the relationship to last, Misfit must be willing to ignore his instinctive drive to end it. Ironically, though, Pal must also get past his own instinctive drive to keep it happening. Only when Pal learns to let go of trying to control the outcome will it be possible for a truly honest relationship to thrive. Trying to manipulate a certain response out of another person has never been the way to intimacy.

Your sex life can easily drift into purgatory. There's a kind of "Why bother?" lethargy that emerges. While there are no guarantees that things will work for you in the long run, they definitely won't work without good communication. You need to talk about what you're feeling—or not feeling—when it's time for bed. When doing so, Misfit needs to resist being insulting, and Pal will need to express his own needs and not just try to be attentive to Misfit.

All couples need to have some activities in common, and in your case it will require concerted effort. Maybe you can volunteer one evening a week at an AIDS clinic and then go to some sort of unusual music performance. By entering into each other's world, you can start to understand each other and help each other become more receptive to the good things a relationship can offer.

MISFIT AND PARTY BOY
★

What's Good: Like Nice Boy, embodies an aspect of gay life for which Misfit has zero tolerance. Misfit has a million reasons why he loathes the gay party life, ranging from the music on through the conversation and activities and the emphasis on appearance and sex and—well, you name it, Misfit doesn't like it. At the same time, Party Boy doesn't like Misfit. He can barely stand to listen to Misfit go on and on so critically about the very things that are at the center of Party Boy's existence. So what's good between you is the relative unlikelihood that anything much will happen.

Still, Misfit gets lonely, and if Party Boy is drawn to Misfit's looks, a little something might develop. To be a good conversationalist, Party Boy might well have a superficial knowledge of a variety of topics, and he might even appreciate the distraction of talking on a more complex level than usual. Misfit might temporarily find Party Boy to be engaging company.

You're unlikely to light up the sky, sexually speaking. But the lack of chemistry and timing to your bedroom escapades will probably be perceived as relatively benign in the big picture of things.

Party Boy is unlikely to leave a major emotional imprint on Misfit's life, and even if Misfit breaks Party Boy's heart, Party Boy will laugh and joke his pain away.

What Needs Work: Misfit feels left out of things, while Party Boy has felt that he's right in the center of all the action. Misfit is still searching for a place to call home, while Party Boy thinks he found it a long time ago. Party Boy's very presence reminds Misfit of the pain and anger he feels over not fitting in with the gay crowd. In an effort to get Party Boy to understand him, he may feel compelled to attack all that Party Boy stands for.

Moreover, Party Boy will have to make an effort to spend at least some time in Misfit's world. However, Misfit does a lot of talking and thinking, and so he's likely to get Party Boy to explore some not-so-happy places in his own mind.

Misfit likes quiet time, and time to himself. Party Boy will go stir-crazy waiting when Misfit goes off to read a book or suggests some nongay social activity. With some types of gay men, Misfit seems like some sort of variation on a Hell's Angel, but Party Boy brings out something subdued and serious about Misfit, who is likely to start feeling like a ponderous nerd.

Actually, you could be a good influence on each other. Misfit sees past Party Boy's laughter to the wound underneath. And whether it's an act or not, a bit of Party Boy's joie de vivre would never hurt Misfit. Sexually, Misfit could stand to lighten up, and Party Boy can have the novel experience of drawing upon his intellect when having sex. But it's rather unlikely that you'll get past your personality differences and learn to appreciate what you might have to offer each other.

MISFIT AND PERENNIAL CLOSET CASE
★★

What's Good: Superficially, you both have your reasons for not being comfortable with your gayness, and you both have your share of internalized homophobia. But somewhere along the way, Misfit *wants* to be comfortable about being gay. Chances are Misfit has some straight friends who know about him. In fact, they've listened more than once as he's ranted and raved about how he doesn't fit in with the gay scene. But Closet Case has straight "friends" whom he isn't out to at all.

Therefore, Misfit will have his fair share of issues with Closet Case. Yet it's also possible that your mutual complaints about the gay world will form an initial bond between you. If this happens, Misfit's nonconformity might help Closet Case realize that coming out as gay doesn't have to mean changing *everything* about yourself. Since Misfit is not a "stereotypical" gay man, Closet Case might feel more comfortable telling the people in his life that he has a boyfriend. He might also feel more at ease around Misfit's friends, since they are fairly likely to not be gay (or at least not exclusively so), and this can be a step in the right direction toward Closet Case's coming out.

If Closet Case *is* able to come out, it can have a good effect on Misfit. Together, the two of you can try to find a niche for yourselves in the gay community. And Misfit's often valid criticisms can help Closet Case to maintain a realistic perspective on gay life as he becomes involved in it. Closet Case hardly tries to force-fit his worldview into the gay milieu, and so he might be open-minded to Misfit's ideas.

If you're both feeling good about yourselves as gay men, you can help each other to come out fully in the bedroom, as well. Whatever Closet Case doesn't want to face about his sexuality—and whatever Misfit faces only intermittently—the two of you might be able to help each other to relax.

What Needs Work: As with other combinations, the very qualities that could make for a comfortable relationship can keep Closet Case very much in the closet. Misfit is unlikely to be the type of gay man who insists that Closet Case comes out, and in fact he might sympathize a bit too much with Closet Case's reluctance to do so. Moreover, since Misfit also is not comfortable with being gay, Closet Case can be a negative influence, and Misfit might take a few steps back into the closet himself.

Either that, or else Misfit will grow to resent Closet Case's closetness and see it as cowardice and complacency. Whatever his difficulties, Misfit is trying to find the truth, whereas Closet Case is content to keep living a lie. Over time, Misfit will regard Closet as one more tepid gay man unwilling to face some of the more daring aspects of life. He'll get angry that Closet Case declares "I love you," but then ten seconds later is afraid to tell anyone about his lover.

There might well be a tendency for either or both of you to experience shame or embarrassment after sex. Ironically, the better the sex was, the more likely you are to feel bad about it afterward. Again, this relates to your internalized homophobia. If this should happen, you both need to talk it out—perhaps in the presence of a counselor.

Your relationship is one more reason why Closet Case needs to come out. Only then can you start to build the honest future together that could bring you both happiness. At the same time, Misfit must remember to work on his own internalized homophobia and his exceptionally harsh judgments of gay men.

MISFIT AND SEXPOT
★

What's Good: Sexpot embodies a common feature of gay life that Misfit has a great deal of difficulty accepting. Misfit simply is not comfortable with a man emphasizing his gay sexuality above all other aspects of personality. Misfit views pure sex as nonarousing, and he thinks it's extremely unimaginative for a gay man to make sex the end-all and be-all of his existence. In a way, Misfit feels that Sexpot needs deprogramming. Simultaneously, Sexpot is not comfortable with having to think so much, and being around Misfit for any length of time will make him feel nervou, and intimidated.

So it's more than likely that any encounter between the two of you will be brief. It's possible to have a fun little quickie together, but that will probably be about it. Even then, Misfit will have to be in an especially needy mood, because what he perceives to be Sexpot's superficiality is likely to be a turn-off.

If you try to make something long-term, technically Sexpot could teach Misfit about giving all his issues a rest and just having a little fun. And the potential theoretically exists for Misfit to encourage Sexpot to live a more thoughtful kind of life. But it's likely to all stay pretty much a theory. You each might experience a passing thought that you'd do well to be more like the other, but it's unlikely that you'll act on it. In fact, you might not even remember much about each other, once things come to an end.

What Needs Work: It's unlikely that Sexpot will get involved with anyone without good sex right off the bat. It's asking a lot of Sexpot to go straight to the opposite extreme—where lovemaking becomes a kind of cerebral experience based on a multifaceted reality. Also, Misfit will need to be willing to meet Sexpot in the middle, so to speak, and strive to let pleasures of the body be nothing more than that.

If you somehow manage to get the sex angle squared away, you'll have to find some sort of activity you can enjoy together. Perhaps it can be something relatively neutral, like having a pet. Misfit can appreciate having a creature to bond with, and Sexpot will find something playful and sensual in your rolling around together with your cocker spaniel.

Sexpot might claim that he wants to become more informed in other areas (and it can be good for him if he does), but Misfit takes a lot of knowledge for granted, and he's unlikely to be the kind of teacher Sexpot needs. Also, while Sexpot may say he wants to live more like Misfit, it's unlikely that he'll be able to do so for any length of time. His desire to be validated by men through sex runs deep, and it will take him a lot of work to get past it.

Asking Misfit to act like a loose man for any duration is equally unlikely. In theory, you can boy-watch together, but your tastes are probably extremely different. Perhaps you can turn this difference into a fun game of sorts ("You think *he's* sexy? Give me a break"). But what's likelier is that you'll each try to convince the other to change his tastes.

If you both are extremely determined to give things a try, be prepared to have a demanding time of it, with many setbacks.

MISFIT AND SHY SNOB
★★★

What's Good: Both of you know what it feels like to be outsiders. Misfit feels this way because of his issues with the gay mainstream, while for Shy Snob it's more a matter of feeling as though people don't like him. On the surface, anyway, Shy Snob might well seem like a "typical" gay man. For the two of you to hook up, Misfit will have to see that there is more to Shy Snob than meets the eye. If Shy Snob is interested in Misfit, he'll have to take a deep breath and do something uncharacteristic: share with Misfit about how alienated he often feels. If he doesn't, he'll have to hope that Misfit somehow notices Shy Snob's hidden depths.

Once you become an item, you can be a positive influence in each other's life. Misfit can learn that even clone boys get the blues, as he discovers just how complex Shy Snob's sense of himself is. And Shy Snob might get the opportunity to alter some of his rigid assumptions about acceptable behavior by letting bohemian Misfit into his life. You'll maintain certain differences, but in ways that both of you are able to tolerate. As long as each of you feels that the other is respecting your space to be yourself, contrasting aesthetics ought to be a minor concern at best—perhaps even a source of humor between you.

Bedroom-wise, things will tend to be on-again, off-again. Both of you have a way of losing your concentration. However, because you're comfortable with yourselves in each other's company, you can pretty much groove past the blah times. If Shy Snob is not in the mood, Misfit probably has a dozen different things he'd be interested in doing, instead.

Socially, you will make a somewhat confusing couple. Others may wonder what you see in each other. Misfit's friends might see Shy Snob as rather unfriendly, with a rather unimaginative demeanor. Shy Snob hasn't many close friends, but his acquaintances might take one look at Misfit and gasp, "What are you doing with someone like *him?*" At times, you both might feel restless for more company, but usually you'll feel pretty good about being alone together. You're one of those couples that develop a kind of private conspiracy, as if you're in on a joke that nobody else knows. You are able to give each other a great deal of emotional support, whereby you both stop feeling guilty for not liking everyone you meet.

What Needs Work: Shy Snob often has somewhat snooty standards, and if he forgets to respect Misfit's right to be himself, he might start pressuring Misfit to become something he's not. Conversely, Misfit might try to make Shy Snob be a little less conformist. While Shy Snob hasn't ever felt deeply accepted in the mainstream gay world, superficially he travels within it and would like to feel more of a connection. His gripes usually have to do with violation of rather conventional social norms. Misfit *wants to* violate some of these conventions. Shy Snob's ideal vacation might be some sort of chichi gay cruise to the Caribbean, while Misfit would rather go backpacking in Madagascar.

You're capable of working through these differences; it's kind of a Patty/Cathy thing. Still, you both need to be mindful of the conflicts you experience along the way and to remember that your differences are part of what makes each of you the appealing man that he is.

You both run the risk of getting so wrapped up in your own minds that you neglect to connect to each other. This is especially important since your connections to outsiders will probably tend to diminish somewhat for your relationship. To no small extent, it's good that you're able to give each other a lot of breathing room. But you both need to remember that to have a truly intimate relationship—and not just one that technically exists—you have to get past what's in your heads and concentrate on what's in your hearts.

MISFIT AND THERAPY JUNKIE
★★★★

What's Good: The two of you can really *talk,* and talk is important to both of you. True, you don't talk about the exact same things. Misfit has an eclectic range of interests, while Therapy Junkie tends to stick to his psychological jargon. Misfit seeks flight away from the gay culture, while Therapy Junkie is probably untroubled by it and, if anything, sees fitting in with it as part of his therapy.

Still, contrasts can often be good—as they are in your case. Because you both express the fruits of your introspection, what you say to each other has enough prerequisite "depth" to be taken seriously. Misfit can expose Therapy Junkie to other, more creative ways of exploring his inner self, while Therapy Junkie can help Misfit to face some of the homophobia-inspired wounds from his past that are holding him back.

The differences you experience are manageable, because there's a shared sense that you're both trying to find yourselves. If there's something in the relationship that concerns one of you, you'll feel comfortable bringing it up. That's because your partner will be willing to listen—to consider the possibility that he can change or improve himself. Trying to get some gay men to do things differently can be like pulling teeth, but you both enjoy trying out new ways of being.

Though sexually you both tend to hold back, if the communication develops over time, you can reach the point where you both feel safe discussing sex. Therapy Junkie can come out of the closet over whatever kink, preference, or fetish he isn't facing, and Misfit might learn that it's okay to be completely physically present with another man. But you're also the kind of couple that can feel intimate simply lying in bed and talking.

Each of you will be able to blend into the social world of the other—albeit for short durations. Misfit is capable of talking the lingo of Therapy Junkie, and while Misfit's friends might think Therapy Junkie is a bit too into all his psychological stuff, they will regard it as a benign background noise as they discuss art or politics.

There is the potential for a mentally and physically stimulating union when the two of you get together. Obstacles toward intimacy will be made easier for being in each other's lives.

What Needs Work: You need to avoid the temptation of hidden agendas. Misfit would love it if Therapy Junkie cooled it with all the psycho lingo, and Therapy Junkie usually thinks that anyone who isn't enmeshed in all kinds of therapeutic activities is "in denial." So you both need to accept each other for who you are and realize that you have something to teach each other. If Therapy Junkie wants to go to a support group while Misfit wants to go to a café, give each other permission to do so. And then *share* with each other what happened—preferably while naked in bed.

Because the way each of you chooses to spend his leisure time is so important, you need to find at least one activity to do together. Ideally, it will be something that involves other people, so that you can make a third—and shared—set of friends. Having a social network in common will help your relationship feel validated. Otherwise, there will be a tendency for both of you to feel that "over here is my life, and over here is my relationship." You'll both start feeling trapped because your relationship will seem like what's *keeping* you from living your lives.

While it's great that the two of you can communicate so openly, remember that talk isn't everything—actions often speak louder than words. There might be a tendency to get little accomplished as you both talk away your days. Moreover, too much talk ironically becomes a way of *avoiding* intimacy—in the bedroom, of course, but also in other ways of expressing your feelings as opposed to your mental abstractions.

But all things considered, you can make a fine couple. You'll tend to bring out the best in each other and both become better men for having been in each other's life.

NICE BOY AND NICE BOY
★★★

What's Good: You shouldn't have much trouble becoming friendly, because you'll feel safe in each other's company. Though you probably don't spell it out, you seem to say to each other, "How nice to meet someone who doesn't get all carried away with all that nastiness and aggression." By smiling and being pleasant and polite, you both feel you're reinforcing important values about living. Other gay man are capable of being courteous, but for the two of you it's what life is all about. Every little "thank you" or "pardon me" is practically an aphrodisiac.

Speaking of which, you can both cut loose with each other in bed. Onlookers would be amazed by how much heat you generate under the covers. What the two of you do is not necessarily exotic, but the spirit behind it is surprisingly porn-ish. You take it for granted that sex is an exception to the rules of decorum you otherwise try to live by, so neither of you feels disconcerted by the experience.

You'll have fun planning your lives together—especially when you agree on how to decorate or divide up the chores. When you don't agree, there will be minor tensions in the air because you both approach conflict passive-aggressively. Even if either or both of you take on a scolding air, it is done half in jest—you are trying to mask your hostility. This has its drawbacks, of course, but it does make for a relationship that is smooth on the surface. But whether you agree or disagree, balancing your budget or picking out wallpaper will seem like something more than it is. You'll feel that this is as deep as life can get.

Some might find the two of you a bit on the dull side, but others enjoy visiting your home, because they can count on having an agreeable time. It's unlikely that the two of you will engage in mind games or detain your guests. The conversation can center around the food being served, the table settings, and so on, so no one will feel insulted.

You both ought to be able to pursue your respective careers with relatively few hassles from the home front. Your orderly, calm, and measured manner of living will probably lend itself to saving money, though you'll also enjoy buying things to beautify your home. When you travel, you like as few surprises as possible and are drawn to group tours—or at least tour guides—to keep things from getting too dangerously spontaneous. If nothing else, you devour maps and tourist brochures to give you a sense of exactly what you're about to do.

What Needs Work: Though your coupling is extremely compatible, what keeps it from being a four-star relationship is that you do not tend to challenge each other out of your complacency aimed at avoiding intimacy. To some extent, life will present you with difficulties that can potentially improve your respective characters. But then again, your shared compulsion to always be nice might make either or both of you try to deny that anything is wrong. And when the tension of this denial becomes strong enough, your relationship is likely to deteriorate.

You speak a silent language together, and a shrewd lift of an eyebrow can speak volumes about your ironic sense of a given situation. Still, you're going to need to talk about *some* things at least *some* of the time that are more complex than the weather or the color of the drapes or whether you should plant begonias. It might even have to get a little—yes—unpleasant. And this type of thing does not come naturally to either of you.

If one of you reaches the breaking point—if you just have to let a toad fly out of your mouth—you're likely to feel extremely guilty afterward and experience an emotional recoil that convinces you more than ever that it pays to be nice. And your partner is unlikely to disagree. Even if he politely says he doesn't mind when you get a little carried away, you know the underlying message is that he hopes you never do it again.

In a way, your ability to know what each other means behind your nice facades is a drawback, because it tends to short-circuit the possibility of truly opening up to each other. The ingredients are there for a big-time romance. What the two of you need to remember is that honesty is more important than always being "nice." In fact, given your inclination to always be polite, you should be able to find ways of expressing yourselves in gentle ways that do not cause the other party to take offense. If you can express your needs, hopes, fears, and desires to each other safely, you can share a wonderful destiny together.

NICE BOY AND PAL
★★★

What's Good: You appreciate qualities in each other that others might find bothersome. Nice Boy will think it's admirable that Pal spends so much time caring for other people, and Pal enjoys the way that Nice Boy always looks on the bright side of things. You might well meet at some sort of volunteer activity, though Nice Boy will be busy spreading sunshine, while Pal will be doing the grunt work. However, Pal is unlikely to resent Nice Boy, because Pal expects that he has to "earn" a place amongst humanity, and if anything Pal might feel more uncomfortable if Nice Boy started infringing on his territory.

You're capable of being friendly with many of the same people and will enjoy commiserating about your loved ones' trials and tribulations. In fact, much of your conversational time will probably be spent talking about other people. If this can be a way of avoiding intimacy, it's also good to know, in the larger scheme of things, that there are people out there who take an interest in the well-being of others. You're the kind of gay couple that can win over the most skeptical of straight neighbors by baking them cakes or mowing their lawns.

Your home will be a hospitable place, though its appearance might be slightly chaotic at times. The two of you tend to always be changing something around—especially if Pal is handy with a hammer and saw. You'll plan your decor or garden with the solemnity of other couples planning their children. If you have pets, they probably get bathed and groomed more often than some would deem necessary.

Essentially, since you both shy away from intense confrontations, your combined energies make for a relationship of *doing*—helping and fixing and planning. If one of you has a long commute to work or has to work on weekends, you accept this as one of life's necessities. It's part of your overall strategy of keeping busy as a couple.

This is not to say that you're all work and no play. After hours, Nice Boy can help Pal to relax sexually. Pal can grow to understand he's worthy of affection and doesn't have to "earn" it. And as this happens, there may even be some interesting fantasies that Pal would like to explore, and which Nice Boy will be willing to accommodate.

You can both do much worse. Moreover, there is something fundamentally rounded and realistic about your pairing that makes you both accommodating toward each other's imperfections of character, as if tolerating bad habits made your relationship cozier.

What Needs Work: You bring out something rather tepid in each other. There's a temptation to get a bit too comfortable in your daily routines. When something major happens to shake you up—ironically, even something exceptionally good—you both may be ill-equipped to deal with it. Neither of you wants to have some sort of round-the-clock encounter group, but minor resentments can become major problems when they aren't dealt with.

For example, as time passes, Pal might grow resentful of Nice Boy's eternal calm. Pal, after all, often runs around like a chicken with its head cut off, while Nice Boy just sits there as serene as can be. At the same time, though Nice Boy admires how helpful and concerned Pal is, he starts to wish that Pal would spend more time with him. (He also does not like it when Pal gets into a foul mood from time to time due to his burnout or frustration.) Unfortunately, you don't particularly inspire each other to confront these issues. You both just sort of hope it all goes away as you go about your routines.

Furthermore, you don't challenge each other to stand up for yourselves. Instead, you encourage each other to keep putting other people first. If one of your straight neighbors invites you to their niece's wedding, but asks that you don't do anything too . . . well, *you know,* that gives away that you're a couple, you're both likely to oblige. You'll spend all kinds of money on the perfect gift and talk about how lovely the bride was, but you may not deal with your resentments. You both could benefit from a partner who encourages you to be bolder.

If you work hard at overcoming your reluctance to express what you really want and need, you can have a truly fulfilling relationship.

NICE BOY AND PARTY BOY
★★★★

What's Good: You make a highly visible couple that many of us are familiar with: the warm, engaging partner, and his more acerbic counterpoint. Despite your superficial differences—including your vocabularies—you both are very connected to your identities as gay men and can bring out the best in each other.

Since you respect each other as gay men, qualities that each of you are lacking can be found in the other. In his quiet way, Nice

Boy can show Party Boy that there is life beyond the latest bitchy barb. Similarly, Party Boy can encourage Nice Boy to cut loose and, yes, maybe even get a little bitchy now and then.

Underneath it all, you share many of the same insecurities. While Nice Boy reacted against his fears by convincing himself that everything was nice, Party Boy did the same thing by pretending everything was fun. And so if you connect as lovers, you will be able to reach each other and get past your respective facades.

To get to this point, you'll need to recognize what you have in common. Nice Boy will need to see that Party Boy can be soft-spoken, and Party Boy will need to see that Nice Boy can be fun. Once you get it together, you will help each other grow just by being yourselves, though of course you'll both have to be willing to learn.

You'll probably develop a rather endearing way of needling each other. Party Boy is no stranger to clever remarks, but when he falls in love with Nice Boy, he'll learn to temper his wit with affection. Nice Boy will relish the chance to be not so nice for a change, and to let a healthy dash of saltiness into his sweet demeanor. Nice Boy can come across as sexier with Party Boy than with many other types of men.

Speaking of sex, Nice Boy can help Party Boy to feel more at ease in bed, and to get in touch with his true sexual desires. Party Boy will respond in kind, displaying a generosity and tenderness that he often tries to camouflage. Part of what makes you vital as a couple is that you really do share more with each other than you do with anyone else.

You make a glamorous and charismatic twosome that others will enjoy spending time with. Your contrasting personalities can make you all the more interesting to observe, because it will be apparent that there's a bond between you that transcends your differences.

What Needs Work: Though to a large measure you are naturally helpful to each other, you both still need to be attentive to the ways in which you try to avoid closeness with men. When Party Boy parties a bit too much, Nice Boy might fall into his passive-aggressive business, silently straightening up around the house while insisting that nothing can possibly be wrong.

In fact, since Party Boy is especially vulnerable to alcoholism and substance abuse, Nice Boy might have to prove just how nice he can be when his lover comes out of rehab. Nice Boy is capable of quiet strength that is well suited to deal with a recovering addict, but so doing is still a challenging task for anyone: (I'm not saying that Party Boy will absolutely prove to be an addict, but I'm saying it's not the strangest thing in the world to happen, either. For that matter, Nice Boy—or any other kind of person—can of course also have problems with substance abuse.)

But yours is not a one-sided relationship. Nice Boy can become a more courageous and assertive man from Party Boy's influence. The problem is that at times you both will forget about the ways you complement each other and focus instead on the ways you annoy each other. This is a normal part of any relationship, but in your case you must be mindful that if you don't talk things out, they can get out of control. Nice Boy will freeze up as Party Boy acts out, and you'll both be made unhappy. Nice Boy has to realize that as much as he doesn't like to face anything "unpleasant," things will get downright nasty if he doesn't speak up when there are problems.

During stressful times, you both must remember that you have defense mechanisms aimed at shutting people out, and that your problems are not one-sided. The world may let Nice Boy be as nice as he wants and applaud when Party Boy does something outrageous, but underneath it all you understand the truth about each other. And that's what you need to bear in mind.

NICE BOY AND PERENNIAL CLOSET CASE
★★★

What's Good: I could not in good faith state that Closet Case has any four-star relationships. But as I have mentioned, some closeted men can be fairly okay as partners, and in fact their ability to maintain relationships can ironically keep them in the closet. If there is a man out there who might actually have what it takes to enable Closet Case to come out once and for all, it would have to be patient and understanding Nice Boy. Thus, I have deemed this to be a three-star relationship.

In a nonthreatening way, Nice Boy can guide Closet Case out into the open air. Of course, other types of men might have less gentle approaches for urging Closet Case to come out. While these techniques can be effective, Nice Boy's approach may take less of a toll on the relationship. If Nice Boy resents having a closeted lover, he will keep the resentment to himself. Nice Boy will be mindful of Closet Case's fears and not overdo things when he first meets Closet Case's family and friends. Closet Case might wish he had a more butch partner to show off, but at least he can count on Nice Boy not to start any fights.

In other words, Nice Boy's tendency to keep things pleasant at the cost of deeper principles can prove useful in this context. And once Closet Case comes out, who knows what heights the two of you might reach together?

You both are extremely concerned about the feelings of other people and are accustomed to making your point in furtive, nondirect ways. While these qualities are a mixed blessing, they will give you quite a lot in common temperamentally. You'll understand when your partner has trouble confronting a situation dead-on and will offer emotional support.

Nice Boy can be quite a tiger in bed, and once he earns Closet Case's trust, Closet Case might face up to the full nature of his sexual urges. If there's a tendency for Closet Case to back off emotionally, then so does Nice Boy in his own way. In fact, you both might appreciate that you have a partner who doesn't get too messy— emotionally, that is—when you're making love.

Much of this good stuff is predicated on Closet Case's willingness to come out of the closet and be who he really is. Closet Case may always find it difficult to tell people he's gay, but life with Nice Boy might make it seem a little easier. In return, Nice Boy will feel the rewards of watching his lover become the man he was destined to be.

What Needs Work: First of all, there's always the possibility that Closet Case won't come out, no matter how much Nice Boy patiently tries to help him do so. Nice Boy will then decide whether to end the relationship or keep plugging along with a closeted boyfriend. As good an actor as Nice Boy can be, he may find himself unable to do the latter, yet he will be scared of all the unpleasant confrontation involved in the former.

In the meanwhile, the tension will be intense, because Nice Boy is losing patience, no matter how much he tries not to show it, and Closet Case will pick up on it. Closet Case will probably try to stay out of Nice Boy's way and avoid him as much possible. You're the type of couple who can split up using just a few words, and even if you both are smiling there will be palpable gloom and despair.

Moreover, even if Closet Case does come out, there will be difficulties. As long as both of you are disinclined to discuss your needs and instead act as if everything is wonderful, there won't be much intimacy in your union. You'll need to develop shared activities (again, Closet Case must come out) to keep your relationship vital. Otherwise, you run the risk of drifting off into the fetid waters of mediocrity.

Closet Case has a lot of self-exploration to do, because he is barely in touch with who he is, and who he turns out to be might not be compatible with Nice Boy. However, if both of you are working on intimacy in your life together, you can develop a solid relationship.

NICE BOY AND SEXPOT
★

What's Good: If you can imagine combining Hawaiian punch with gin, you might have an idea of what it's like when Nice Boy meets

Sexpot. They just don't go together. Though Nice Boy is far too polite to ever say it, he resents Sexpot's behavior and might even find it morally offensive. In privacy, Nice Boy can be a bit of a Sexpot himself, but he has that funny way of not quite being cognizant of his sexual nature, so he will not recognize the similarity. Also, his fundamental lack of confidence makes him assume that Sexpot would never be interested in someone like him. Nice Boy might even be a bit tongue-tied in Sexpot's presence, which Sexpot might misinterpret as some profound attraction on Nice Boy's part. But probably Nice Boy is simply overwhelmed and flustered by Sexpot's demeanor.

As if this weren't enough, Sexpot is unlikely to be attracted to Nice Boy, though he might derive cruel pleasure out of leading him on. If you do get together physically, things might heat up more than Sexpot bargained for, and there might be a brief period of attraction. If such is the case, you'll both get to experience some fairly good sex.

The parting of ways will probably barely register with Sexpot. Nice Boy might surprise himself by getting upset, and even a little angry. But he'll lick his wounds and soon enough decide that things didn't work out because Sexpot just wasn't very *nice*.

What Needs Work: If you become seriously involved, it will be an uphill climb all the way. Sexpot will need to work extremely hard at reminding himself that he need not always connect to men sexually, and that it's possible to enjoy a man's company without so much as flirting or insinuating. Nice Boy will need to remember that he tries to deny much of the wildness inherent in the life experience, and that what he doesn't like about Sexpot is something he'd do well to start embracing in himself.

But all this depends on your willingness to try, and while it's possible that such will be the case, it is far from a sure thing. Sexpot's way of being festive and outgoing does not inspire Nice Boy's confidence, and so his sexiness is unlikely to rub off on Nice Boy. And Nice Boy will bring out a kind of emotional horniness in Sexpot, who will want to shake Nice Boy out of his complacency and feel the kind of intense connection to a man that he craves. Despite Nice Boy's willingness to be sexually playful, he does not give Sexpot the kind of all-encompassing urgency he thinks he needs.

You have dramatically different ways of avoiding the pain in your lives, but the differences tend to pull you apart rather than complement each other. You probably do not have any hobbies or activities in common, nor are you drawn to the same types of people. Unless you're willing to make your relationship a full-time job, it's doubtful that you'll be good for each other.

NICE BOY AND SHY SNOB
★

What's Good: Nice Boy may try to reach out to Shy Snob, and Shy Snob might even be touched by his doing so and try to respond in kind. But before long, Shy Snob's need to retreat into himself will conflict with Nice Boy's need to keep everything harmonious. In theory, you both can be good for each other, in that Shy Snob can teach Nice Boy about having his own space, and Nice Boy can show Shy Snob how to extend himself socially. But it's far from a certainty that things will ever get that far.

When making love, Nice Boy will try to reach out to Shy Snob, who will respond with a superficial insistence that nothing is wrong—or else make up some excuse about why he's so distracted. But Shy Snob is not always nice, and before long his moodiness or distance will scare Nice Boy away. If Shy Snob is feeling especially superior, he might even enjoy putting Nice Boy down, just to watch Nice Boy's facade crumble.

And that's about as good as it gets.

What Needs Work: If you decide to have a relationship, Nice Boy will become surprisingly snippy. But it will be in a small-minded, nitpicky way; Nice Boy's friends will feel that he's changed for the worse. Shy Snob will fluctuate between brooding avoidance and insults hurled like arrows into a bull's-eye. Nice Boy will act as if nothing were bothering him, which will make Shy Snob feel all the more angry and frustrated.

When Shy Snob is feeling superior, Nice Boy will have a way of smilingly cutting Shy Snob down to size. When Shy Snob feels he's worse than other people, Nice Boy will try to cheer him up, but not know how. His pleasantries will sound like a foreign language to Shy Snob, whose reasons for despair are much too complicated for any pleasant platitude from Nice Boy.

Both of you will become somewhat afraid of confronting the other. You'd both be shocked to learn this, however, since each of you will be convinced that it's the other one who's the bully, always putting you down and never seeming to understand anything you say.

The sex will probably dwindle down to nothing. Unlike some couples, though, you won't get much comfort out of hugging or holding hands, instead. You'll both feel fundamentally inadequate to meet the other's needs, and in the brooding silence you will both ache for freedom. Only the bravest of souls can do the work necessary to make this a happy relationship.

NICE BOY AND THERAPY JUNKIE
★★

What's Good: Therapy Junkie talks about things much more intricately—and much more negatively—than Nice Boy is accustomed to. Still, if Nice Boy is willing to listen to Therapy Junkie and not dismiss all of his issues with pat little sayings, Therapy Junkie might feel that Nice Boy is a sympathetic soul. And if there is a mutual attraction, things might work fairly well.

The basis of your relationship will largely be that Therapy Junkie needs to get better, and that Nice Boy will try to give him patience, understanding, and love. If this is as far as things go, the relationship is destined to be unstable. But if along the way Nice Boy starts getting in touch with some of his own less than ideal memories, you might be able to redefine your relationship into something more mutual and sturdy. Some of Nice Boy's niceness might rub off on Therapy Junkie, who may start to learn that there's more to life than carrying a grudge.

Certainly the sex can be one positive aspect, provided that Nice Boy can be patient with Therapy Junkie's reluctance to open up. Nice Boy must also not take it personally when Therapy Junkie closes back down once he does open up. In his own way, Nice Boy can be somewhat distant, so Therapy Junkie may not mind it when Nice Boy pleasantly shuts down.

Nice Boy will not pry into Therapy Junkie's therapy, not so much because he respects Therapy Junkie's privacy, but because it involves icky stuff. In return, Nice Boy can enjoy feeling like the one who has it together, because in many other combinations Nice Boy often privately feels inadequate.

What Needs Work: You tend to be judgmental of each other. Nice Boy thinks that Therapy Junkie is overly critical, and after a while Therapy Junkie thinks that Nice Boy is in denial. You'll have conversations in which Therapy Junkie is superficially talking about himself, but is actually talking about Nice Boy. Nice Boy will not take the hint, and Therapy Junkie will never be certain if Nice Boy is simply dense or is purposefully avoiding the issue. At the same time, a moralistic, insistent undertone will creep into Nice Boy's seemingly superficial discussions of the weather, or who at work ordered salad for lunch. He will seem to be saying, *"This is what life is all about, not all the therapy stuff you keep talking about."*

You both have to remember that while you can be a positive influence in someone else's life, in the final analysis it is up to that person to change. Therapy Junkie needs to develop patience for Nice Boy and learn that just because a relationship doesn't feel perfect at all times it doesn't necessarily mean it should end. And Nice Boy must develop a sense of humor about his lover's being a bit of a mess.

Since you're both somewhat disconnected from your sexual natures, you'll want to have a lot of honest discussion about sex. Start at the beginning: how you felt growing up gay in a homophobic society, how you felt the first time you had sex with a man, and so forth.

You need to partake of an activity together regularly. It should get you out of the house and integrated into the world; watching the same TV shows will but reinforce the distance between you. If it's something physical, like a sport or a hike, so much the better, because you need to get away from your battle of the psychological, and the tendency for each of you to believe he is 100 percent right in his approach to life.

PAL AND PAL
★★★

What's Good: You're likely to turn to each other as a kind of last resort. Pal doesn't like himself much, so he's not initially attracted to someone who reminds him of himself. Since Pal sees people as either givers or receivers, he feels that in a relationship he's supposed to perform a lot of chores and favors, and in return his partner is supposed to be sexy and romantic. However, if the two of you do decide to be practical and give things a chance, you'll have a pretty good time of it.

You'll be in sympathy with each other as you go about being helpful and jolly and good sports. You won't nag each other about spending more time on the relationship or to stop always having to *do* something when at home. You can perform various tasks and errands *together* and so have someone to hold hands with when you drive over to the soup kitchen or agree to perform in drag for an AIDS fund-raiser. When your moods turn foul, you'll each have a partner who understands why.

Both of you are afraid of being alone for any length of time, so having a partner who feels the same way can paradoxically help you to overcome this fear. By having someone around all the time, you may start to realize that it's not all it's cracked up to be, and that you can indeed stand a few moments of privacy here and there—you might even crave them. After a while, the endless stream of people coming and going from your home might dwindle to a moderate level.

Sexually, you both assume that you exist to please your partner. At first, it will be a little like the old vaudeville routine: "After you." "No, after *you*." "No, I insist, after you," etc. Assuming this doesn't cause you to break up, sooner or later one of you will have to take the lead, and things should be able to work themselves out. You both have a lot of affection to give and will appreciate having each other to get next to on those long winter nights.

As you become closer, you can begin to trust each other enough to open up about your lack of self-esteem, your age-old fears that nobody likes you, and the self-deprecating humor that you use as a defense mechanism. You'll take comfort in having a mate with so many similar feelings and experiences.

What Needs Work: You both are inclined to a type of masochistic buffoonery, and you run the risk of turning into a rather sad, pathetic couple who perform nightly installments of their zany unhappiness for the benefit of a nonpaying audience of guests. Since you both actively seek flight from pain, you can be a negative influence on each other when it comes to drinking too much, or not attending to daily necessities such as getting enough food and sleep.

You should set aside time in each day to be alone together. The good you can accomplish in each other's life is predicated on the assumption that you aren't just running around in two separate directions and treating your relationship as merely a way of avoiding loneliness. *Talk* to each other. Find out how each of you is feeling—about himself, about his partner, about the direction of his life in general. If your lives don't have a direction, it's time to get one. Where are you headed together? What is your relationship *about?* These are questions you'll need to answer if you want to have a partnership that brings you happiness, rather than simply exists.

Speaking of sex, it's a good example of the kind of black-and-white, either/or thinking you engage in. For example, can two bottoms find happiness together? Yes, providing that they stop assuming that people always have to be one thing or another. So take turns. Find other ways of having sex. Remember that the sex role you've assigned yourselves is not necessarily what you prefer so much as what you think you're supposed to do to please someone else.

You can be good together, provided that you remember that relationships take work—and it begins with working on the self. Be true to your own selves, and not to what you think will make other people like you.

PAL AND PARTY BOY
★★★

What's Good: You're in sympathy with each other's energy; in a way, Party Boy is like Pal's wild yet sophisticated big-city cousin. (And this is true even if Party Boy lives in Smalltown, USA.) When you become kissin' cousins, you combine your efforts to derive happiness—or at least keep away the blues—by being around people. Pal can pull out all stops in getting your home ready for the festivities, and Party Boy can be an even more outrageous host, knowing that Pal is there to clean up the mess.

There is of course a downside to all this: It has a lot to do with avoiding intimacy. But you're both inclined to be defensive men who lash out at those who criticize you, even when they're trying to be helpful. So if you're both ready to pull your lives together, you are each the type of man whom the other might just listen to, because you understand what makes each other tick. If substance abuse is a problem for you both, you're the kind of couple who can go into recovery together and give each other a lot of strength and support.

If you are in fact ready to settle down, neither of you has to worry about life being dull. Together, you can make even a simple evening of watching TV seem exciting. Party Boy can make devastating quips through a TV movie-of-the-week, and Pal can serve up big gooey sundaes. You bring out an appealing mischievous quality in each other. Even in spiritual or therapeutic settings, there's a healthy irreverence that you lend to the activity.

There's something important that you may learn from each other: you're both already likable and interesting men, and you don't have to do all the extra stuff you do to impress people—Pal by doing favors, and Party Boy by being a million laughs. At the same time, Pal can help Party Boy learn that helping people can be fun (as opposed to getting them loaded or putting them down). Party Boy can enable Pal to realize that life is to be enjoyed.

The sex may take a while to develop a rhythm, because it may take a while for the two of you to get serious about your relationship. On the surface, there may be a lot of oohing and aahing, but you both tend to give *performances* in bed. Pal wants to please, and Party Boy wants to show how wickedly decadent he is. As the love and trust develops, you can get past all that and start figuring out what things you really do enjoy together. Until you reach that point, your energies are compatible in that you intuitively understand why your partner is giving the performance he's giving. So it's possible to at least feel *comfortable* together before you become truly intimate.

What Needs Work: You both already live too fast, and the potential is there to encourage each other to live even faster. Whether or not you drink too much, there's a tendency to do *something* too much— even if it's just spending too much money—and you need to work on keeping your relationship stable. The key is finding your own stability inside yourselves by getting in touch with the things you do to avoid experiencing closeness.

You could benefit by taking one day a week off from all the stuff you do. Don't drink or call people or go places or do things. Just sit around the house together for an afternoon. Talk or make love, if you feel like it. If any chores are done, have Party Boy do them; let Pal be waited on for a change. Otherwise, don't do any chores at all. Just learn to be together. If you're both very into improving yourselves, meditate or write in your journals. Otherwise, watch a video or play cards. Learn that mundane can be okay—that you can survive it.

Even during the rest of the week, you might want to impose a few ground rules. For example, in the evening after work, Pal can only perform three chores. Or Party Boy can only sarcastically put down Pal three times a night. Sexually, be patient with each other—you've both been hiding from yourselves a long time. Learn to talk about how you feel about sex, what about it brings you pleasure, and what about it makes you afraid.

You can forge something together that's solid, because you're temperamentally compatible. At the same time, this compatibility can lead you down destructive paths if you don't work on getting past your fears and insecurities.

PAL AND PERENNIAL CLOSET CASE
★★

What's Good: You're a gay equivalent of a straight couple who rather humorlessly tolerate each other for fifty years because you needed to work on the farm and raise your kids and save your pennies. Pal is busy being everyone's pal, while Closet Case is looming about the house reading his newspaper and making sure the shades are drawn so the neighbors don't get the "wrong idea"—or more accurately, the right idea. There's a kind desperation in your getting together, as if to be single were a fate worse than death.

As devitalized as your relationship might be, it is at least constant, and probably there is relatively little arguing. Though you are together because each of you is afraid to be alone, you bring each other at least some moments of genuine comfort. Pal would of course prefer a partner who's more comfortable with himself as a gay man, but he can keep himself so busy minding other people's business that he barely has time to think about it.

Since Closet Case is heterosexist—he's ashamed of being gay because it doesn't match his heterosexual ideal—he gives a pretty good

imitation of a straight spouse. Around the house, he can be as attentive and annoying as any husband or wife. So it does feel like a
"real marriage." Sadly and ironically, that you don't act married once
you leave the house can strengthen the bond between you—it's
your tragic little secret.

Your sex life is probably lackluster. There's too much mediocrity
between you to make an effort toward real passion. As long as Pal
feels "useful," he won't mind too much. Anything too intensely
intimate might frighten him, because it would be so unfamiliar. And
Closet Case can take comfort in that the relationship isn't all that
great, because it reinforces his belief that coming out isn't worth it.

What Needs Work: Once again, Closet Case needs to come out.
Only then can your relationship take on a vital dimension that inspires Pal to get out of his own rut and deem himself worthy of
something truly intimate and romantic and sexy. Otherwise, Pal will
go about his busy, fearful way.

As part of the coming out, the two of you could join a social
group. Closet Case can also grow more comfortable with himself
by accompanying Pal on some of his activities. The gay-related ones
will of course help Closet Case feel more at ease about being gay.
But even if Pal is helping some elderly straight widow, Closet Case
can experience firsthand a straight person not minding or caring that
he's in a gay relationship.

You could also stand to develop a decent sex life. Go ahead and
invest in some porn or fancy gadgets. Closet Case needs to feel free
to explore his sexual nature, and Pal can channel his helpfulness into
this endeavor, rather than just pretending there isn't a problem.

When one partner is firmly in the closet and therefore accustomed to lying, you likely don't know all kinds of things about each
other. You need to start having honest communication. Even if
you've been living together for years, it's possible that you know
relatively little about each other, especially since Pal often keeps busy
at the cost of paying attention. Take some of those personality quiz-
zes together. See a marriage counselor. And don't be too shocked
if either or both of you are seeing other people on the sly. There's

nothing wrong with having an open relationship, provided that you're honest about it. Otherwise, what's so great about lying to someone for fifty years? Is that really all that either of you want out of life?

PAL AND SEXPOT
★

What's Good: Pal might well be attracted to Sexpot—*lots* of guys are attracted to Sexpot—but it's unlikely that Sexpot will feel the same way. He might be momentarily distracted by Pal's attentiveness, and he won't mind it when Pal takes him out to an expensive restaurant. But Pal simply doesn't project enough sexual energy to engage Sexpot's attention for long. In theory, Sexpot can relate to the fantasy of having a sexually awkward sugar daddy, but in real life he'll believe he can do a lot better.

Perhaps the best that can be said about this match is that Sexpot might acquire a trinket or two from it, and since Pal probably never realistically believed he could keep a guy like Sexpot, he'll drown his sorrows in busywork and move on.

It's possible for Sexpot to learn from Pal about helping others as an alternative way of connecting with people, and that Sexpot could teach Pal a thing or two about how to have fun. But for this to happen, Sexpot must think Pal is interesting, and this probably isn't going to be the case.

What Needs Work: Something devastating needs to happen to Sexpot for him to be in a receptive enough frame of mind to take a chance on Pal. But as Sexpot heals from his grief, he will need to reprioritize his life if he wants to continue to feel good about being with Pal. Otherwise, before long it will be business as usual, and he'll feel restless and bored (and perhaps even degraded) by being with Pal.

If the two of you are toughing it out, you need to work hard at breaking the habits that keep you from being intimate. Pal must regularly affirm that he is worthy of being loved for who he is, and not for the things he does to help people. Despite Sexpot's allure, he is not intrinsically "superior" to Pal, and Pal should not feel "unworthy" of him. All relationships involve give-and-take, and if Sexpot were getting nothing out of being with Pal, he would probably have already moved on.

Also, Sexpot must work hard at finding ways of connecting to men other than through sex. He needs to realize that love is never something to be taken lightly, and that it comes in many forms—including Pal's way. Pal is eager to please Sexpot in bed, and that ought to account for something. Sexpot must remember that sex has often been a way for him to avoid getting close to men, and letting them get to know who he is as a person.

You can learn a lot from each other, but it's unlikely you'll give each other the chance to do so. Too much work is required to make either of you feel safe or engaged for long.

PAL AND SHY SNOB
★

What's Good: You're on very different wavelengths and will probably not last long as a couple. Shy Snob cannot even begin to imagine living the way Pal does. It seems so glaringly obvious to Shy Snob that Pal is trying to get people to like him, and such emotional transparency is repugnant to Shy Snob. Doesn't Pal realize that people are using him? And look at these people he associates with—doesn't Pal have any standards whatsoever?

Pal might be nice to Shy Snob, but Shy Snob will respond with cool politeness at best. Pal very much brings out Shy Snob's superiority complex. He'll think that Pal is lucky that Shy Snob even deigned to say "No, thank you" to him. If the two of you bed down together, Shy Snob will feel violated and unclean. Pal has so little finesse, after all. Indeed, the encounter might inspire Shy Snob to stay away from men for quite some time afterward, just to recover.

Shy Snob is not always mean-spirited, and sometimes he's even a warm and helpful person to be around. But unlike Pal, he believes that helping people is not necessarily doing them any favors. Shy Snob is quite self-sufficient, thank you very much, and he feels that if *he* can take care of himself, *anyone* should be able to. So he also does not understand Pal's fear of being alone and is quite out of sympathy with it.

Since Shy Snob is smart, he knows not only how to scare Pal away, but (if the mood strikes him) how to do it in a way that hurts Pal's feelings big time. And mind you, this is what's relatively "good" about this relationship.

What Needs Work: As with Sexpot, Shy Snob is likely to pursue something with Pal only if he's been humbled. When Shy Snob is feeling inferior, he might well be grateful for Pal's presence in his life. But once he's feeling better about himself, he's likely to think he's "too good" for Pal. And for Pal's own good as much as his own, he'll end things. If Pal doesn't get it right away, Shy Snob will be angered and insulted: Imagine someone like Pal thinking he could be partners with someone of Shy Snob's caliber!

If you both are willing to make your relationship a full-time job, you can try to build something together. Pal will need to develop a great deal of self-confidence in order to communicate with Shy Snob as an equal and not be swayed by Shy Snob's mood swings. Otherwise, Pal will fluctuate between feeling like a nurse who ministers to Shy Snob when he's feeling low, and a slave who is all but spat upon when Shy Snob is feeling superior. Pal needs to realize that Shy Snob is essentially insecure and not as different from Pal as he likes to act.

Shy Snob has to understand that even though Pal may not be the most imaginative or stimulating person he's ever met, his intentions are sincere, which is more than can be said for Shy Snob in certain moods. Also, Shy Snob must realize that he can be intimidating, and that Pal might well have more charisma than Shy Snob is seeing. Additionally, Shy Snob must remind himself that he, too, can be hard to get close to, and that maybe he's lucky to have Pal in his life.

But for all this to transpire, you both should expect a great deal of turmoil along the way.

PAL AND THERAPY JUNKIE
★★

What's Good: If Therapy Junkie projects anything, it's that he's in need of help, and Pal is certainly willing to give plenty of that. The problem is that the type of help Pal is willing to give is not the type of help Therapy Junkie is looking for. Pal shies away from introspection and may not understand some of the things that Therapy Junkie is talking about. Of course, this will not stop Pal from *trying* to be helpful. If Therapy Junkie says, "My mother never loved me," Pal might say, "I see your radio's broken. I know where you can get it fixed." Moreover, Therapy Junkie is likely to deem Pal to be "codependent" or an "enabler."

Nevertheless, if there's a strong attraction between the two of you, it's possible to make things work. However out of sync Pal's responses might be to Therapy Junkie's needs, in the broad sense it is a *response,* and Therapy Junkie (who so often feels that nobody cares) might be flattered on general principle.

Therapy Junkie also wants to feel understood, so Pal will probably have to do some homework on the issues that Therapy Junkie discusses—Pal may have to read books or attend meetings. He will be frightened of doing so, because it's new information, and he doesn't relish having to explore himself. However, if he does, it might prove beneficial both for himself and for the relationship. So Therapy Junkie can help Pal get on the path to exploring his own issues.

If this happens, Therapy Junkie will be in the novel position of being a kind of teacher instead of student. It will be Pal who seems to need more help. By reversing roles, so to speak, you both can learn about new aspects of yourselves and new kinds of risks you can take to be emotionally present for another man.

How you live, whom you associate with, and what you do in bed will probably need to be created as you go along. Your existing patterns are not conducive to intimacy and are not very compatible. As long as it can be framed as a growth exercise, Therapy Junkie will be willing to change. Pal will need to feel that it's another way of helping someone—in this case, helping his partner to have a happy relationship. You'll both need to explore yourselves—and each other—to see what feels good and what doesn't. Just bear in mind that your goal should be intimacy and not avoidance.

What Needs Work: The success of your relationship is contingent upon both of you being willing to change. Pal needs to seriously understand that how he's living just doesn't work. Therapy Junkie needs to realize that there comes a point in which he simply must *start* living and stop thinking that he has to endlessly work on himself before he's ready to embrace what life has to offer. Given your druthers, you would probably not have fallen for each other. Pal would like a less complex lover, and Therapy Junkie would like a more complex lover. So you both need to be willing to work with what you have.

Therapy Junkie thinks too much, while Pal often does not think enough. When there is tension between you, both of you need to remember that you're both right and both wrong.

You need to avoid being critical of each other. This doesn't mean that you should never point out things you want to change about the relationship. But remember that both of you function from somewhat stilted perspectives. Neither of you is the world's greatest expert on how to be happy or get close to people.

Each of you needs to let go of a lot of preconceptions about life, love, and who you are as gay men for your relationship to work. This can be extremely beneficial, but it will take a lot of commitment and courage. If you both can strive to improve your characters and resist being disappointed when your partner doesn't seem to be working on himself in the same way, you can build something together that takes you into surprisingly interesting places.

PARTY BOY AND PARTY BOY
★★★

What's Good: If there's an obstacle to the two of you getting together, it's that either or both of you might assume that the other guy does not have serious intentions. Like two people walking aimlessly down the street, each one thinking the other knows where he's going, you can get into a vicious cycle in which you assume he just wants to have fun, so you act as if that is all you want, too, so he acts as if it's all he wants . . . well, you get the idea. But assuming someone takes things to the next level, you have a lot going for you as a couple.

Obviously, you both like to get down and boogie. If you have disagreements about how to spend your time, it will be more a matter of whether you should go to party A or party B. Neither of you is going to say, "Can't you stay home tonight and watch PBS with me?"

Whether you have access to the party circuit or do what you can in a small town, you have the stability of partnership while still having lots of fun meeting men, dancing with them, and—if you have an open relationship—even fooling around with them. So you get to have the best of both worlds: security and freedom. You can stay together without getting bored.

Sexually, you share the same sensibility. You probably like to keep the dance music thumping away while you make love, so that you can be reminded of bars and drinking and whooping it up. If you're both too tired (or inebriated) to do much, you both understand.

Hopefully, you boogie within a reasonable budget. If you don't, at least you'll both be equally to blame and can figure out together how to resolve your monetary crisis. (But please stick to legal ways of making money.) If either because of financial, emotional, or physical strains, the party comes to an end, you'll have quite a shared history to fall back on and should be able to help each other to adjust.

Given all you have in common (and the fact that some men find you a bit much to take), you should be able to build up enough trust to work on your intimacy issues together. And you should be able to find new, more honest ways of dealing with your pain, as well as new ways of relating to each other as gay men.

What Needs Work: While the two of you obviously are a lot alike, it doesn't mean that you'll always be a good influence on each other. Partying is not a bad thing, but when it becomes the *only* way you know how to relate to men, something is not right. If you both can maintain a sense of humor about it all and not take it too seriously, then you can have a great time. But if exhaustion, substance abuse, mind games, or dishonesty creep into your party activities, things can get gruesome in a hurry.

You both should work on cultivating other ways of spending time together—as well as other ways of spending time with friends. It doesn't mean you can *never* party, just do it a bit more moderately. You should be able to relax in each other's presence—and relax around other gay men—without loud music and bright lights and cocktails. If you can't, you're ultimately not going to be able to bond with each other. The only way you know how to try is through an essentially artificial setting. It will be as if you live in a kind of limbo until music begins.

It can be fun and lively to get bitchy with each other, but it can cross over into real nastiness. Hurtful words, of course, take their toll in a relationship—even when Party Boy A can throw it right back at Party Boy B.

You might assume that you can always kiss and make up. But since your sex is probably not as deeply gratifying as you both like to pretend, it may not be powerful enough to eliminate the pain you cause each other. The only way to get past the destructive elements of your relationship is to work on becoming more well-rounded gay men who are able to experience honesty and intimacy in a variety of ways.

PARTY BOY AND PERENNIAL CLOSET CASE
★★

What's Good: Assuming that Closet Case is willing to socialize after dark in discreet gay settings, the two of you might be able to build something together. Needless to say, Party Boy would appreciate a lover who isn't afraid to be seen at more public events. But unless you're to be the poster couple for a huge gala event, there might be a way you can work through these things.

Being in a hedonistic setting can bring out the animal in the nerdiest of humans, and even Closet Case might find himself getting into the party spirit, dancing and acting sexy and bold. In fact, drinking and carrying on in a darkened bar might be the one way that Closet Case lets down his inhibitions. Since Party Boy places little importance on the nonparty world, he may not mind that much if he has a boyfriend who isn't out to the people in his life. As long as Closet Case can boogie when the music starts playing, Party Boy can be fairly well satisfied.

Closet Case holds back when it comes to sex, but then, so does Party Boy, albeit for different reasons. So fair to middlin' sex can be experienced as the hottest thing since Carmen Miranda. Neither of you is really being honest, but nobody's being hurt (or at least not intentionally). For Closet Case in particular it's better than being home alone, since it's giving him *some* connection to his gay identity.

Hosting a party will be problematic if Closet Case is at all nervous about who's invited, and who might know whom at his office, and so forth. However, if the "wrong" person is there, it might be good in the larger scheme of things for Closet Case to have been slightly outed.

What Needs Work: Though you can both do worse, your respective personalities tend to reinforce patterns of nonintimacy. Closet Case can stay as closeted as can be, because he can get his gay jollies off at parties and dance clubs. Party Boy gets the idea that the only way to have a good time with his lover is to keep on partying. You don't by nature challenge each other to confront your Intimacy Blockers.

When the only way Closet Case feels comfortable being gay is when he's under the influence of booze or drugs, he is making himself extremely vulnerable to alcoholism and drug addiction. Party Boy is unlikely to be aware of the seriousness of the situation and will deny that it's a problem when confronted with it. At worst, your relationship could set in motion financial ruin, mental cruelty, even accidental or intentional violence.

Allegedly, what the two of you really have to offer each other is sex. But since this sex ain't all it's cracked up to be, it doesn't help you get past the bad times as well as you keep hoping it will.

To have a good relationship, you have to have an honest relationship. As long as Closet Case is closeted, this is more or less an impossibility. But Party Boy will not help matters if he continues to hide from his own issues by trying to dance them away. You both need to find new ways of enacting your gay identity in order to build intimacy together.

PARTY BOY AND SEXPOT
★★★★

What's Good: Obviously, it isn't difficult to imagine how the two of you might end up in bed together, and perhaps that will be the end of that. But if Sexpot is able to touch something vulnerable in Party Boy, a deeper attraction can develop. Party Boy intuitively understands that Sexpot not only wants to be lavished with attention, but that he wants to be lavished with *exciting* attention. Going to all the hot spots will endear Party Boy to Sexpot.

Though Sexpot enjoys attention from all men, he'll be surprisingly faithful to Party Boy (in public, at least) and will enjoy making out with him as other men watch enviously. Party Boy will feel as if he's found a living embodiment of his most cherished fantasy, and he'll make sure Sexpot knows it. Sexpot will feel loved and respond in kind.

Party Boy is not necessarily unattractive, but Sexpot stands out more. Physically, there's a glamorous contrast between the two of you that adds to the adulation you receive when you go out together, and which makes the relationship between you more exciting. Even if you have similar physiques and you both show off your bare chests when dancing, you'll make sure that you come across differently to onlookers. It might only be that you make a point of dancing differently. But you want the world to know that your differences blend together beautifully, like peanut butter and jelly.

Party Boy is a vocal bed partner, which Sexpot appreciates. Sexpot wants to be told that he's the best lay in the world, and Party Boy will gladly give him the desired impression. Party Boy is actually somewhat out of touch with his sexual desires, but Sexpot has a large bag of tricks (so to speak) to share with him. And so Party Boy might discover that he likes certain things that he did not necessarily think about before. As you sex life evolves, you might find yourselves getting exclusively into some sort of uniform fetish, or other type of role play.

Neither of you likes to think much about the serious side of life. But if fate forces you to do so, there's a strong foundation in place. You might surprise each other by how much you can be there for each other during troubled times. And as you grow as human beings, you may just find that the source of your shared attraction goes much deeper than the surface.

What Needs Work: Life in the fast lane can take its toll in all sorts of ways. There's a temptation for both of you to abuse your bodies as you show yourselves off to the world. Poor health and irritability can make for some stormy moments. Sexpot probably works out (or in any case is body-conscious), but when he gets attached to

Party Boy, he might start getting careless with himself without meaning to. (And of course the potential is there for substance abuse.) You'd both do well to set aside some "down time," in which you can rest, regroup, get a little fresh air, stretch the ol' body— you know the drill.

Your relationship functions well in all the superficial ways, and this is nothing to take for granted. Squabbles over someone's appearance or where to hang out have caused many a breakup. Nonetheless, over time you both should develop more of an inner life if you want a relationship that's truly satisfying. Party Boy needs to discover how to communicate in nonglittery settings, and Sexpot needs to discover how to get close to men when outside the bedroom. All those mundane or unattractive things you both like to claim you are not are, in fact, a part of who each of you is. And it will be challenging to maintain a relationship over time when it's aimed at ignoring about 80 percent of reality.

Party Boy needs to be honest with Sexpot about what really works for him in bed and what doesn't. Sexpot needs to be mature enough not to be devastated when he hears that something he's been doing is not the end-all, be-all he thought it was. And Sexpot needs to learn that his lovemaking, though highly competent, is indeed within the human realm, and not the superhuman. It doesn't make who he really is inside go away, just as Party Boy's fun and games don't obliterate his inner nature, either.

PARTY BOY AND SHY SNOB
★★

What's Good: If Shy Snob thinks Party Boy has good taste and a lot of style, he might just be intrigued. It won't hurt matters if Party Boy takes Shy Snob to ritzy gallery openings or upscale music clubs. Like Sexpot, Shy Snob is hurt and offended when men don't want to take him to the best or most interesting places, but while Sexpot is seeking validation of his sexuality, Shy Snob desires to validate something more intangible inside him. He wants a man to say, in effect, "I see that you are a man of rare quality and sensitivity, so I will expose you to the beauty you deserve."

If Party Boy drinks too much and sings off-key in public or takes Shy Snob to visit some drunk, boring couple, Shy Snob will be permanently turned off. Party Boy will need to be on his best behavior with Shy Snob—which may not be such a bad thing for Party Boy.

If Party Boy survives this initial trial by fire, Shy Snob will appreciate that Party Boy likes to get out and do things. Shy Snob doesn't have many people to do things with and is embarrassed to be seen in public alone. So he'll like having Party Boy around to take him places.

Some people may wonder what Party Boy is doing with Shy Snob, because he's so much less outgoing than Party Boy. Even when Shy Snob feels inspired to relate to others, there's often something off-putting about it, because he isn't trying to fit in so much as set himself apart. Still, contrasts can be interesting in a relationship. As long as things don't turn nasty, people will at least be fascinated by the two of you, as if in suspense over when the secret of your attraction will be revealed. It will be good for Shy Snob to spend more time around people, and it will also be good for Party Boy to have Shy Snob's tempering influence. Party Boy may start to see the superficiality of many a party moment.

What Needs Work: Shy Snob is accustomed to spending a lot of time alone, and he will grow profoundly tired trying to keep up with Party Boy. When Shy Snob "vants to be alone," Party Boy should let him and not take it personally.

Shy Snob often gets full of himself when he's around people for any length of time. Party Boy should be prepared for how caustic and critical this seemingly "shy" man can be. In a battle of sarcasm, Party Boy should be prepared to lose. Even if Shy Snob seems to quietly take it when Party Boy berates him, sooner or later he will open his mouth, and a six-headed, fire-breathing dragon will pop out.

Though each of you senses that the other has something to teach him, you are coming from extremely different viewpoints. Shy Snob loves time to himself, while Party Boy is fairly terrified of it. Shy Snob senses that Party Boy is running away from himself, but since he at least is doing it with flair, Shy Snob will not be totally critical of him. Still, after a while Shy Snob will find it difficult to have much respect for Party Boy. He'll want deep conversations that Party Boy technically can follow but lacks the patience to engage in for any length of time. Party Boy will come to regard Shy Snob as kind of an oddball, and anything that makes Party Boy have to stop and think too much is likely to be met with scorn.

If both of you work hard at being honest with each other, you can learn to embrace in you own selves the things you fear most. But don't expect it to just happen by itself.

PARTY BOY AND THERAPY JUNKIE
★★★

What's Good: Since at least some of Therapy Junkie's pursuit of psychological well-being masks his fear of becoming his own man, his personality has a Peter Pan dimension that can merge surprisingly well with that of Party Boy—who, in his own way, doesn't want to grow up. Therapy Junkie can provide good fodder for party chat, since he tends to be up on the latest developments in self-wellness. He's like one of those "interesting guests" you can pay to have come to a party, only he does it for free.

Party Boy won't be very interested as Therapy Junkie launches into one of his spiels, but at least Party Boy knows how to *act* like a good listener. And anyway, past a certain point Therapy Junkie really just wants to hear himself talk, so as long as Party Boy doesn't seem rude, Therapy Junkie will be fairly content. Also, there are all the people that Party Boy can expose Therapy Junkie to, and at least a few of them are bound to be good listeners, too.

You're two different people, but in ways that can be beneficial to you both. Therapy Junkie needs to lighten up, and Party Boy can certainly show him how to do so. In return, Therapy Junkie can demonstrate to Party Boy that it's possible to explore less than rapturous memories and still function through a day of life. If Therapy Junkie can convince Party Boy that some sort of therapy group is "fun," Party Boy might even get up the courage to attend and start to explore some of his own issues.

Your respective friends might wonder what each of you sees in each other, but you both like to engage people in conversation, so neither set of friends will dislike your partner outright. Underneath it all, you both crave acceptance from other people and feel that you didn't get much of it while growing up. In contrasting ways, both of you are still reacting to wounds to the soul you received in the past. This can form a bond between you, and if the attraction is strong enough, it might get you past your differences so you can explore your common ground.

What Needs Work: After a while, Party Boy might think that Therapy Junkie is neurotic and a drag, while Therapy Junkie will believe that Party Boy is in major denial about his unhappiness, and perhaps his use of drugs and alcohol. You both need to remember the qualities that draw you together that transcend all of that. You fell in love with what you both were, not what you weren't. If you both are working on improving your own character, the defects of your partner will be in perspective.

As with certain other combinations, the two of you have different social worlds, and so you should each create your own set of friends and find at least one activity you can do together. It might be especially useful for you to volunteer for a worthy cause. Party Boy probably attends a lot of fund-raisers, but he could benefit by actually making phone calls or running errands himself. It can bring a healthy groundedness into his life. Therapy Junkie will find it useful to get out of his head and realize that people out there have to live with some pretty serious problems. And when the two of you work together in a love relationship, the sense of reward you feel for helping other people will be that much stronger.

Given your perpetual boyishness, neither of you enjoys accepting adult responsibility for your actions. Emotional upsets tend to be seen as someone else's fault, and since you're boyfriends, you each have a convenient person to blame everything on. You can also be irresponsible with finances. Party Boy has difficulty comprehending that a bill collector can actually be taking it all seriously, while Therapy Junkie will feel that morally he doesn't have to pay up because the bill collector is being so *mean*. You need to work on yourselves so that you can enjoy a mature, man-to-man way of life.

PERENNIAL CLOSET CASE
AND PERENNIAL CLOSET CASE
★★

What's Good: You certainly understand each other. There will be no arguments along the lines of "When are you going to explain to your parents about me?" You'll both be meticulously careful not to out each other and, without a second thought, will take turns sleeping on the couch when relatives visit. So in a limited sort of way, the issue about coming out will seem to be "resolved." After all, there isn't any discussion about doing things differently.

When any two lovers share a secret, it can make them feel closer. You'll find your mutual closetness poignant, and over time, erotic. There's nothing all that kinky going on in this; it's just that most people eroticize the circumstances of their sexuality. It might even get to where you can't perform sexually unless the shades are pulled down. In any case, your intimate encounters are nonthreatening because you both hold something back. If ultimately this keeps you from being your full selves, you find the arrangement manageable day to day.

Since you aren't public about your relationship, you probably spend a fair amount of time apart. If you attend work or family functions alone, it can make your time with your partner seem extremely special. At times you'll feel like a tragic couple from an old movie.

Chances are you both are quite busy with your careers. One of the "reasons" you can't come out probably has to do with your job, and so by being extremely dedicated to it you can justify staying in the closet. So probably you can build a stable financial future together.

What Needs Work: A great deal of lethargy and despair hangs like a dark cloud over your relationship. You both may try to deny that it's there, but it is. You can keep humming along in this purgatory for years and try to convince yourselves you're happy. But about the happiest you get is how other couples feel when they're becoming cordially estranged. You always feel as if there's this *distance* between the two of you that you just can't get past.

At times, you both think that if only you felt totally comfortable in the relationship, you might start to come out to people. After all, why tell everyone about this other guy if you're going to break up soon? Besides, there's enough that feels unsettled in your relationship without having to deal with all your nutty relatives . . .

Ironically, the truth is just the opposite. If you come out, then you might actually start to feel closer. Maybe you won't, but you'll never have the level of intimacy you want while you're both refusing to come out of the closet. By hiding who you are from the world, neither of you is getting used to your own skin. You aren't getting a sense of how you handle various people knowing who you are. When you're unfamiliar with your own self, it's unrealistic to expect that you can connect to somebody else.

If you love each other, that's a lot right there. You don't have to go it alone. Figure out how you can help each other to come out and start living honest lives. One way or another, you'll both start to find real happiness if you do.

PERENNIAL CLOSET CASE AND SEXPOT
★★

What's Good: For this coupling to work, Closet Case has to keep Sexpot excited. Maybe Closet Case has a lot of money or he travels out of town a lot, where he feels less inhibited about being gay. If he's being shown a good enough time, Sexpot might be willing to be discreet and not dwell on the fact that Closet Case is essentially ashamed of him. (Though even in the best of arrangements, Sexpot will be unable to resist teasing Closet Case by *almost* outing him.) Closet Case will feel macho, as if he were this incredibly powerful man to have gotten himself a kind of kept woman.

If Closet Case hasn't much money, he should expect to work overtime if he wants to keep Sexpot around. Plus, when he comes home, Closet Case shouldn't expect dinner waiting on the stove. Sexpot will expect to be treated to a bit of fun, to make up for having to wait around for Closet Case.

This may not sound like much of an arrangement, but it's a familiar enough one from a million different movies. And since Closet Case doesn't feel that gay relationships somehow "count" as much as straight ones, the sheer familiarity of the arrangement will ironically make it seem more "real" and "solid" to him. It's not as esoteric as more egalitarian gay relationships, and it helps him feel like more of a "traditional" man.

It isn't the sort of arrangement likely to last a lifetime; either or both of you will probably get bored before too long. But neither of you invested much emotionally, so you both got what you wanted from it. Closet Case is not a fully expressive sexual partner, but Sexpot might be able to show him a thing or two just the same. And so Closet Case might get more in touch with his sexuality— and perhaps this will help him to eventually come out.

What Needs Work: This is another situation in which Closet Case gets to have his cake (among other things) and eat it, too. He needs to come out if he's going to find real intimacy, but why should he go through the hassle when some hot stud is willing to put out for him? By being a kind of sugar daddy to Sexpot, Closet Case also helps reinforce Sexpot's belief that the only way to bond with a man is through sex.

Even if you both use the L-word, on some level there's a sense that you're using each other, and so you both might think you're being very "modern" somehow by not falling prey to cheap sentiment. But underneath it all, you're both afraid of your own shadows—you're afraid of what might happen if you tried to achieve a more fulfilling relationship.

Sexpot deeply craves validation from men, and he might think that since Closet Case isn't out, he's somehow "more" of a man than a gay man who is out. But there's actually something rather emotionally tepid about Closet Case, because he's burying so much of his true self (which might be much more passionate).

Closet Case must face who he is as a gay man, and Sexpot must realize that he uses lying naked with a man as a kind of defensive armor. Only then will it be possible for the two of you to have a deeper understanding of yourselves and each other.

PERENNIAL CLOSET CASE AND SHY SNOB
★★

What's Good: Shy Snob has a critical nature, and for him to think a closeted man is worth pursuing, that man will have to have a great many extraordinary qualities to make up for being closeted. It will also not hurt if Closet Case has some exceptionally convincing story for why he can't come out, since Shy Snob has a good nose for dishonesty.

You both will have your reasons for keeping each other at arm's length, but since you're doing it to each other, at least it won't seem unfair. And since you're both a bit afraid of closeness, it might seem as if you've found a practical solution for finding a partner. Over time, the arrangement is likely to feel more like a friendship, but there are worse things in this world than having a close friend.

When you get carried away sexually, you both tend to feel awkward or embarrassed afterward. You probably have sex relatively infrequently, and when you do, it's as if your partner isn't really there. And in a sense, neither of you is fully present. But since Closet Case wishes he weren't gay, and since Shy Snob on some level wishes there were no such thing as sex, *period,* neither of you will mind that much. (Of course, sometimes Shy Snob will get into one of his other kinds of moods, and he will crave Closet Case with a surprising degree of intensity.)

Privately, Shy Snob might wish that Closet Case would come out, and he might even drop a not-so-subtle hint along these lines. But Shy Snob doesn't like feeling emotionally entangled, and he also doesn't like losing arguments. So after a while he will keep his resentments to himself and appreciate the time alone that living with a Closet Case affords him.

What Needs Work: Closet Case thinks that coming out isn't worth it, and Shy Snob often thinks that associating with the human race isn't worth it, and your relationship together will tend to confirm your respective hunches. It won't be some incredibly painful disaster that warps you both for life (you probably won't get involved enough for something like that to happen). But it will be disappointing, especially so since Shy Snob has a violent hatred of mediocrity, and Closet Case must have had a lot to offer for Shy Snob to invest in knowing him.

Even if Shy Snob starts working on his intimacy issues and makes a real effort to connect to Closet Case, he won't feel very satisfied. Because as long as Closet Case is denying who he is, he isn't connecting with anyone. Closet Case can put a fair amount of feeling into his relationships, but Shy Snob is acutely sensitive and will not be convinced. This will encourage Shy Snob to hold back (since it never takes much for him to withdraw emotionally), and the whole thing will become a depressing cycle. After a while, you both might grow dangerously accustomed to things as they are. And the next thing you know, years can go by, and neither of you feels much of anything.

It might well take a major crisis for something to give way. Whatever it is, and even if sharp words are exchanged, on a deeper level you both will feel relief that it's finally over. The only way for things to end more happily is for Closet Case to come out and Shy Snob to start getting close to people.

PERENNIAL CLOSET CASE AND THERAPY JUNKIE
★

What's Good: It's doubtful that the two of you will get together for long. But your breakup might involve an interesting conversation that ends with both of you saying, "I'm glad we had this talk," and hugging.

Closet Case has a kind of complacency about himself—an unwillingness to change—that will drive Therapy Junkie up the wall. You might think you're mentally connecting, but you're not. Therapy Junkie is trying to get at the truth about himself (albeit in somewhat stilted ways), while Closet Case is happy to keep living a lie. Still, being around someone like Therapy Junkie might compel Closet Case to talk a little more about himself, and maybe this type of self-reflection will help Closet Case to come out eventually.

The sex will lack passion because both of you have sexual secrets—urges that you do not share with the world. But if you both can have a sense of humor about it, you might be able to look back on it as a comical disaster.

When you break up, Therapy Junkie will have fresh fodder for his analyst, and Closet Case might comfort himself by thinking that Therapy Junkie was more than he could handle, so it wasn't his fault. And that's about all that can even pass for "good."

What Needs Work: Closet Case's preoccupation with self-protection probably translates into other areas of his life. Therapy Junkie will feel that Closet Case is a demon from his past, some ultra-cold and selfish parent or whomever who never gave Therapy Junkie validation. To take a man so preoccupied with the psychological implications of things and to have him paired up with a man who's ashamed of being gay . . . well, you don't have to be a genius to see all the built-in booby traps.

Therapy Junkie will tell story after story about how important coming out has been to him, and all about how it has changed his life on so many levels. That may well be true, but the information is so complex it overwhelms Closet Case. Therapy Junkie has to understand that the kind of self-examination he thrives on is something that Closet Case is frightened of.

Conversely, Closet Case tends to develop a rather condescending attitude toward Therapy Junkie. Closet Case must remember that he himself is living a dishonest life. He is hardly in the position to be criticizing how another gay man is trying to get his life in order.

Since this is the last of these matches that involves Closet Case, it is with both relief and impatience that I state for the last time that Closet Case needs to come out. As he gets in touch with who he really is—and as he lets the rest of the world get to know this man, too—he'll also start to understand and appreciate the complex, baffling, fascinating Therapy Junkie in his life. And if Therapy Junkie is learning to live more spontaneously, he might be able to help Closet Case through the real-life struggles he faces as he comes out. But it will be an extremely challenging struggle for you both.

SEXPOT AND SEXPOT
★★★★

What's Good: It's somewhat unlikely that one Sexpot will fall for another, as neither of you welcome competition in the attention department. But if you do, yours will be a strong, passionate union. You'll especially enjoy flaunting yourselves in public. Dancing barechested to show off your hot, sweaty bodies will become a kind of rite of marriage. You both fall more deeply in love as you ponder how hot you both are to look at. Probably you wouldn't mind posing for erotic photos together, or making a video. If one component of intimacy between gay men is not being ashamed of one's sexuality, the two of you have that one down pat.

No doubt you'll want to go places together to flaunt your ultra-perfection as a couple. If you don't have much money, your looks can be a passport, and you can get yourselves invited to all sorts of sojourns. You'll pick out your clothes for a night on the town the way other couples pick out names for their children.

Certain shoes will be on the other foot, and it will be good for both of you to see what it's like to feel jealous (for example) when someone else is coming on to your man. Such experiences have the potential to humble you and teach you how to treat people more humanely. Sexually speaking, you not only do your usual great performance, but are given a great performance in return. You learn that it can be at least as noble to receive as to give.

Yours will not be the deepest relationship in history, but you'll have the chance to experience a lot of pleasure together. Perhaps the bond between you will be so strong that you can start to explore other, less superficial aspects of yourselves when the novelty of being together starts to wear off.

What Needs Work: There will be a tendency to compete with each other. You're both used to being the center of attention, and though sharing the spotlight with someone can be thrilling in a different way, it will take some adjustment. You both need to develop other ways of feeling good about yourselves, anyway, so this can be a good time to start. Try to have other things about yourselves to be proud of, so that if someone is making a big deal about how cute your husband is, it doesn't make you resentful.

When things go wrong in your relationship, it might be hard to hold it together. Ending a relationship is not necessarily a bad thing—indeed, but it can be a good thing—but in your case it's likely to end out of sheer incompetence. You're both so used to being able to glide by on surface values that when problems arise, neither of you has much problem-solving experience to fall back on. To have the inner strength and wisdom to find a solution, you both will have to be in touch with other aspects of yourselves.

One pursuit you should find helpful is spending time with male friends. Whether they're gay or straight, it will help you to learn what it's like to have men in your life in a nonsexual context. The sex between you will seem more special because it won't seem like part of a larger continuum of endless flirtation and sexual possibilities. There's nothing wrong with being sexy—in fact, some gay men could stand to be more like you—but you guys need to go a bit in the other direction.

You not only love each other, but you like who each other is as a person, so the foundation is there to build something important together. Don't be afraid to explore yourselves more fully as gay men—remember, you have each other to do it with.

SEXPOT AND SHY SNOB
★★

What's Good: Shy Snob is not a man who takes many chances, so it will be largely up to Sexpot for the two of you to get together. Sexpot is used to being the pursued, but if there's something about Shy Snob that strongly attracts him, he might just swallow his pride and be on the pursuing end for a change. He shouldn't have that much difficulty getting Shy Snob to take notice, given Sexpot's obvious assets. Still, Shy Snob will need to be in one of his more social moods to take things beyond a glance or two. And over time, he'll need to feel that Sexpot has more to offer than sex. If Sexpot has ever had the urge to talk about a good book he read recently, this is his chance.

You understand each other, in that you both know what it's like to tell someone no when he doesn't seem good enough. But you are also puzzled by each other. Sexpot doesn't understand how Shy Snob can spend so much time alone, and Shy Snob doesn't see why someone with as much to offer as Sexpot would squander himself on men so obviously unworthy of him. More so than many other couples, you alternate between thinking you've picked the right partner and thinking you've picked the wrong partner.

And yet, all these complications might be good for both of you. Shy Snob needs to engage himself in the muck and mire of human interaction, and Sexpot needs to see that his sexuality alone will not be enough if he's trying to relate to another man.

The sex will be good some of the time. When Shy Snob feels like being physical, he can ignite with Sexpot to create something fairly out of this world. But when Shy Snob is not in the mood, Sexpot will be perplexed and even hurt that his usual magic spell isn't working. Again, something beneficial can emerge from this challenging situation. Sexpot can be reminded that a relationship requires more than good sexual technique, especially if Shy Snob can explain how he's actually feeling and can reach out to Sexpot with tenderness and understanding.

What Needs Work: When Sexpot is being candid, other men might be amazed to learn he's had his heart broken, too. There's a good chance that the man who broke it was a Shy Snob. Whether or not Shy Snob is technically as handsome as Sexpot, he gives off an aura of quality that attracts Sexpot. Moreover, Shy Snob seems unreachable, and Sexpot loves a good challenge. The mixed signals he gets from Shy Snob alternately elate and depress him. One minute he'll feel that he's getting through to Shy Snob—that he's getting the validation he craves. But then Shy Snob seems preoccupied and unfriendly, and Sexpot's worst fear will seem to be confirmed: that in the final analysis, men don't want him.

Sexpot is not accustomed to being scorned, and if the relationship dies, Sexpot will do what he can to make sure Shy Snob hurts as much as he does. Shy Snob sometimes likes to think he doesn't feel things the way other people do, but he'll be shocked into thinking otherwise before Sexpot is done being cruel to him. And yet, despite all the potential for pain—or maybe because of it—you will always know in your hearts that getting together was important.

Yours is the kind of relationship with very high highs and very low lows. You can feel better than you ever knew you could feel, only to suddenly feel worse than you thought possible. Shy Snob wants to guide Sexpot into a deeper world, and Sexpot wants to make Shy Snob feel loved. If you can hold on to your lofty goals, and—just as important—work on improving yourselves, the road to happiness might still be bumpy, but it will finally get you where you want to go.

SEXPOT AND THERAPY JUNKIE
★★★

What's Good: This is a surprisingly good combination. As Marvin Gaye would have said, Therapy Junkie needs sexual healing. There are ways he wants to explore himself sexually that he isn't giving himself permission to pursue. All of his therapy and encounter groups do not bring him to the point where he can let loose. More than he may realize, his shame over this sexual secret is what's holding him back. Sexpot is just the ticket for getting Therapy Junkie beyond all this. With Sexpot's loving instruction, Therapy Junkie can liberate himself. This does not mean that all of Therapy Junkie's problems will go away. But it will do much toward making him feel integrated, adult, and empowered.

There's good stuff in store for Sexpot, too. As with Shy Snob, Sexpot senses that Therapy Junkie has something to teach him. But unlike Shy Snob, Therapy Junkie will be eager to do so. He'll find himself in the unusual and healthy position of helping someone else as Sexpot learns to trust him and starts to share about his past in ways he seldom does with anyone. He may even show Therapy Junkie virtually unrecognizable photos from his geeky past, when he wore braces and glasses. As with any relationship, the two of you need to work on yourselves if you want to find happiness with someone else. Yet in your case, just being together accomplishes this in many ways.

Lovemaking will be a solemn yet exciting part of your commitment to each other. The two of you might even join a sex club that specializes in whatever it is you do as a couple. In contrasting ways, you both will be startled by how emotionally gratifying it is to have sex together.

From Therapy Junkie's influence, Sexpot will feel more confident about pursuing other interests. Whether it be going back to school, studying sculpture, or starting a fossil collection, Sexpot will be delighted in himself for finding a broader range of interests. Therapy Junkie, in his own way, will start to feel turned on by living and can learn to let life just happen a little, without always having to analyze it to death.

What Needs Work: Assuming there's a strong mutual attraction, you'll try to blend into the other's world. This will be good for both of you, but you'll need to be patient with each other. Therapy Junkie is a bit of a square when compared with Sexpot, and Sexpot is a bit of a dunce when compared with Therapy Junkie. But if given a chance, Therapy Junkie can prove himself to be a cool dude, and Sexpot will be able to hold his own conversationally at any self-help workshop. So be prepared for a period of adjustment, and know that it won't last forever.

Develop some sort of activity you can do together—something unrelated to either therapy or sex. The more mundane, the better. In different ways, you both need to feel more connected to the everyday world. Plan a garden or redecorate your apartment or take a course together in financial planning. Learn how it feels to be part of the crowd.

Remember that even though you both will teach each other a lot, you both still have a different frame of reference to fall back on. Therapy Junkie can become a much more skillful and intense lovemaker, but he will still tend to live inside his head. Sexpot can become much more introspective and thoughtful, but he will still gravitate toward hedonism. Don't expect each other to change completely. Don't expect your partner to turn into you.

If you remember to be grateful for all you've meant to each other, you can get past the times in which you feel restless or annoyed. You would do especially well to remember that many of your life-long habits were aimed at keeping you away from other people. So when your partner is not living up to your expectations, take a look at what your expectations are about.

SHY SNOB AND SHY SNOB
★★★

What's Good: You truly understand each other. There will be no need to apologize for feeling socially out of place. It will be taken for granted that these things happen. You give each other permission not to like most of the people you meet. Neither of you has to worry about seeming overly critical, as you do when you're around other types of gay men. This can have a positive effect. Once given full license to let fly whatever it is you're actually experiencing, you both might get a great deal of pent-up negativity out of your systems and start to feel more generous toward others. (Of course, sometimes things will still not go well with other people, but you'll still have each other to fall back on.)

Just as important, you can openly share all your thoughts and ideas about life. If one of you has a theory that human destiny is controlled by fluctuations in the rotation of the moons of Jupiter, you can talk about it with the other without fear of ridicule. Even when you're not in sync, you intuitively understand the effort, taste, and judgment that went into your partner's arriving at a given con-clusion and can respect it. Getting together simply to talk can be like a powerful narcotic, because you both have so few people you can share your ideas with.

When it comes to sex, you can be quite forgiving of each other's lapses—those times when sex seems so utterly remote from anything that could interest you, because it involves being close to another person. Since you both know what this feeling is about, you won't take it too personally when your partner falls into it (or at least not if you are mature). At the same time, when the sex is hot and ravenous, you don't realistically expect it to always be that great. If one of you wants to do something completely different when it's over, the other one won't make a big fuss about it. The major exception to any of this would be if one of you withdraws emotionally in a manner that strikes the other as unesthetic or insensitive.

You won't have many friends together, but you will probably have a few tolerable acquaintances with whom you occasionally socialize. These people will sense that what you share together is on a whole other level and will not try to get too close to you. Whether you talk about the weather or the meaning of the universe in a group setting, something about it will not lend itself to closeness with other people. But you will have each other.

What Needs Work: While it's nice that you're able to find another gay man who shares your difficulties in getting close to others, remember that ultimately it would be even nicer if you *could* get close to others. There's no need to be critical of yourselves, but see if you can encourage each other to take small steps toward getting out of your respective social ruts. Little things such as calling so-and-so back when you don't feel like it can be a big step for the Shy Snob. Be there to encourage and reward each other for each small step you take.

It's not uncommon for couples to have sex less often over time, but the two of you can get to this point rather quickly. Within a remarkably short period, you can feel as though you've been married for fifty years. There's something good in this, of course. But the downside is that you both could benefit by taking a few more emotional risks. Talk openly about the things that really turn you on in your fantasies, invest in some porn, see a sex therapist—do what it takes to keep lovemaking a vital aspect of your relationship.

Tension will result when one Shy Snob feels overly criticized by his Shy Snob partner. It may even turn into a kind of unspecified contest, in which you both keep tally of who got to put down whom the most. See if you can temper your remarks with positive feedback. Your partner is a smart guy, so probably his idea isn't all bad, and you should give him a bit of credit for it. (This isn't a bad rule to follow when dealing with people in general.)

Finally, remind yourselves that life is not simply about saving face or holding on to one's pride. How much we give of ourselves will count for much more in the long run. See if as a couple you can take some sort of generous action regularly. Volunteer at an organization or help someone you know who's in need. As you reach out to others, learn to reach out as a couple, as well.

SHY SNOB AND THERAPY JUNKIE
★★★★

What's Good: You're not exactly on the same wavelength, but you're close enough. Therapy Junkie has lots to share about his latest self-discoveries. Shy Snob's knowledge base is more rigorous and eclectic. Something that Therapy Junkie thinks is a profound insight will be a kind of so-what bit of common sense to Shy Snob. Therapy Junkie will usually be the one who does most of the talking, while Shy Snob will be like a sage, who approves or disapproves of what Therapy Junkie is sharing. Shy Snob will appreciate the attention and respect he gets from Therapy Junkie, who will value Shy Snob's wisdom. Even if Shy Snob is younger than Therapy Junkie, he will function as the older person in the couple.

This somewhat nurturing role on the part of Shy Snob will carry over into the bedroom. Therapy Junkie will be open about how important it is to his healing as a gay man that he be able to experience passion and tenderness, and in a quiet way Shy Snob will communicate that by helping Therapy Junkie to heal he also is trying to heal himself. It will not quite be the intense kind of sex life that Therapy Junkie can benefit most from, but it will be comfortable and safe for both of you.

When Shy Snob is not in the mood, Therapy Junkie will be understanding, especially if Shy Snob says that sex is bringing up his childhood issues. Over time, Therapy Junkie might reply that getting rejected is bringing up *his* childhood issues. But even if you end up parting ways, there will be a lot of talking things over, and the end will be perceived as the next step in your respective quests for self-growth.

Shy Snob can help Therapy Junkie see a universe beyond the rather monolithic worldview he's adopted. And Therapy Junkie can provide an emotionally safe way for Shy Snob to extend himself to another person.

What Needs Work: Shy Snob has a keen sense of what's going on with people on the inside, and he can use this ability to hurt other people. He will often be tempted to make fun of Therapy Junkie. Shy Snob won't be vulgar about it; he'll say a few words in his low-key way that make Therapy Junkie look like the fool of the century.

Over time, Therapy Junkie will realize that though Shy Snob may know a lot, he's also just another messed-up human being. Since Therapy Junkie tends to think that everyone but himself has all the answers to life, his admiration of Shy Snob is based partly on immaturity. Your relationship is not emotionally incestuous, but when Therapy Junkie sees Shy Snob's flaws, it will be a bit like an adolescent realizing his parents aren't perfect. Therapy Junkie will want to rebel against everything he's shared with Shy Snob, who not only doesn't have it more together than other people but might even be more messed up than other people. Therapy Junkie will need to remember that no one twisted his arm to put his trust in Shy Snob.

Shy Snob might get bored with Therapy Junkie. He likes to dissect things, too, but he feels that Therapy Junkie goes overboard, and that much of what he obsesses over is trivial. Shy Snob has a low threshold for staying involved with people, and when Therapy Junkie gets on his case for something seemingly unimportant, Shy Snob will want to retreat.

You both need to remember that you have work to do on *yourselves,* if you want to find intimacy in your lives. Your partner isn't perfect, but neither are you, and underneath it all there's a fairly similar fear of trusting others. With patience and love, you should be able to help each other get past these fears.

THERAPY JUNKIE AND THERAPY JUNKIE
★★★★

What's Good: You both use a lot of the same buzzwords in your conversations and so can speak a kind of shorthand to each other. At the same time, communication can get lengthy and complex as you explore circles within circles of the dynamics of your relationship. But you both enjoy the process. You can go to a lot of the same therapeutically oriented activities together. A weekend seminar on self-growth can seem like a romantic getaway.

As you talk and talk and talk, you might actually start to learn more about yourselves. To an outsider, there's a lot of hyperbole to sort through, but somewhere in the midst of it all there're bound to be some real insights. It will mean a lot to both of you when these moments happen, and your relationship will be strengthened.

As you learn about yourselves and each other, you might even start to figure out your sexual needs. Given the foundation of trust you've been building together, it ought to be possible to work out together what you both like to do in bed. If nothing else, the information will probably be received in a mutually nonjudgmental atmosphere.

When problems arise, you'll be better than many other couples at facing them. Expressing what's making you uncomfortable should be relatively easy. Quite often, either or both of you will be willing to try changing your behavior or attitude, because you both are open-minded to change. Like most people, you are often tempted to blame your problems on your partner, but you've trained yourselves to understand that the source of and solution for our problems often rest within ourselves.

You'll probably have a network of people that are part of your Therapy Junkie world. You'll confide in them quite a lot about your relationship, because you welcome input from others as well as the chance to share. This should help give you more insights into your relationship. You won't have to worry about becoming an overly private, closed-off couple. And you'll share with other couples some of your own ideas about what works and what doesn't, based on your own victories and defeats as a couple.

What Needs Work: Therapy Junkies are in the process of becoming. They feel as if they haven't quite grown up or found themselves yet. And so when two Therapy Junkies get together, there's always the possibility that one of them will eventually take off in some radically different direction from the other. The activities or beliefs you had in common may become sources of contention when they no longer seem important to either or both of you.

In particular, it is possible that you will not be compatible sexually, once you both come to terms with what you like to do. There might well be a way you can compromise, but be prepared to face some challenges under the sheets.

Over time, you experience the rude awakening that not every little aspect of life goes back to childhood trauma. To paraphrase Freud, sometimes a bill is just a bill. Though it will be good for you to realize this, it might threaten the stability of your relationship, because it was built on assumptions that won't be adequate for getting you through life.

Though it's good to open up to people about your relationship, try to keep some things private. What you see on the soaps is only too true. All kinds of creeps out there will try to break you up. Additionally, there needs to be a core of specialness—memories and feelings that belong only to the two of you.

You both tend to live in your head and hide from your feelings. It isn't so much that you talk *about* your feelings as that you try to talk *away* your feelings. Remember that what brings you together is not your unhappy childhoods but the spontaneous feelings of love and joy that you have for each other in the present. Feelings don't have to be scary. As you've proven to each other, they can be positive and warm. Remember to share them with each other.

PART THREE

. . .

MALE
BONDING

IN THIS FINAL SECTION OF THE BOOK, we'll take a look at issues beyond the OWTAs that apply to *all* gay men trying to figure out how to be happily in love. First, I've provided you with a section called "OWTAs at a Glance," which pretty much summarizes everything that's been said so far about your OWTA.

Then we move on to "The OWTA Limits." There are suggestions about becoming a fully realized gay man that apply to all OWTA types. I call this process the *Second Coming Out,* because in a way you have to come out all over again—not just as this abstraction called "gay," but as a fully fleshed-out human being. This section leads us to "Letting Him Be Him," whereby the man in your life also becomes all he can be. I call this the *Third Coming Out,* because here you are proclaiming to yourself, your partner, and the world at large that this man in your life is who he is and that you accept him as an integral part of who you are.

Next, we discuss "How to Become a Couple," "How to Be a Couple," and "How to Stay a Couple." In other words, the process doesn't end with taking the leap into couplehood. You need to know how to be together day to day, as well as how to stay together when times get rough. But sometimes staying together isn't possible or it's not in your best interests, and so we then move on to the bittersweet section called "How to Break Up," followed by "Final Thoughts."

OWTAs AT A GLANCE

■ ■ ■

So THAT YOU DON'T HAVE TO KEEP FLIP-flopping through the entire book, I've made it easy for you and listed how you rank with each of the other OWTAs, using the four-star system. I then provide a series of brief statements that sum up your OWTA type in so many nutshells:

- *Overriding Relationship Pattern:* How you relate to men, regardless of the OWTA you're paired off with. Not what you truly believe love is, but what you *seem* to believe love is, given your behavior.
- *Internalized Homophobic Statement:* This is the message that you take with you through life, and it reflects the shame you were taught to feel about being gay and that keeps you from finding intimacy.
- *Unconscious Relationship Statement:* This isn't something you literally say to yourself but it is what you communicate to other men, even though you probably do so unconsciously.
- *Defensive Breakup Statement:* The type of thing you're likely to tell yourself when a relationship ends, rather than face the complex truth. This helps keep you emotionally closed off from intimacy in the future.

BLUE COLLAR GUY AT A GLANCE

with Blue Collar Guy: ★★★★
with Creature of Habit: ★★★
with Discriminating Shopper: ★★
with Hyper-Romantic: ★★★
with Misfit: ★★★★
with Nice Boy: ★★
with Pal: ★★★★
with Party Boy: ★★
with Perennial Closet Case: ★
with Sexpot: ★★★
with Shy Snob: ★
with Therapy Junkie: ★

Overriding Relationship Pattern: "Love" means being told you are masculine. Like your straight-male counterpart, you seek out partners who validate your manliness—or more to the point, what you *think* it means to be a man, which is often quite limited. You are less attracted to men who don't seem to give you this validation. It apparently does not occur to you that you might find happiness in a relationship that honored your "feminine" side (which is a part of you, anyway) or that bypassed these male/female dichotomies altogether.

Internalized Homophobic Statement: "I'm gay, but I need to prove that I'm still one of the guys."

Unconscious Relationship Statement: "I want a relationship because it's what people do, and it's how I express myself as a man."

Defensive Breakup Statement: "We broke up, but at least I still have my manly pride."

CREATURE OF HABIT AT A GLANCE

 with Blue Collar Guy: ★★★
 with Creature of Habit: ★★★
 with Discriminating Shopper: ★★
 with Hyper-Romantic: ★
 with Misfit: ★★★
 with Nice Boy: ★★★★
 with Pal: ★★★★
 with Party Boy: ★
 with Perennial Closet Case: ★★
 with Sexpot: ★★
 with Shy Snob: ★★★★
 with Therapy Junkie: ★

Overriding Relationship Pattern: "Love" means finding someone who leaves you alone, yet somehow is willing to always be there for you. You seek out men who won't interfere with or question your set routines. You're not unlike a straight man who gets married for the sake of getting married, but has no intention of adapting himself to his partner and resents it if his partner attempts to get him to try something new.

Internalized Homophobic Statement: "I'm gay, but I keep very busy to prove that I can still be a productive member of society."

Unconscious Relationship Statement: "I want a relationship that simplifies my life. Dating and going out to bars throws me out of my routine."

Defensive Breakup Statement: "We broke up, but it's just as well. I have a lot to do around the house, and the busy person is the happy person."

DISCRIMINATING SHOPPER AT A GLANCE

with Blue Collar Guy: ★★
with Creature of Habit: ★★
with Discriminating Shopper: ★★★★
with Hyper-Romantic: ★
with Misfit: ★★★
with Nice Boy: ★★
with Pal: ★
with Party Boy: ★★★★
with Perennial Closet Case: ★
with Sexpot: ★★★
with Shy Snob: ★★★★
with Therapy Junkie: ★★★

Overriding Relationship Pattern: "Love" means someone who looks and acts like your fantasy ideal. As long as no one's ever good enough, you won't have to take any emotional risks. When you do get involved, you seek out men who reinforce your rather cold, calculating standards and who do not challenge you emotionally. When straights say that gay relationships don't seem as deep as straight ones, it's possible that they were observing one of yours.

Internalized Homophobic Statement: "I'm gay, but as long as I don't find the perfect man, I won't ever have to fully face the fact that I am."

Unconscious Relationship Statement: "I'm going to find every possible excuse not to get involved with you."

Defensive Breakup Statement: "We broke up, thank God. I *knew* he wasn't good enough for me."

HYPER-ROMANTIC AT A GLANCE

with Blue Collar Guy: ★★★
with Creature of Habit: ★
with Discriminating Shopper: ★
with Hyper-Romantic: ★★★
with Misfit: ★★
with Nice Boy: ★★★★
with Pal: ★★★★
with Party Boy: ★
with Perennial Closet Case: ★★
with Sexpot: ★★★★
with Shy Snob: ★★★
with Therapy Junkie: ★★

Overriding Relationship Pattern: "Love" means finding the first man willing to get involved with you, and staying with him forever. You're rather like a child who wants to play house, and you seek a man who won't question how overly simplified and fundamentally inadequate your approach to relationships is. Because you're willing to drop everything for the latest guy, you think he should be, too. If he isn't, you'll decide he doesn't "love" you.

Internalized Homophobic Statement: "I'm gay, so I'm not entitled to happiness. I should be grateful for whatever shabby opportunity comes along."

Unconscious Relationship Statement: "I want to glom on to you so that I don't have to face any more loneliness ever."

Defensive Breakup Statement: "We broke up, and my life is over. Why doesn't anyone love me? I'll never be happy again. Unless maybe that guy standing over there is available . . ."

MISFIT AT A GLANCE

with Blue Collar Guy: ★★★★
with Creature of Habit: ★★★
with Discriminating Shopper: ★★★
with Hyper-Romantic: ★★
with Misfit: ★★★★
with Nice Boy: ★
with Pal: ★★
with Party Boy: ★
with Perennial Closet Case: ★★
with Sexpot: ★
with Shy Snob: ★★★
with Therapy Junkie: ★★★★

Overriding Relationship Pattern: "Love" means finding a gay man who isn't into the stereotypical gay culture. You are deeply embarrassed by the typical gay preoccupations because you feel they stand for something essentially asexual and milquetoast about the gay life. You turn off to any man who turns out to be "gay-acting," and you make an incredibly intense play for any man who seems "straight enough" for you, as if your life depended on it.

Internalized Homophobic Statement: "I'm gay, but I wish I weren't, because straight men are so much better than gay men."

Unconscious Relationship Statement: "You can't ever say or do anything that seems 'too gay,' or else I'll leave you."

Defensive Breakup Statement: "We broke up because my boyfriend turned out to be such a typical gay man, with such a namby-pamby personality."

NICE BOY AT A GLANCE

with Blue Collar Guy: ★★
with Creature of Habit: ★★★★
with Discriminating Shopper: ★★
with Hyper-Romantic: ★★★★
with Misfit: ★
with Nice Boy: ★★★
with Pal: ★★★
with Party Boy: ★★★★
with Perennial Closet Case: ★★★
with Sexpot: ★
with Shy Snob: ★
with Therapy Junkie: ★★

Overriding Relationship Pattern: "Love" means being pleasant with each other while Mr. Sunshine shines and the birdies go tweet-tweet. It means *not ever* getting upset or annoyed or unhappy with each other. You want a man who does not question your niceties and lets you keep everything at room temperature at all times, and you will run from a man who wants something more honest than that.

Internalized Homophobic Statement: "I'm gay, so I'm kind and sensitive, and like a little elf it is my role to make everyone else happy."

Unconscious Relationship Statement: "Let's get together so that we can pretend that everything is wonderful."

Defensive Breakup Statement: "We broke up, but everything happens for a reason."

PAL AT A GLANCE

with Blue Collar Guy: ★★★★
with Creature of Habit: ★★★★
with Discriminating Shopper: ★
with Hyper-Romantic: ★★★★
with Misfit: ★★
with Nice Boy: ★★★
with Pal: ★★★
with Party Boy: ★★★
with Perennial Closet Case: ★★
with Sexpot: ★
with Shy Snob: ★
with Therapy Junkie: ★★

Overriding Relationship Pattern: "Love" means finding a man who lets you "earn" a place in his life by doing him favors, just like everyone else you encounter, only in his case he lets you have sex with him. You don't think much of yourself, but you don't like to dwell on this. Instead, you seek out men who will let you go about your busy dance that is aimed at manipulating how others respond to you and keeping them emotionally distant.

Internalized Homophobic Statement: "I'm gay, so I have to do twice as much as everyone else to get people to like me."

Unconscious Relationship Statement: "Let me take care of you, whether you want me to or not, because otherwise I don't know what to do with myself."

Defensive Breakup Statement: "We broke up. Here, let me help you with that."

PARTY BOY AT A GLANCE

> with Blue Collar Guy: ★★
> with Creature of Habit: ★
> with Discriminating Shopper: ★★★★
> with Hyper-Romantic: ★
> with Misfit: ★
> with Nice Boy: ★★★★
> with Pal: ★★★
> with Party Boy: ★★★
> with Perennial Closet Case: ★★
> with Sexpot: ★★★★
> with Shy Snob: ★★
> with Therapy Junkie: ★★★

Overriding Relationship Pattern: "Love" means finding a man who completes your social life. You want to keep living the same way, laughing and drinking to avoid your pain. So you want a man who can laugh and drink beside you, preferably with lots of other people around. You're afraid of quiet, so you won't want a man who challenges you to be still and pay attention. A lover can take you from high to ultrahigh, so hopefully you'll never hurt again.

Internalized Homophobic Statement: "I'm gay, so people used to make fun of me, but I pretend I'm *nothing* like that anymore and do whatever it takes to kill my guilt and shame."

Unconscious Relationship Statement: "Let's get into this sports car together, drive at two hundred miles per hour, and never slow down, because if we did, I'd be unhappy, and we can't *ever* have that."

Defensive Breakup Statement: "We broke up, as if I care. I can take it. Nothing gets *me* down."

PERENNIAL CLOSET CASE AT A GLANCE

with Blue Collar Guy: ★
with Creature of Habit: ★★
with Discriminating Shopper: ★
with Hyper-Romantic: ★★
with Misfit: ★★
with Nice Boy: ★★★
with Pal: ★★
with Party Boy: ★★
with Perennial Closet Case: ★★
with Sexpot: ★★
with Shy Snob: ★★
with Therapy Junkie: ★

Overriding Relationship Pattern: "Love" means finding a man who lets you deny that you love men. He could be the greatest guy in the world, but if he wants an out relationship, you'll let him get away. Though you're very controlling, it's usually going to be up to the other man whether anything develops. He has to decide whether he can tolerate a closeted arrangement. So your fate is *less* in your hands than it is for other types of gay men.

Internalized Homophobic Statement: "I'm gay, but maybe I'm not *really* gay. Maybe it will go away or I can change or no one ever has to know."

Unconscious Relationship Statement: "No one must know about us, but I'm lonely and horny, so please tell me you won't mind keeping what we have a secret."

Defensive Breakup Statement: "We broke up. At least he promised not to tell anyone about us."

SEXPOT AT A GLANCE

    with Blue Collar Guy: ★★★
    with Creature of Habit: ★★
    with Discriminating Shopper: ★★★
    with Hyper-Romantic: ★★★★
    with Misfit: ★
    with Nice Boy: ★
    with Pal: ★
    with Party Boy: ★★★★
    with Perennial Closet Case: ★★
    with Sexpot: ★★★★
    with Shy Snob: ★★
    with Therapy Junkie: ★★★

Overriding Relationship Pattern: "Love" means being told by a man that he wants to spend every second of his life looking at you and worshiping you and being driven out of his mind with passion by so much as a single touch from your pinkie. In fact, if you had your druthers, every man you encountered would tell you this (yes, including the straight ones). Should a man respond less enthusiastically, you are deeply wounded and move on to the next devotee.

Internalized Homophobic Statement: "I'm gay, so the only value I have to other men is my body, and the only way I can feel accepted by men is through sex."

Unconscious Relationship Statement: "I don't have to love you, but you have to love me. In fact, what would make me happiest is if you love me and I can't stand you."

Defensive Breakup Statement: "We broke up—I mean, I broke up with *him.*"

SHY SNOB AT A GLANCE

with Blue Collar Guy: ★
with Creature of Habit: ★★★★
with Discriminating Shopper: ★★★★
with Hyper-Romantic: ★★★
with Misfit: ★★★
with Nice Boy: ★
with Pal: ★
with Party Boy: ★★
with Perennial Closet Case: ★★
with Sexpot: ★★
with Shy Snob: ★★★
with Therapy Junkie: ★★★★

Overriding Relationship Pattern: "Love" means finding a man who tells you how great you are and never makes you do anything you don't want to do. You are unhappy when you can't control other men's responses to you, because you might look bad or be rejected, so you withdraw to "save face." You're afraid that you're unlikable, but you show off against this fear and act as if you're simply better than other people.

Internalized Homophobic Statement: "I'm gay, but I'm just as self-sufficient as a straight man, and I'm so strong and self-possessed that I don't need anybody."

Unconscious Relationship Statement: "I want you to be like a genie in a bottle and appear or disappear, depending on my mood."

Defensive Breakup Statement: "We broke up. It was *his* loss, not mine."

THERAPY JUNKIE AT A GLANCE

with Blue Collar Guy: ★
with Creature of Habit: ★
with Discriminating Shopper: ★★★
with Hyper-Romantic: ★★
with Misfit: ★★★★
with Nice Boy: ★★
with Pal: ★★
with Party Boy: ★★★
with Perennial Closet Case: ★
with Sexpot: ★★★
with Shy Snob: ★★★★
with Therapy Junkie: ★★★★

Overriding Relationship Pattern: "Love" means resolving all of your childhood traumas with a nontoxic, noncodependent, nonaddictive man who lives in nondenial, nonguilt, and nonshame, and whom you can help (in a noncodependent way, and with healthy boundaries) work on his own issues. In truth, you are much more horny than all this, but you're afraid to just let go and live. You think all men are your father—or your childhood bully, or whomever.

Internalized Homophobic Statement: "I'm gay, so the shaming voices in my head are more powerful than I am, and I'm still a little boy because being a man sounds scary."

Unconscious Relationship Statement: "You are an abstraction in my ongoing investigation of how much progress I am making toward psychological wellness."

Defensive Breakup Statement: "We broke up. But I'm getting better. I *am*, aren't I?"

THE OWTA LIMITS
YOUR SECOND COMING OUT

■ ■ ■

IF YOU'VE READ THIS FAR AND ARE thinking (for example), "Well, no wonder my last relationship didn't work, because I was a Shy Snob and he was a Blue Collar Guy," I'm glad you've gotten something out of this book. But at the same time, please don't use the OWTAs as an excuse. While some personalities *tend to* bring out the best or worst in others, it doesn't mean they *have to*. Remember what OWTA stands for? The OWTAs are mere *appearances,* disguises gay men wear to keep people from knowing who they really are. Often, these performances become quite habit-forming, and it's difficult, even painful, to get past them. But we can learn to keep them under control, emphasizing the positive qualities of them—and sometimes even getting past them altogether.

In Alcoholics Anonymous, people talk about being *recovering* alcoholics, rather than *former* alcoholics. The idea is that you're always an alcoholic, but you can be getting better, as opposed to getting worse. In a way, that's how the OWTAs might be for some people. You can be a *recovering* Discriminating Shopper or Nice Boy or whichever type fits you. If you seem to go from one OWTA to another, depending on the relationship you're in, then maybe you can be a recovering all-OWTA, or some such.

The point is that as gay men we need to hold ourselves accountable for the things that go right or wrong in our intimate relationships. When straight men try to get away with saying, "I can't help it if I'm uncomfortable with intimacy, because I'm a guy," someone is usually there to tell him he's full of it. Sure, it often might be *harder* for straight men than straight women to handle intimacy, but it doesn't means it's *impossible*.

Gay men also find intimacy tough, but (as I mentioned earlier), because they are marginalized, they often learn how to be subversive, like disempowered women, and to hide their fear of intimacy behind a manipulative disguise. In many ways, it can be liberating to be a gay man, because you get to pick and choose which aspects from the male and female worlds you want to adopt as your own. But in other ways, without realizing it, we can take on some of the more limiting aspects of being a man and being a woman.

The male part of being a gay man is often discounted in gay circles. Somehow, when gay men get together, they often think they need to emphasize the allegedly "female" side of their natures. But we are capable of acting "just like straight men." All that male energy is a *part* of who we are.

Years ago, I knew a gay guy whose nose would crinkle and snort as he talked in terms of "darling this" and "honey that" and was so flamboyant he made Auntie Mame seem like Dan Rather. He worked for his family's trucking business, and when you called him at work, a deep, macho voice would say, "Acme Trucking." After you identified yourself, you'd hear him snort, and in a much higher voice he would say, "Well, hel*lo,* darling . . ."

He was a dear man, wonderful fun to be with, and I still miss him (sadly, he died of AIDS). Yet in more recent years, I've thought about how easily he blended in with the macho atmosphere at work. I see it as more than just a cute joke many of us can relate to from our own experience. It's telling for what it says about this gay man—or millions of others just like him. The world of straight men was not all he was about, but it wasn't *that* far removed from his frame of reference. He could partake of it when he had to. (In fact, as I recall, he wasn't out to his family.) All kidding aside, he was more convincing as a straight man than he would have been as a woman. If I met him at his job, I might have assumed he was straight, whereas if he did drag, I would never have believed for a second he was a woman. One of the most outrageously "queeny" men in town, full of bitchy put-downs toward the straight world, he could draw upon a different aspect of his personality and pass for a straight man.

Gay men often try to disassociate culturally from straight men—for political reasons, because of unhappy experiences, or perhaps from a little bit of both. Interestingly, however, the personal ads are filled with men who claim that they are "straight-acting" and are seeking someone similar to themselves in this regard. Gay male porn is extremely pro-straight-male. Frequently, the ultimate fantasy is seen as seducing a straight man. The models in adult videos (unless being presented as "boys") have muscular bodies and are depicted in stereotypical male pursuits: the military, the gym, the sports locker room, the truck stop. They frequently are police officers, drill sergeants, truck drivers, or firefighters. For all of our joking and political rhetoric, when it comes to fantasy ideals, we want to watch a trucker and a cop in action—as opposed to a florist and a ballet dancer. It is extremely doubtful that anyone would watch a video entitled *Hot Times at the Beauty Salon.*

It has been said that when a human being engages in a sexual fantasy, he or she is trying to connect with some part of him- or herself. If this is true, then a lot of gay men are trying to connect to their "male" self when they engage in supermacho sex fantasies. Five minutes later, many of these same men will be putting down straight men as homophobic, sexist pigs, without being cognizant of how they are contradicting themselves. Yet on some level, it would appear that the straight male and the behaviors and values he stands for are not totally foreign to the gay experience; they are simply subverted into other realms. And like most forms of subversion, these qualities are then acted out in unconscious ways.

The gay male experience is *somewhat* different from the straight male experience, but it is far from being its *opposite.* Straight and gay men have in common many of the same agendas regarding the importance of sex and a fear of the "feminine" world of feelings and intimacy. Perhaps the major difference is that gay men are less aware of this part of themselves than straight men, because gay men tend to subvert it. We like to convince ourselves that our dislike of "feminine" intimacy only comes out in our sex fantasies, as if this were some coincidence totally unrelated to everything else about ourselves.

Not only do we wrestle with intimacy as men, but being gay teaches us to doubly fear closeness. From an extremely early age, we start lying to ourselves and to everyone around us, and we have virtually no role models to guide us into adulthood. We also seldom have champions. When gay children are made fun of, there's usually no one who stands up for them, because the widespread belief is that the kid would be better off not being gay, so does it really do any harm to try to tease him out of it? Well, of course it does. We grow up being told in a million different ways that being gay is simply *wrong,* impossible to defend.

Then along comes puberty, and we find out there's a gay rights movement, and we tell ourselves that we're "out" now, and we try approaching one of those man creatures for love and tenderness— only he's been through all the same shaming crap. As men, we already have one strike against us in the intimacy game. As if that weren't enough, we attempt intimacy with *another* man. Then to top it off, this other man probably also has withstood a great deal of shame and disconfirmation over being gay.

What can we do about it? Well, on a political level, we can change our laws, norms, and values, so that gay children are taught to be proud of who they are and can one day have a legal gay marriage if they choose. But interpersonally, what we do is pretty much up to us as individuals. If our lovers confront us with emotionally charged information, we can't hand them a card that says, "Please call my family to get a response to this. They took away my dignity as a gay man, so I can't relate to what you're saying. It's simply too painful and difficult. But maybe my mom or dad can help you."

It's unfair because we're not the ones who screwed ourselves up. But nevertheless, we're the only ones who can change things in our lives. We can ask our jailers to free us in a legal and political sense, but we can't expect them to free our souls. That we have to do ourselves.

Obviously, we all need to give each other a great deal of emotional support. But there's a rut we fall into. Being gay goes against the grain of society, so when a man comes out as gay, we must applaud him to let him know that not everyone thinks it's wrong; some of us think it's pretty cool. But where to draw the line? Some gay men go on to realize they're really into leather or foot worship or threesomes. And again, we need to applaud and say, "Right on, Joe or Chuck or Bob. You do whatever makes you feel good."

But what about the gay man who says, "On the night of our second anniversary, as my lover was baking us a cake to celebrate, I sneaked out for a quickie with the guy next door, because I feel like my lover is suffocating me. I'm just not into this commitment thing. As far as I'm concerned, my lover's the one with the problem."

Should we still applaud? After all, this is a gay man apparently figuring out what he's into. Monogamy really isn't for everybody, yet I wonder if that's the point here. Maybe this guy needs to be held accountable for what he's doing. Apparently, he got into a relationship without believing in being faithful, which slight detail he neglected to tell his lover, who's expecting him home for their anniversary. It's not so much a question of morality as that here is a man who seems to be lying to minimize the possibility of intimacy. He needs a partner who wants an open relationship—or maybe he shouldn't have a partner at all. But he's found something comfortably dishonest. He's found a way to avoid intimacy while also avoiding the loneliness of being alone.

He's having his cake and eating it, too, yet I would submit that the cake doesn't taste all that good. It's like a mediocre cake-mix cake with artificial preservatives and too much canned frosting on the surface to camouflage the mediocrity of it. It's certainly a common cake—all kinds of men, straight or gay, would seem to bake it.

Straight people who are friendly with gay men often feel awkward saying anything in these kinds of situations, because they don't want to risk sounding antigay. But amongst gay men, there's often an unspoken rule that if it has to do with love or sex and a gay man does it, it must be okay.

However, if as gay men we are to free ourselves from the emotional straitjackets society has put us in, maybe the time has come to stop applauding. The choices we make when it comes to sex and intimacy are not simply "right" or "wrong" on some monolithic level. Instead, they reflect complex natures whose aims often are at cross-purposes with themselves. And so it is fitting that we take responsibility for these actions. I'm not suggesting we lose our sense of humor. Our love mishaps can still become funny party stories. But I am saying that we can start to look deeper at ourselves and think about how our choices indicate a flight toward or away from intimacy—both with ourselves and with others. Rather than just say, "It's right on that I do this, because nobody tells *me* what to do"—which declaration, I should point out, sounds exactly like something a straight man would say—maybe we can say instead, "Gee, a lot of the things I do seem to make me less close to people, and I wonder why this is."

This ability to look inside yourself for complex and sometimes painful but ultimately liberating answers is what I call your *Second Coming Out*. Regardless of your OWTA type, you can take some basic steps to set in motion this Second Coming Out, in which you can be out not just as gay, but as a multidimensional human being who may or may not choose intimacy, but who is *capable* of having intimacy in his life:

TAKE THE "STRAIGHT MAN" TEST

Is what you're doing an expression of your true self or is it aimed at keeping yourself in a kind of semidishonest rut? One way of figuring it out is to ask yourself what people would think if you were a straight man saying or doing whatever it is that you're saying and doing.

For example, if a gay Blue Collar Guy says, "I like to feel like a real man. I only do guy-type things. When I come home from work, it's TV and a six-pack of beer. My partner brings me dinner and massages my feet. Then I give him what he's been waiting for all day long." Gays and supportive straights are likely to say, "Good for him. He's living proof that a gay man can be just as masculine as a straight man. If this is what works for him and his partner, all the more power to them." But if a straight man said this, many people would be deeply offended by his male chauvinism, and how he was using his partner to validate his masculinity.

A Creature of Habit says, "I had to kick my new boyfriend out of my apartment last night because he rearranged my bottles of cologne, and I felt so violated." Gays and supportive straights are likely to say, "I don't blame you. Who you are is very important, and another person has no right to be crossing those boundaries." But if a straight man said this about his girlfriend, people would think he was cruel, selfish, and a great big fuddy-duddy.

A Discriminating Shopper in his forties is told that a guy at the office would like to go out with him, and he replies, "Thanks but no thanks. Alfred's a nice guy, but he's in his thirties, and I only date guys in their twenties." Gays and supportive straights are likely to say, "That's cool. You're into what you're into, and it's good that you're in touch enough with yourself to know what turns you on." But if a straight man said this about Alfreda, people would call him a pig.

A Hyper-Romantic says, "I met this guy last week at the bar. I've called him three or four times a day since then, but he hasn't called me back." Gays and sympathetic straights might feel sorry for Hyper-Romantic and try to explain to him that he's being naive and setting himself up to get hurt. But if a straight man said this, people would say that he sounds like some sort of psycho stalker and should be put on Prozac.

A Misfit says, "I met this guy who I thought was interesting. Then I got to his place, and it turns out his home is this shrine to Barbra Streisand. He's got Streisand posters, framed autographed pictures of Streisand, Streisand CDs, books about Streisand, framed magazine articles—you name it. It was such a turnoff I had to leave. I like *real* music, not that synthetic showbiz crap." Some gays and sympathetic straights might be a little hard on Misfit and wish that he could be more comfortable with the gay world. Still, many people would still say they understood. Even gay men who are into Babs might think there was something a little too *too* about it all. But if a straight man said this about a girl he had dated, people would think he was incredibly insensitive and full of himself.

A Nice Boy says, "I had to end my relationship with my boyfriend because he kept trying to get me to talk about what he said were the problems in our relationship. And I just can't deal with all of that. If you don't like being with me, then go be with someone else, but I can't stand big, nasty confrontations." Gays and sympathetic straights would say, "Here is a very gentle soul who knows who he is and what works for him. He asserts his needs with other men and so has healthy boundaries." But if a straight man said this, people would call him a coward and say that it was mean of him to so coldly shut another person out.

A Pal says, "A guy I've met said he would like to see me today. I told him I had to pick up my nephew at soccer practice, plus I said I'd help my mother with the table decorations for her party this weekend, *plus* I have to rehearse my song and dance for the AIDS benefit, *and* I told my ex's ex that I'd loan him fifty bucks. The guy ended up changing his mind. What a jerk. I mean, I can't help it that so many people depend on me." Gays and sympathetic straights would say, "Good old Pal. What an asset he is to the gay community, almost like a mascot, always doing things to help others. I guess this guy who called him just wasn't right for him." But if a straight man said this about a girl who called him, people would say he sounded like a lunatic headed for an ulcer and a heart attack, and that he obviously had a lot of issues to sort through about getting his priorities in order.

A Party Boy says, "Some bozo I met at the bar last weekend called and said he wanted to go out tonight. *Tonight,* when it's only the biggest circuit event of the year! And he didn't even know it was happening. I mean, hello? We are living on planet Earth, are we not? Then he keeps me on the phone for like a century and a half as he goes on and on about how he just broke up with someone and could use someone to talk to. I had to say, 'Darling, we've all been there.

Get over it.' I mean, can you *imagine?*" Gays and sympathetic straights would say, "Good old deliciously wicked and witty Party Boy. The things he gets away with saying! He's *such* a scream, and *so* much fun." But if a straight man said this about a woman who had called him, people would think he was a grade-A son of a bitch.

A Perennial Closet Case says, "I have a lover, but I can't let my family know. It would *kill* them." Gays and sympathetic straights would not all agree he should stay in the closet, but everyone would bemoan the homophobic, heterosexist world that keeps men like him from freely expressing themselves. But if a straight man said his family couldn't know about his female partner (maybe because of her race or religion), many people would be far less sympathetic and think this guy was just a flake.

A Sexpot says, "I live for sex. I love it all kinds of different ways. I can never have too many sex partners." Gays and sympathetic straights will say, "Good for him. As long as he's being safe and everyone's having a good time, what's the harm?" But if a straight man—or for that matter, a straight woman—said this, people would be far more judgmental and more inclined to say the person needed to see a therapist for his or her "sex addiction."

A Shy Snob says, "I need a lot of space to myself. A lot of people simply offend me. I don't know how to talk to them. I'm really happier alone." Gays and sympathetic straights would say, "Here's a man with rarefied tastes who is simply too sensitive to be in the world. It's no wonder he has trouble being around people." But if a straight man said this, people would say he was rather pathetic, and that something must have happened to him to make him so afraid of people.

A Therapy Junkie says, "Growing up, all my parents did was shame me. It's no wonder I can't get close to anyone as an adult after the way they warped me for life." Gays and sympathetic straights would agree that this gay man certainly has the right to sing the blues, and that it's tragic that he has indeed been scarred for life. But if a straight man said this, people would assume he was trying to alibi why he screwed around so much, and that he needed to grow up and take responsibility for his actions.

You get the idea. Now, am I saying that it's morally wrong for these gay men to act as they do? Am I saying that the standards to which straight men would be held accountable are right or wrong? No, that isn't the point. Whether these gay men change their behaviors is up to them. But it's a revealing, thought-provoking, and humbling exercise to think about the things we say and do as gay men and compare it all to what's expected of straight men. Maybe some of the habits we fall into could use a little shaking up, because they reinforce patterns aimed at keeping people away from us. And in some cases, our behavior may contain a great deal more traditional male arrogance than many of us "sensitive" gay guys would like to admit.

LISTEN TO FEEDBACK FROM OTHERS

Other people do not know everything about you, and you are not obligated to do anything as they would like. Still, when people tend to say the same things about you and tend to respond to you in similar ways, something is going on that might well be worth noting. For some people, this is common sense. But often in the gay world, there's this idea that goes something like "For eighteen years I had to listen to people telling me what to do and how I should be, and now that I'm out, no one's ever going to make me be anything again."

Great—don't be what other people want you to be. But you can pay attention to what your interactions with others seem to tell you. If men seem to turn off to you on the second date, it isn't that there's a hex upon you; there's probably something you're doing that turns them off. Part of getting to know ourselves is being willing to accept the feedback we get from others.

Blue Collar Guy might be told he's too bossy, Creature of Habit might be told he's too set in his ways, Discriminating Shopper might be told he's too picky, Hyper-Romantic might be told he's unrealistic, Misfit might be told he's overly critical, Nice Boy might be told he's too nice, Pal might be told he needs to mind his own business, Party Boy might be told he needs to sober up and slow down, Perennial Closet Case might be told he needs to come out (amen), Sexpot might be told he's more than just a body, Shy Snob might be told he needs to get off his high horse, and Therapy Junkie might be told he needs to grow up. Not bad advice, if you ask me.

Remember that you're trying for your Second Coming Out. You want to manifest all you can about yourself as a human being and get past the limitations of your OWTA. If people never tell you what they think of you, you might try asking them. And don't just have them say, "I think you're great." Probe a little. If someone's being really stubborn about saying anything less than perfect about you, say something like "If you were given a hundred thousand dollars to come up with something negative to say about me, what would it be?"

If you're afraid of finding out what other people think of you, that ought to tell you something important right there. And you say you want a happy relationship? Good luck finding one, if you can't listen to a little constructive criticism.

I'm not saying that you have to turn your life into some twenty-four-hour-a-day encounter group. (Though Therapy Junkie would no doubt think that was fun.) But it would never hurt you to meditate a bit on the impression you make on others. This is not to make you become what other people want you to be, but to help you to engage in more productive behavior that gets the real and best you across to people.

EMBRACE YOUR PAST

By this I don't mean you have to try to love unpleasant memories. But it would be helpful if you could accept the person who lived through them as a part of who you are now. I don't mean some sort of "inner child" exercise, where you pretend there's a four-year-old living inside you. I mean that the so-called nerd or the frightened gay guy or the socially inept one who managed to survive high school is still a part of who you are now.

Depressing thought? Well, look at it this way. Because gay men are usually put down so much growing up, and because we have no road maps to help us develop sound personalities, we tend to more or less reinvent ourselves. We want to escape the painful identity of our youth, and our new gay self can to a large measure be whatever we want it to be. Unfortunately, our inner resources (since we lack role models and guidance) are often lacking, and so we fall into new kinds of ruts and patterns. Because the process is idiosyncratic, we often don't realize that we haven't changed as much as we'd like to think. (Especially if, as per above, we seldom get any feedback from others.)

We might think that changing our address, name, social set, or hair color makes us into a totally different person. But it doesn't. And part of the fear of intimacy experienced by a gay man involves a deeper fear of facing those parts of himself that he knows are still there. He's afraid that an intimate lover will find out these things about him, and then . . . and then what? Hurt him the way the neighborhood bullies did? Or is it really just that the gay man doesn't want to be reminded of those times at all, and anything that makes him feel that way again seems too painful to face?

I have important news for you: When you were growing up in Podunk or wherever, you did a remarkable job of taking care of yourself. With no one to guide you, you managed to juggle around all sorts of levels of hurt and shame and secrecy and emerge from it saying, "I know who I want to be." There is *nothing* to be ashamed of. If anything, you should feel proud of how strong and life-affirming you were. You not only survived a great deal of psychological torture (and maybe even physical abuse), but you kept on having goals for your future and managed to laugh and fool around and have fun.

So Blue Collar Guy, yes, you still have some "effeminate" traits. Creature of Habit, you still have a wild, untamed nature. Discriminating Shopper, you still have the capacity to love and commit. Hyper-Romantic, you still have the courage to be alone. Misfit, you still have those telltale signs of gayness about you that make you a part of a large, growing, and vital movement. Nice Boy, you still have the anger that can set you free. Pal, you still are looking to be loved. Perennial Closet Case, you still know you're gay. Party Boy, you still are sensitive and bright. Sexpot, you still have the inner beauty no one understood. Shy Snob, you still have a heart that craves love. Therapy Junkie, you still have everything you need to grow up; it's waiting inside you and ready when you give the word.

Sorry if I got a little New Age-y there for a minute, but it's true. Who you were back then might well have been much more than you realize. You believed the propaganda of the homophobes and internalized their antigay sentiments. So to come out as a full human being, you need to accept within yourself and share with the world all the different facets of who you are. This should be the case especially when it comes to having a relationship. If you have a partner but are keeping about 75 percent of your personality hidden from him, what's the point?

As you learn to think about yourself in a more multifaceted way, you might also want to give attention to that man lying next to you in bed, trying to be a good sport as he clicks on the remote control and waits for you to finish reading this book . . .

LETTING HIM BE HIM

YOUR THIRD COMING OUT

...

Now that you're learning that being yourself ain't half-bad, you're ready to start sharing with another man. I don't just mean sex or talking about yourself. Sharing is also being there for the other guy's needs. In our technologically sophisticated society, it's become unpopular to talk about how we can be there for each other. That's because moment to moment, we simply don't need other people all that much. Today I paid my bills by using my Touch-Tone phone to punch in my debit-card number. I got gas for my car by putting my credit card into the automated pump system, and I got cash from an ATM. For entertainment this evening, I could listen to CDs, watch a DVD, or surf the Internet. Unless I want to, I will not have to directly connect with a single human being to get through my day.

This independence and individuality transfer into our interpersonal relationships. More traditional societies still place much importance on kinship and community ties. In such societies, who you are as a person largely depends upon how well you connect with other people. It is believed that your family or tribe or village is what makes you who you are. In our society, we tend to say the opposite. We're keen on saying that no one can change another person, that no one can change himself until he is ready, and so on.

All of this may well be true. But sometimes, we throw out the baby with the bathwater. We forget that while we may not be able to *change* another person, we can at least *help* another person. In intimate relationships, we can help our partners to become their best possible selves. We can't do all the work for them, but we can offer love and support and sometimes even advice and favors. To have a happy relationship, not only do you need to strive to be the best possible you, but your partner must also strive to be the best possible him. This doesn't just mean letting go of your control issues—those parts of you that wish he looked different or had a different job (although, of course, you need to get beyond all that). But in *letting* him be him, you can constructively *help* him be him. That's right. A good relationship isn't just about having someone around so you don't get lonely or horny. It's also supposed to involve helping each other.

If you and your partner are concealing important things about yourselves from each other, your relationship is not destined to be close. And since there are not the legal incentives to stay together, a devitalized gay relationship is probably going to end before long. That it ends is not necessarily bad; why stay in a dull, listless partnership? Yet ironically, as gay relationships get a bit more acceptable, a non-intimate one might well last for years and years, just as mediocre-to-miserable straight relationships can drag on and on.

Whether your crummy relationship comes to a merciful end or holds you prisoner for a lifetime, wouldn't it be better to have a relationship that is intimate, vital, and nurturing? You can have a partnership that simply technically exists, or you can have one in which both partners honestly can say, "I am a stronger, wiser, and happier man for being in this relationship."

So help your partner to become himself and to get beyond his OWTA-ish tendencies. At the same time, let him help you. I am calling this the *Third Coming Out*. After establishing that you are not only gay but a full-fledged human being, you now can pronounce to yourself, your partner, and the world at large that as an adult you are able to get beyond yourself and take an active interest in another person's happiness and well-being. As a gay man, you are generous of spirit and extend yourself into the intimate realm of giving your

lover your heartfelt support. Here are some of the important steps
to take in your Third Coming Out:

ASK QUESTIONS

This may seem like the most basic common sense, but instead of
assuming you already know something about your partner, ask him
about it. To some extent, all people are guilty of making assumptions
about others. To get through a day of life, we can't go around asking
people about every little thing all the time. We need to assume that
we have some sort of built-in understanding of the situation at hand.
Our assumptions might be based on our past experience with this
person, our experience of other people who remind us of him or
her, or what we ourselves would be going through in that person's
place. At other times, we are not interested in the other person so
much as in protecting ourselves, and we let our emotions or "gut-
level" instinct tell us what's going on.

Yet whatever assumption we are making, we need to realize that
we might just be wrong. And in intimate relationships, people have
to make fewer of these assumptions and ask more questions of their
partner, or else major misunderstandings can develop.

In particular, people who very much want to control their social
interactions (such as gay men who fit into an OWTA category) are
less likely to ask questions and more likely to make assumptions
about their partners. By assuming you already know the answer,
you don't have to get out of your personality rut and risk intimacy.
You can keep on pretending you're a Nice Boy or Pal (two types
especially prone to assuming and not asking) and try to control your
partner's responses toward you by "helping" him. Even the relatively confrontational Therapy Junkie often assumes that his partner
is "in denial" or "acting out his childhood issues" when perhaps
such is not the case.

Let's say your boyfriend tends to be late whenever you meet for
an engagement. You can assume you know why this is and decide
it's because he doesn't really like you or is passive-aggressive or is
seeing someone else. Or you can ask him about it. Maybe, just

maybe, it turns out that he's always late for *everything,* and it really has nothing to do with you.

If your boyfriend doesn't seem interested in sex anymore, you can assume you know why this is, or you can ask him about it. If he's standoffish around your family, you can assume you know why, or you can ask him. Why doesn't he like to dance or go to old movies? Why can't he remember to take out the garbage? Why doesn't he want to live with you? Whether a big thing or a small one, you need to get out of your comfortable rut and learn to ask questions.

Now, here's the tricky part. Your boyfriend also is a guy, and so he may not be all that great himself at this intimacy stuff. So if you ask him about something, he might just say, "I have to think about that for a while" or "I dunno" or "You ask too many questions." Regarding the lattermost, if it seems as if *all* you're doing is needing to find out this or that and it never lets up, there's probably something deeply wrong with the relationship. Either you're much too insecure to be ready for a relationship just now, or there's something fundamentally out of sync with your combined personalities.

But assuming that you're asking questions wisely and moderately, remember that timing is important. If you're getting glib answers from your partner, it might have to do with when or where you're asking the questions. With all due respect for spontaneity, no one likes to be zapped with a major issue ten seconds before a movie starts or in the middle of making love by candlelight or just after announcing he's had the worst day at work ever. Or maybe he's busy doing something. Gay or straight, men often have this way of wanting to do one thing at a time, and whether he's fixing the car or sewing sequins on his gown for Halloween, he may not appreciate being interrupted.

You shouldn't keep things bottled up inside, and if you're "afraid" to confront your partner, there's something seriously wrong with your relationship. But assuming that you have basic confidence in your ability to communicate with your partner, remember to be a little patient, and be willing to wait for a day or two here and there for the right time to talk. If he says he needs to think about how to respond, believe him. Some people genuinely do prefer to think for a while before commenting on something important. (But then get back to him in about a week if he still hasn't commented.)

If he says he doesn't know or simply shrugs and seems disinterested, again it might be that he needs to think it over, and this is his way of saying this. But if he really is trying to worm his way out of dealing with whatever it is you brought up, you have several options. You can try probing a little by asking another question or so, or giving him a little hint to get started with ("Well, is it because you don't find me sexy anymore?"). You can also try requesting that he think about it, and that you'd appreciate knowing his answer within a few days.

If he's truly too defensive, going so far as to get angry with you, your relationship is in serious trouble. You're involved with a man who isn't interested in addressing something that's important to you. If such is the case, there isn't much you can do, other than to try couples counseling or to break up. (You could also of course continue in what would seem to be pretty much a loveless arrangement, but I wouldn't recommend that.)

LISTEN

When your lover talks, listen to what he has to say. You may not agree with him, but you need to realize that this is how things look from his point of view. If you aren't interested in what your boyfriend has to say, why are you involved with him? You must not want an intimate relationship—or at least not with him.

Listening is harder than it seems. Just because you hear the words, it doesn't mean you understand them. It's always a good idea to briefly summarize what your partner has just said, to make sure you got it right: "So, if I'm hearing you correctly, you're saying that when you're working overtime, you aren't in the mood for sex." Remember, it's what he actually says, not what you *think* it means. Now, if you disagree with him or think he's full of it, you can always say so: "Then why is it that even when you don't work overtime, you still don't want to have sex?" But first, it should be established that you did at least hear him. (And you'll notice, too, that in the example I just gave, you're still asking another question, and not just making an assumption.)

What he says might put your mind to rest; maybe there really was something simple going on, and now you know what it was. But maybe what he says is devastating. Maybe he says something like "Every time you touch me I am repulsed" or "I'm involved with someone else." If such is the case, you can break up then and there and cut your losses, argue and get your frustrations out of your system, or you can give *yourself* a little time before responding and say something like "I need to think about what you just said."

REMEMBER

Assuming what your partner tells you is not something that makes you want to break up with him, you need to remember what transpires in your conversations, and the resolution that the two of you decided on. I don't want to make too many broad statements about gender, yet my personal observation is that men are much more conveniently forgetful about these sorts of things than women. I think it's because of the way men are raised. Often someone is there to pick up after them, and so men (even, yes, gay men) often think that whatever is said or decided on, they can pretty much do whatever they want, anyway.

This is not the way to have a happy, intimate relationship. It's difficult to believe after a while that your boyfriend "loves" you when he never seems to take anything you say seriously. If your partner says that he doesn't like to be touched in a certain way, don't touch him that way. If supposedly the two of you have resolved to share the household chores (instead of one of you doing most everything), then both of you need to live up to your word. If five minutes or three days after your talk, things go back to the way they were, something is wrong. One of you or both of you aren't really interested in intimacy, because you aren't really interested in taking your partner seriously.

The same goes for the deep and complex stuff you talk about. If he says, "It's painful to talk about my mother, and I'd rather you didn't bring it up again," *don't*. Wait for when he does. If he says,

"I don't do that in bed because it goes against how I define safer sex," honor what he has to say. If what he's requested goes intensely against your needs or who you are as a person, then you might want to think twice about getting involved with this man. If you don't like who he is, how do you expect to feel close to him?

If what he wants strongly conflicts with what you want, hopefully you can work out a compromise. Then try out the compromise. If you feel it isn't working, then talk some more. But remember that you can't mold another person into being what you want. Nor can you just blindly assert your male privilege, as if your boyfriend doesn't have the same rights you do. Or rather, you can, but don't expect a relationship that lasts long—or at least not one that's happy.

OFFER TO HELP

As important as it is to acknowledge your partner's right to call the shots in his own life, there's a completely different trap that gay male couples sometimes fall into. When someone isn't trying to be totally controlling, he might go to the opposite extreme and adopt the ultramodern viewpoint that since he can't control another person, he might as well have nothing to do with him. People in our society (whether gay or straight) have become a bit too independent-minded. We're often a bit too eager to say, "Oh, well, that's his problem," and leave it at that. After all, it's up to the other person if he's going to have friends or find a lover or make more money; what can *you* do about it?

True as it may be that no one can or should assume responsibility for another adult's life, an unwillingness to help out at all can indicate another type of control amongst gay men: wanting to keep everyone out of your life so that you never have to experience any sort of emotional messiness. That way, you can watch TV, weed your garden, or screw around town without anyone hassling you. In other words, you can be a stereotypical man.

Since gay men often feel emotionally rejected by their families or peers when growing up, they sometimes tend to become rather cold and unsympathetic when they see someone else in need. Beneath the "sensitivity" they sometimes project—or even the jokes or complaints about desperately wanting a lover—is often a strong desire to be left alone. This might be why so many gay men walk away from the opportunity for a real relationship. As the old saying goes, you can't give to another person what you never got yourself.

Well, that old saying may not be completely true. Maybe you can make an effort to care about other people, anyway. If you think about it, your boyfriend is supposedly someone you love. It's only natural that you should offer to help him. Not only will he appreciate your concern, but you'll be healing something in your own life at the same time. When your actions state that you are a loving and caring person, people will respond to you accordingly.

However, notice that I say you should *offer* to help. Don't assume that your boyfriend wants or needs your help—or more to the point, that he wants the particular kind of help you're willing to give. His take on the situation might be different. But offer to help. Offer to be there for him emotionally, and even to run an errand or two or to go with him to some important confrontation, or whatever the challenge is that he's facing. If he has problems relating to an aspect of your relationship, offer him your patience and strength. If he's working on improving himself as a person, be there to listen to his insights. Suggest a good book he might read. Again, don't force anything on him. But make the offer.

If your boyfriend deeply resents your offer to help, you might want to reconsider getting involved with him. If you haven't tried to control his life, but have merely made a few suggestions, he is being unreasonable if he feels you are "invading his space" or "not giving him room to breathe." In sum, he's being a rather stereotypical man, without the veneer of politeness he might give you if you were a woman. He may claim to want a partner, but apparently he wants one only in theory.

Additionally, because we often react against the straight world, many gay men get defensive about how they conduct their lives and think they must at all times exhibit "perfect" behavior that reflects the new moral order for which we stand. Everyone is always supposed to know precisely how to handle everything all the time, and if someone does something a bit skewed now and then, it is unforgivable. So heaven forbid someone should "cross" somebody's "boundaries" and be a bit of a butinsky.

Nobody's perfect, and when two people are truly close, either or both of them will occasionally make a mistake and say something that seems a bit too personal or "none of their business." If it's happening all the time, then that's a valid concern. But if it happens only every now and then, it should be forgivable and tolerable. If it isn't—or if it never even happens—then maybe you're not as close as you think you are.

Offering to give of yourself to another person is an important dimension of an intimate relationship. It's what makes it different from a casual sexual encounter. If you don't want to give of yourself, you might be happier sticking with casual sex, because you'll make a mess out of any relationship you attempt.

HONOR DIFFERENCE

Life would be so much simpler for you as a gay man if your partner was *exactly* what you wanted him to be. Some gay men are attracted to men who seem very unlike themselves, but this difference is usually about appearance. A short man wants a tall man, or vice versa. Or maybe the difference sought has to do with age or sexual roles.

But even if you're a short, chubby, twenty-year-old top who seeks a tall, thin, fifty-year-old bottom, it's possible that underneath it all you want someone who's going to be like you. After all, if the man in your life likes all the same music, foods, TV shows, and hobbies that you do, if he shares your beliefs about family and friends and travel and sleep, your life together will be a breeze. You won't have to make any compromises or changes. Or so it seems.

To some extent, all couples obviously look for common ground. Heterosexual and lesbian couples can also get all gooey when both parties have the same favorite song or like tuna fish with grape jelly. Yet sometimes it seems that these happy little coincidences have a special meaning for gay men and get taken way out of proportion. Since both people in the couple are men, they both may want to live as hassle-free and change-free as possible.

Even if your partner also prefers Joan to Bette, there will be moments in which you are *not* alike. Your personal habits, deeply ingrained beliefs, ways of emotionally responding to certain situations, priorities, and ways of thinking might well be unalike. You of course need to have some things in common, but past a certain point, you won't. And when you realize this, there may be a temptation to change each other. You can't really change someone else, but there's even more at stake here. If you're trying to make him be more like you while he's trying to make you be more like him, your relationship will turn into a battle of wills, which is not how one usually describes a happy, intimate relationship.

Another common trap is to *ignore* the differences. You say to yourself something like "I hate drag, and my boyfriend just told me he does drag regularly. Well, maybe he didn't really just say that. Maybe he's exaggerating. Maybe he means he did it a long time ago. Maybe by 'drag' he means something else. Maybe I should just forget he ever said this. After all, what difference does it make, when we're still so right for each other?"

The problem is that if you really have strong feelings about cross-dressing, it may well be a problem that you can't just sweep under the rug. You need to talk about it—and, yes, ask questions about it. Ultimately, you need to realize that difference can be good. That having a partner with a contrasting point of view can open you up to new ideas, new interests, new information about yourself.

If a couple is like the Bobbsey Twins, they seem awfully dull, don't they? So honor difference as a positive influence in your life. Let your boyfriend be the best possible him. Don't try to make him into you, and don't deny or ignore the parts of him that are unlike you. You want to be a positive influence in his life and help him to feel more relaxed about being himself. You don't want to turn into another person who does not validate his right to be himself. As a gay man, he's experienced enough of that already. And as you honor your differences, you can learn and grow at the same time. But you need to ask questions, and not to pretend you understand something you don't. That's dishonest, and therefore not intimate.

HOW TO BECOME
A COUPLE

■ ■ ■

THERE ARE TWO WAYS OF GOING INTO A
relationship. One way is with ignorance and desperation. You think
that having *any* relationship will be better than being single, and the
less you know about your partner, the better. Too much information
might cause the little bubble to burst, and you'll be back at square
one, alone with your pathetic, single self.

I'm going to take a wild guess and assume that you already know
about that way of having a relationship (or something close enough).
So instead I'll talk about the other way of building a partnership:
the wise, sensitive, and patient way. In this approach, the two men
sit down together (or lie down, as the case may be) and do this
peculiar thing called getting to know each other before making a
commitment.

How much time does it take? How long should you know each
other before living together (if that's the next step)? It's really up to
both of you. I know of a happily married male couple who moved
in together the second time they met, and who recently celebrated
their tenth anniversary. Though this is probably the exception to
the rule and I don't recommend it, it does go to show that you
can't live your life around rules. Probably it's going to take a bit
longer for both of you to be ready. Shall we say at least six months?
From a gay perspective, that can seem like a long time, yet I know
a straight man who said to me a while back, "I've only just started

to connect to my girlfriend. After all, we've only been going out for six months."

In the final analysis, it's not a matter of how long you've known each other but how *well* you know each other before making a commitment. Whether it takes a weekend or a year, the point you want to get to is where you both are comfortable with what each other wants and can bring to the relationship. Here are some of the most important things you need to figure out:

WHAT DOES EACH OF YOU
WANT FROM A RELATIONSHIP?

You might be saying, "Well, what do you *think* we want?" But it's not always that simple. Even when it comes to sex, you may want it every day, while he wants it once a week. If you think that's not going to be a problem, you are in for a surprise. Let's say you both make a list of ten things you want from the relationship (which is not a bad idea, by the way). Number one on your list is that you want someone who will listen to you, and this is not on his list at all. *His* number one is that he wants someone he can travel with. A match made in heaven? I think not.

As we were saying not a moment ago, difference can be good. For example, you may recall that though Sexpot and Therapy Junkie have very different approaches to life, their differences often compliment each other. These two men can challenge each other in a healthy and manageable way. The ways they are unalike can be a source of personal growth. (Indeed, you should feel free to refer back to the OWTAs when trying to determine whether difference is good.) But a good place to start is to see how a given difference makes you *feel*. Sexpot and Therapy Junkie stand a fairly good chance of being excited by their differences.

However, in other instances, you might feel extremely uncomfortable to learn what your partner wants from a relationship. You get a sinking feeling inside that you try to ignore, but that doesn't go away. Much of your relationship is spent silently and perhaps only semiconsciously trying to ignore or work your way around these differences.

Sometimes the biggest disappointment is learning that your partner doesn't have any particular goals. He just sort of assumes that a relationship is something to want, and that he'll live happily ever after once he meets the "right man." Or maybe you are most distressed to realize that *you* don't have any particular goals. You just don't like being alone or are jealous that so many of your friends are married. If that's really all your desire for a partner is about, it's no wonder that you don't seem to have much luck fulfilling it.

Before you can ask someone to share your life, you need to have a sense of what your life is being lived for. Who is this man in the mirror whom you want some other man to know and love and cherish? Do you even understand who he is? If you don't, how can you expect that someone else will? Moreover, do you like him? If you don't, why should somebody else? If you don't enjoy your own company, why inflict it on another person?

Your goals can be fun and silly, but you might also want to think about serious stuff, such as someone you can have good communication with. Furthermore, it never hurts for a long-term relationship to have a purpose beyond the two people involved in it. Some couples find that raising children gives them this larger purpose. But if kids aren't your thing, maybe it can be working for charitable causes or writing a book together or saving your money to travel around the world. No matter how enraptured you are of each other at first, that feeling will go away. You'll need something else to sustain the relationship over time.

Is there such a thing as having too much in common? Realistically, this probably won't be the case. There will be at least some differences between you. But it's also a matter of what the common ground is. If number one on both of your lists is "Find a partner who doesn't guilt-trip me for shooting smack," I'd say you have a problem. But as long as what you have in common isn't something that's going to harm either of you or doesn't seem to reinforce your worst habits ("Someone who will spend all his free time watching TV with me"), it probably won't be a problem.

WHAT ARE YOUR DAILY LIFESTYLES AND HABITS?

As you may already have learned through bitter experience, it's often the little things that drive a couple apart. Legally married people have sometimes gotten divorced over things like squeezing the toothpaste tube from the middle, and a gay couple doesn't even have the legal arrangement (or at least not yet) to make it a bit more difficult to split up. So it can be challenging to maintain a gay relationship when you don't share basic habits or ways of living. We find ourselves thinking, "Why should I stay with this jerk who snores when I don't have to?"

Gay men such as the Discriminating Shopper can take these matters to an extreme and decide that no one is exactly perfect, so there's no one worth pursuing. Obviously, within limits, differences can be discussed, accepted, perhaps even compromised. Where do you draw the line between a workable and nonworkable difference? It's largely up to the two of you. If you like different types of music or movies, it shouldn't be too big of a deal—unless of course one of you is a musician or film critic. Some nonsmoking gay men are not troubled by dating a smoker, but others genuinely are. Again, the key might well be how the discovery of the difference makes you feel. Do you find yourself thinking that this difference might be a constructive learning experience, or does it make you feel full of dread and a secret desire to change the other man?

In any event, you'll want to know such things as if you're "morning" or "night" people, how you like to spend your evenings and weekends, whether either or both of you are spiritually inclined, do you tend to sit still or move around a lot when at home, your tastes in clothes, furniture, food, films, books, and so on, and of course your practices in the bedroom. Some gay men very much want what a traditional marriage has to offer: a ceremony, rings, and of course children. Other gay men don't want to model their relationship on what heterosexuals do and expect a more casual relationship. This doesn't just mean whether it's an open relationship (although needless to say that is no slight detail), but whether you see the other man as very much being your "husband," or something a bit less formal such as a "partner" or "lover." Some gay men want all the gooey romantic stuff all the time, and some gay men don't.

You also need to realize that two-person relationships are reflexive. In other words, what Person A says and does can significantly influence what Person B says and does—which in turn influences Person A, and so on. If you get out of the shower dripping wet and dance sexily around the room, you really have no right to sing the blues if your partner comes on to you. Why didn't he know you weren't "in the mood"? Well, because the signals you were putting out indicated that you very much were in the mood. If you're grouchy all the time, that may just be why your lover is emotionally withdrawing from you. If you've bounced a check again after promising a million times not to do so, that might just be the reason why your partner doesn't feel like making love. While we do not have total control over another person, we can and do influence the behavior of the people in our lives. So be aware of how your habits and his habits can influence each other in ways you hadn't considered.

You first need to be aware of what your differences and similarities are when it comes to how you live your lives day to day. Then, you can decide whether you can make things work. You may decide that you want to be a couple, but you don't want to live together. You may decide to live together anyway and try to work through your differences. Or you may decide to split up. But in any of these cases, if you're both making informed decisions, in the long run you'll both emerge as winners.

WHAT CAN EACH OF YOU PROMISE, AND WHAT CAN EACH OF YOU NOT PROMISE?

It's easy to assume at first that "everything will work itself out." But you might want to ask yourselves and each other at the start what you can realistically expect from yourselves and from each other. You both may say you want a monogamous relationship, but can each of you promise to be faithful? Do either or both of you get restless and bored quite easily when it comes to sex? If so, it might just be that despite your best intentions, neither of you will end up being faithful. Instead, you'll lie to each other, and ironically your relationship will very much be a "marriage just like any other."

If you want more than that, you might try being honest at the get-go. Maybe you can say something like "In theory, I've always believed in monogamy. To date, the longest I've ever dated a guy has been four months, so I don't know if I can stay faithful to one person longer than that. I'm willing to give it a try, but if I find myself getting bored, one thing I can promise is that I'll talk to you about it and see what we can work out. Maybe we'll be able to explore more kinky and exotic territory, to liven things up. Or maybe we'll decide to try an open relationship. Maybe we'll even decide to split up, although I hope not. But that's what I can promise and not promise."

There are other things to consider promising besides sex. Can you promise to always speak up when your partner is doing something that makes you unhappy? Can you promise to pay the bills on time, even though you've never done so before? Can you promise to stop smoking, so that your lover doesn't have to take care of you when you develop health problems or doesn't become a widower at an early age?

The list can go on and on—though see if you can limit it to about ten promises each. You also should make a list of ten things you feel you *can't* promise. There are no right or wrong answers here. There also are no simple rules to follow as to what is acceptable. That's for the two of you to work out. But it will be extremely useful to know these types of things about each other in advance.

HOW WILLING IS EACH OF YOU TO COMPROMISE?

In a relationship, a willingness to compromise means that you are honoring your own needs, yet also the needs of your partner. It means that you take your partner seriously, that you can listen to him when he expresses what he needs and—just as important— remember what he said a week or five years ago. Where there is no compromise, there is no real desire to know or understand each other. You're having a relationship simply for the sake of having one.

Stereotypically, men are less willing to compromise than women, and I regret to say that my experiences have taught me that gay men are no exception to the stereotype. In fact, since most of us have already been hassled and put down and told what to do quite a lot, we might even be less willing than many a straight man to compromise, and more willing to walk away to avoid having to do so. We work hard to become the people that we are, and the last thing we want is to have to change in order to please another person.

Obviously, you should not feel obligated to compromise on everything. Maybe you truly disagree with your partner on an important investment or career matter, and it is wise to hold steady. If your partner says, "I want to start drinking a quart of gin a day," it is *not* in your best interests to reply, "Could you make it just half a quart?"

But there's a large and varied gray area in which compromise is possible: how late to stay up on weeknights, how often to have sex, who does what chores, how you spend vacations and holidays, and so forth. Perfection is impossible; inevitably, you will argue with your partner at some point over either or both of you being unwilling to compromise on something. Still, if it seems as if you disagree on virtually everything and are seldom willing to consider the other person's point of view—or if one of you is willing to do so, but the other isn't—your relationship is probably going to make you both unhappy.

As you get to know each other and become familiar with your various similarities and differences, note not just whether the differences get ironed out, but *how* they get ironed out. Are you willing to consider new ways of doing things, or not? And your partner— does he welcome or fear compromise and change? Are compromises reached fairly easily, or is it like pulling proverbial teeth? Can you reach compromises with humor and respect, or do you feel drained and angry at the end (even if a compromise was found)? Some men (gay or straight) are extremely defensive about considering that they could be doing anything differently, and if you or your partner is such a man, be prepared for some rough weather—and the likelihood of splitting up. Or maybe even worse, being one of those miserable couples that stay unhappily together.

HOW TO BE A COUPLE

...

AT THE END OF A MOVIE, IT SAYS, "THE End." But in real life, the "movie" doesn't end with someone saying, "Let's go steady" or "Let's move in together." A relationship is a day-to-day, minute-to-minute enterprise. Even if technically you don't break up on a given day, either or both of you can say or do things that will take their toll in the long run. Perhaps you've made the naive mistake of thinking, "At last I'll be happy," when you've "finally" found a lover. Well, a few weeks or months or years down the road, you may whistle quite a different tune.

Couples often say they broke up over money or sex, as if to suggest that had there been more money or more (or less) testosterone, they'd be well on their way to celebrating their golden anniversary. In the final analysis, however, the problem isn't so much money or sex but how it is dealt with. Breaking up can be a good thing. Maybe underneath all the hyperbole, the two of you discover you just plain don't *like* each other. But sometimes couples split up simply because it's assumed that nothing can be worked out, when maybe it could.

In particular, male couples may have problems with talking things out. Their male training teaches them not to express much of themselves. Plus, the homophobia of our society, which might well be internalized, tells gay men that their relationship somehow does not matter the way a straight relationship does. And so when a relationship is on the skids—even if it's your *own* relationship—you might think to yourself, "This is no big deal. Let's just break up and get it over with. Why go through a lot of unpleasant fuss? It's not like this was some sort of 'real' marriage." Also, as we were saying not long ago, gay men might be even more defensive than straight men, because they've had to fight that much harder to forge a place in the world for themselves, and so feel that much more threatened when someone says, "I don't like the way you do something."

To maintain a healthy relationship, you'll want to examine at least three likely areas of conflict: *conflicting needs, hiding of needs,* and *refusal to change.* Whatever the problem supposedly is, underneath it all it is likely to be one or more of these three simple things.

CONFLICTING NEEDS

You've had to struggle simply to become yourself as a gay man, and so disagreements can sometimes seem more important than they are, because they represent all those voices from your past saying, "You have no right to be you." While male couples can raise children, oftentimes they don't. And so without the distraction and perspective that having children (or some other united purpose) can often provide, conflicts over what color the living room curtains should be can escalate into major issues. After all, it's the *principle* of the thing.

Of course, not all conflicts are over trivia. Sometimes what each of you wants from a partner might not be compatible. For example, what a Blue Collar Guy wants might simply not mesh with what a Therapy Junkie wants. When the two of you are truly coming from different perspectives that are unlikely to mesh well, you might well be better off chalking it up to a learning experience and moving on (unless you both have the patience of Job).

But whether or not the issue at hand is minor, it can be *perceived as* major, depending on the symbolic meaning we assign it. Let's say there's a couple named Bob and Joe. Bob tends to be absentminded and forgets to readjust the car seat after he drives Joe's car. Joe can think that this is symbolic of the way his parents ignored his needs all through his childhood, whereby Bob becomes another "obstacle" to Joe's psychological well-being. Or Joe can decide that Bob really is absentminded, plain and simple. Maybe Joe can make a little sign that reads: "Please put the seat back the way you found it."

In other words, it might be possible to work through your differences. It won't happen overnight. One half-hour-long conversation is not going to solve everything forever. But it might be worthwhile to consider that even if something seems less than ideal, you might be able to get past it as a couple. If the most you're ever willing to do is say "forget it" the minute a conflict of needs emerges, you are certainly entitled to live your life as you choose. However, the next time you criticize straight men for being "closed-minded" or "afraid to face their feelings," you might consider taking a look in the mirror.

HIDING OF NEEDS

In your childhood, you might well have felt all alone, even if you were in a room crowded with relatives, because there was this dreaded secret you were carrying inside you. The message has often been that the things that gay men experience are not important. Yes, we give you permission to be gay—provided that you do not do anything so distasteful as *talk* about it. So you've probably grown accustomed to being secretive. In recent decades, there have been a number of books called things like *How to Be Your Best Friend.* Many gay men don't need to read such a book. They already know how to keep themselves company all too well. Even if your OWTA type is outgoing (such as Pal or Party Boy), there's that great big pile of experience, ideas, and feelings that is For Your Eyes Only.

You may have thought that once you had a lover, all this would change. You'd suddenly become this open person who feels safe sharing virtually everything with that One Special Man. What may have happened instead is that you found yourself identifying more with your mother or womankind in general. You started having a whole new set of secrets, as a million and one things a day that you didn't like about your relationship were kept very much to yourself. Like a good housewife, you tried to find subversive or passive-aggressive ways of getting your point across.

Maybe you've done this other routine where you never speak up about anything that's bothering you, but your boyfriend is simply supposed to know that (a) something is, and (b) exactly what that something is. It's as if you're starring in a movie and the audience can see all of your subtle nuances that passive-aggressively telegraph what's on your mind.

If you don't feel comfortable sharing your needs with your partner, that ought to tell you something right there. True, as a gay man you might have difficulty sharing your needs with anyone, and if that's what the problem is, you need to find ways to boost your self-confidence. But if you find that it's *harder* to share your needs with your partner than with other people, it could be that you're with someone who really isn't right for you. If you find yourself having to mentally rehearse every little thing you want to say to your partner, as if preparing in advance for all the ways he might discredit your words, there would not seem to be much trust in your relationship. You fear your partner's negativity, anger, perhaps even his violence—but in any case you do not feel that he honors your needs.

Hiding your needs from your partner can become a vicious cycle. Because you don't share what's really going on with you, you feel less close to him, and he becomes more likely to say or do something that seems "insensitive," which makes you less likely to share with him—and so on. If you're thinking, "I want a relationship so bad I'll just pretend I don't have any needs and become whatever my partner wants me to be," then think again. No matter how hard you try, your actual needs will have this funny way of making themselves known. Whether or not your relationship lasts, you'll put yourself—and your boyfriend—through a lot of needless pain by being dishonest about who you are.

REFUSAL TO CHANGE

When you become aware of conflicting needs in your relationship, it doesn't mean you have to give in to your partner, nor does it mean that you have to meet in the middle. As we were saying not long ago, some issues should not be compromised. So refusal to compromise is not always the point, whereas refusal to *change* often is.

"Refusal to change" can of course refer to behavior. No matter how many times your boyfriend asks, you refuse to do anything about your snoring—or financial irresponsibility or whatever the problem is. What can even be more annoying over time, you might promise to change, but then five minutes later be right back to your old tricks.

Assuming that whatever you do or do not do that bothers your partner really is a habit worth breaking, you may not be able to change completely right off the top. Old habits can be hard to break. But if you refuse even to make an effort, it can signal that underneath it all you have little respect for your partner. You do not honor him as a human being in his own right. Instead, you want a relationship in which you get to call all the shots and will never be held accountable for any of your actions.

Ultimately, refusal to change is about a refusal to listen. It's deciding that you already know everything there is to know, and nobody can tell The Great You anything. Nobody messes with *you*. If this doesn't sound like the worst stereotypical male behavior, I don't know what does. You should not be expected to change everything about yourself, and if it seems as if that's what your partner wants, he must not really like you very much. But assuming this is not the case, you should be able to accommodate new information—to at least *consider* another point of view or possibility.

The Creature of Habit is of course notorious for not wanting to change, but in one form or another all the OWTAs can get pretty much set in their ways. However your refusal to change manifests itself, it will be extremely difficult to have a happy relationship. With little social pressure to stay together as a male couple, your relationship will probably fall apart. Even worse, you could have a sick, bullying arrangement in which one partner feels he has no rights at all.

You might eventually decide you're better off being single—not because you like being single, although some gay men genuinely do, but because it's less painful than getting involved. Do whatever you think is best, but realize that it isn't necessarily always the other guy's fault that things don't work. Realize, too, that if you throw up your hands and say, "I just can't change," you might be selling yourself short.

HOW TO STAY A COUPLE

■ ■ ■

THERE'S A LOT OF DISAGREEMENT IN the gay community on whether a gay relationship should be modeled on its heterosexual counterpart. The debate transpires on many levels: political, psychological, cultural, even theatrical. I'm not here to offer any easy answers to it. Moreover, I don't think it's wrong to break up or to decide to remain single. But if you are a gay man who *wants* a long-term, happy relationship (and the choice is up to you), I see no way around imbuing your relationship with certain qualities that might just happen to be similar to the ways that straight couples maintain long-term, happy relationships.

Maybe in the final analysis, it's simply how *humans* would seem to do certain things, as opposed to gays versus straights. Moreover, what's good for the goose is good for the gander, as it were. If some thriving gay relationships "break the rules" by being sexually open, then certainly some successful straight relationships have similarly broken the rules. Not all straight relationships are about 2.2 children and white picket fences. Flipping the coin over, some gay relationships *are*.

So when I discuss the qualities that go into a long-term, happy relationship, please don't think I'm simply trying to turn gay relationships into straight ones. Studies indicate that couples, gay or straight, need to manifest certain conditions to stay together: *ongoing commitment, two is better than one, honesty is the best policy, taking action,* and *going with the flow.*

Notice that I keep saying "long-term, *happy* relationships." As some of us know from the relationships we've observed, two people can be together for fifty years and be pretty far removed from happy. That's usually because neither party is bringing much intimacy to it.

ONGOING COMMITMENT

There's really no getting around this one. If you really, really, really want to stay together, you have to be very, very, *very* committed to staying together. According to this philosophy, even if someone is unfaithful or there are all kinds of money problems or drug problems or you don't get along, you *still* don't consider splitting up to be an option. I'm not saying I agree with it. (I especially don't agree with it when the relationship is abusive.) I'm just saying that if you want to stay together no matter what, you don't get divorced. It's that simple. The choice is yours.

Religious taboo is sometimes what prevents straight couples from getting divorced. For a gay couple, the conviction to never split up will have to come from a deeply held personal belief. It's unlikely that your feelings for your partner will be enough, because those feelings are likely to change many times over.

Some pretty crummy things can happen when a couple refuses to split up. There can be years of just plain misery for all concerned. Staying together guarantees only the long-term part of the equation, not the happiness aspect. But for some couples, staying together no matter what means always finding a constructive alternative to splitting up: therapy, financial counselors, treatment centers—doing whatever it takes. It's not for everybody, but it works for some people.

TWO IS BETTER THAN ONE

Another condition that encourages the possibility of a long-term, happy relationship is when the two people involved genuinely enjoy each other's company. This doesn't mean you never get angry or annoyed with each other, or that you never appreciate a short break.

But if *most* of the time you're happier to be doing things with your partner than you would be doing them by yourself, chances are you have a good thing going.

By the way, "happy" here doesn't mean a fear of being alone. It doesn't mean that if he leaves the room for five seconds, you suffer a psychotic breakdown due to your fear of abandonment. It does mean that your life experiences truly are enhanced and made more meaningful with your partner by your side.

Whether it's going to a movie, visiting friends, shopping for clothes, hiking in the woods, cleaning the garage, or vacationing in Rome—not to mention that slight detail of experiencing an orgasm—you genuinely prefer doing it with your partner than by yourself. You're capable of enjoying these things by yourself—you're not just clingy and insecure—but it's better with your boyfriend. If a business trip temporarily separates you, you really do miss him. You don't find yourself thinking, "At last, an entire weekend of freedom!"

If you do find yourself coming more to life when he's away from you, it would appear that your relationship is holding you back more than it's helping you grow, and making you more unhappy than happy. You should reconsider your relationship and either take steps to improve it or end it.

HONESTY IS THE BEST POLICY

There needs to be trust in a long-term, happy relationship, and trust is not possible if the two people involved are not being honest with each other. If you say you're going out for a newspaper and your partner thinks you're really going to diddle around in the alleyway with some stud, it doesn't sound to me as if Happiness has just knocked on your door. Maybe your partner is paranoid and insecure; but maybe he has perfectly good reasons to be suspicious of you.

If monogamy just doesn't work for you, be honest about it from the start. If you don't *know* if monogamy is for you because you've never had a live-in relationship before, be honest about that. Don't say you've had more boyfriends than you have really had. On the other hand, don't say you've had "a few" sex partners when you've had a thousand. These lies will come back to haunt you. Not the way it happens on the soaps, where some lover from the past appears to blackmail you. But you'll trip yourself up in the middle of a sentence, and your boyfriend will lose a lot of his respect for you. Not only that, but if having had few or many sex partners is part of who you are, it will show itself in one form or another—in how you conduct yourself in the bedroom, or even in other, extremely subtle ways.

Who you really are will leak through, whether you like it or not. If you say you don't have a bad temper, but you do, your boyfriend will learn that you not only have a bad temper but that you lied to him. You're better off telling him up front you have a bad temper. He may walk away, but he's likely to do it once he finds out you lied to him, anyway. And by telling the truth, maybe you can figure out why you lose your temper, what sorts of things set you off, and perhaps grow as a person while you try to work things out in your relationship.

Once you're together, you still need to be honest, no matter how painful or inconvenient it sometimes is. If he asks you, "What's been bothering you lately?" and you reply, "Nothing," no matter how big your smile is, he'll know that something really is wrong. Not only that, but he'll be hurt that you're excluding him from whatever it is.

The truth doesn't guarantee happiness. But on the other hand, dishonesty sooner or later guarantees misery. Be courageous enough to want the best out of life, and always tell your lover the truth.

TAKING ACTION

This may seem ridiculously obvious, but some gay couples don't seem to know that if there's a problem in the relationship, you have to do something about it. Of course, any sort of couple can be in denial. But for gay couples, there often is an additional sense that their relationship is just this sort of secondary thing happening off to the side that is not as important as a straight arrangement. Gay unions (at this time) are not legally sanctioned except in Vermont, and for some couples this makes their relationship seem diminished. Also, of course, there are all the antigay messages we've been taught about feeling ashamed of who we are, or that we can discreetly couple but cannot go about "flaunting" ourselves.

So some gay couples feel they have no idea what to do or whom to turn to for help if anything should start to go wrong. They may also feel that it doesn't matter much if the relationship does end. After all, it "only" involved a couple of gay men.

Still other gay couples feel that they've fought so hard to be in a relationship at all that they just don't want to hear any bad news about it. Whatever problems they are experiencing will simply have to go away. I have especially noticed this among younger couples, who often assume that their first crush must be their one and only love throughout their lives. It isn't just that they aren't facing their problems; it's that they don't even want to believe there *are* any problems.

Failure to take constructive action when there's emotional, sexual, or financial turmoil in your marriage is not the crime of the century. Indeed, it is all too common. Men in particular often get into complacent ruts in relationships and resent having to pay attention and change things. But if you don't try to fix the problem, sooner or later it will cause you and your partner a great deal of unhappiness—quite likely more than if you simply dealt with it in the first place. Yes, doing something about it means that ending the relationship is always a possibility. But ending an unhappy, problematic relationship can mean finding a happy one with someone else. And there's always the possibility as well that you won't have to end the relationship, but will instead find a way to solve the problem and find happiness with your current partner.

GOING WITH THE FLOW

It's important to take action, but it's just as important to realize that some things can't be fixed. I don't necessarily mean breaking up. I mean that even if you stay together, fate deals us whatever it deals us, and sometimes we have to live with it. If your partner loses his job, you can't get it back for him. If he has an incurable disease, you can't cure him. If you lose all your money, you can't just make it reappear. If one of you has deceived the other, you can't turn back time and make it so it never happened.

In other words, you are not Samantha Stevens. Not even for ten seconds; not even for one second. At times a decisive action can change the outcome, but at other times neither of you can do anything. You have to just ride it out, roll with the punches, and go with the flow. If, that is, you want to stay together. If you want to split up over this massive, dramatic change, you always have that option. But if you want to remain a couple, be prepared for situations that you can do nothing about.

Actually, you *can* do a few things. You can let your partner know that you're there for him. You can caress each other. You can hold his hand while he cries. You can buy a lot of candy and eat it off of each other's body. You can do whatever it takes to bring love and faith and good cheer into each other's life. But you won't be able to fix everything.

HOW TO BREAK UP

...

THIS BOOK IS ABOUT FINDING INTI-
macy. But what if Mr. Right starts feeling like Mr. Wrong? If you
do decide to break up, it can be a positive or negative experience.
There are many ways of having a negative breakup. Putting all the
blame on your ex, flaunting your newly claimed sexual freedom in
his face, withdrawing from humanity, and trying to convince yourself you aren't gay are probably the most common.

Unless there never was much feeling there in the first place, a
breakup is bound to be extremely painful. Though it usually hurts
more to be the dumpee than to be the dumper, both parties can be
expected to suffer. And so it's natural to go a little nutty when things
don't work out. But the thing about these negative breakups is that
over time they fester inside you and make you that much more
afraid of emotional intimacy in the future. You've broken up, but
you haven't really worked through anything. You're just shoveling
more depression and disappointment onto the heap and becoming
an ever more unreachable gay man. Even years later, you aren't
comfortable dwelling on the breakup. It never becomes a source of
wisdom or a funny anecdote.

By contrast, a positive breakup is an experience that you can look
back on without feeling angry or hurt all over again. Sometimes, time
simply does heal us and gives us a more enlightened perspective.

But it can move slowly, and in the meantime, five or ten years go by, and you're still not truly ready to try again.

The key to having a positive breakup is intimacy—both men being honest about who they are. In fact, even if the other man is being dishonest but *you're* being true to yourself, you can still have a positive experience breaking up. A positive breakup requires *facing the facts, facing your feelings, appropriate catharsis*, and *self-honesty.* Remember that "positive" doesn't necessarily mean "sweetness and light." It's going to hurt, no matter what. But you can turn all that pain into a wellspring of wisdom and strength for the future.

FACING THE FACTS

Breakups can be a lot easier when you feel that you understand why things ended. Whether it's your idea to call it quits, his idea, or a mutual decision, if you realistically take stock of things, it shouldn't be that unthinkable a possibility. If the breakup does come as a total shock to one of you, you need more than ever to sit down together and talk about why this is happening. If your partner refuses to do so, then you can think hard by yourself and start making a list of all the things that went wrong.

If one of you feels that despite the problems you should tough it out and try to make things work, one (to paraphrase Jacqueline Susann) is not enough. However painful it may be, it must be understood that without mutual consent, the relationship can't continue. No matter how much you or he wishes it weren't ending, it *is.*

Hopefully, you can at least see that there were serious problems in the relationship. Some key questions you can ask of yourself—or of your partner—when considering a breakup include the following:

- Are you more unhappy than happy being in the relationship?
- Do you feel worse instead of better when you see him, talk to him, or have sex with him?
- Are you staying in the relationship just because you're afraid to face the pain of splitting up?

- When you consider such options as couples counseling, do you think to yourself, "But I don't want to make it better. I'm tired of this and I just want out"?
- Are you passive-aggressively taking little steps to end it all, such as insulting your boyfriend, saying or doing things you know will embarrass him in public, and in general showing him your worst side so that he'll take the hint?
- Does making an emotional commitment to a different man sound mighty appealing?
- Are there approximately 150 million different things about him that you can't stand?
- Do you find it extremely difficult to talk to him about the things that bother you?
- Does even thinking about your boyfriend piss you off?

If you answered yes to all of these questions, you probably have a relationship that's beyond repair. You both deserve better than a crummy relationship. If you answered yes to only some of these questions, it might be worth a try to fix it. But remember, it needs to be a mutual decision. And remember that the breakup will still be painful, even if it's for the best.

FACING YOUR FEELINGS

No, you aren't perfectly fine. Even if you're the one who instigated the breakup, you're likely to feel hurt, betrayed, and abandoned. After all, if he really *had* loved you, why didn't he put up more of a fuss when you ended things? And why is he already going out with someone else? Or even if he's not dating a new guy, why is he able to function through a day of life? Didn't your relationship mean *anything* to him?

Of course, some other part of you knows better than all this. But you might as well be honest with yourself and admit that whoever did the breakup, you feel like hell. Not only that, but the person you were likeliest to turn to for the past six months or ten years is your ex, so you feel doubly wounded. If your relationship was all-encompassing, you may have few if any people to turn to for support. Even if you do have friends, a great deal of pride is at stake. You want to bitch about what a louse your ex was, but you don't want to do it too much, because you don't want people to think you're *that* upset about it. (Plus, of course, you may tend to sweep your hurt under the rug if you have internalized shame over being in a gay relationship.)

As restrictive as our society is, it does permit people to be bitter and brokenhearted when breaking up with a partner. Take advantage of the opportunity to let things hang out a little. If you're lucky, you might get a free dinner or a small gift out of the whole thing, should a fellow human being take pity upon you. More important, facing your hurt will help you to heal—sort of like the way a stinging antiseptic helps a cut to heal. You have to put up with that little wince of pain in order to get better.

Remember that you're bemoaning the loss not only of the relationship or the constant presence of this other man in your life, but who you were in the relationship, as well. Even if the role you played was rather demented, it did at least become a familiar part of your day, and now you can't do it anymore. This is another void in your life that you have to deal with.

APPROPRIATE CATHARSIS

To experience catharsis is to get something out of your system. It can be extremely healthy to shout or run around the block or give someone the finger. On the other hand, catharsis can be taken too far. No, you don't have the right to inflict physical or emotional abuse on another person, even if you think it will help you feel better. You don't have the right to beat up your ex or tell him something deeply cruel and ugly like "Every time I've looked at you for the past three years, I've wanted to puke."

But without causing any serious harm to yourself or to another person, do what you need to do to feel better. Remember that your first responsibility right now is to yourself, and within a certain perimeter all truly is fair in love and war. Depending on your OWTA type, an appropriate catharsis can not only help you heal from the relationship, but it can be a watershed moment in your development as a human being. For example, if Nice Boy tells his ex to fuck off, it might be the single most decisive action he's ever taken toward becoming a more integrated individual. A scene in public might help Perennial Closet Case to come out.

As gay men, we suppress so much of ourselves that even if we've told people that we're gay, we might still be extremely reluctant or embarrassed to come out as three-dimensional human beings who feel all the same things that nongay people feel. Don't be afraid to let your human imperfections show, and to let the world know that you, too, sometimes need to get a little something off your chest.

SELF-HONESTY

As the smoke clears, have a heart-to-heart talk with yourself. Rather than saying "good riddance to bad rubbish" and hating his guts forever, be honest enough to consider what *you* brought to the relationship that was problematic. Did he do things that made no sense? Did he contradict himself? Did he lie to you? The answer is yes to all three; otherwise, you wouldn't have broken up. But the tricky part is that *you* also did things that made no sense, contradicted yourself, and lied to him.

There's such a thing as righteous anger. It's the anger we feel when something truly unfair has happened to us—usually something way beyond our control. You lost a loved one in a hate crime, or you lost a limb because of a drunk driver. You've been sued or arrested or got fired for something you didn't do. In these sorts of situations, you have every right to be angry—for the rest of your life, if need be. And from this type of anger, something positive can often be achieved. You sue right back or you get a law changed or you help other people who are going through something similar.

But unless it was this type of extreme situation, your breakup with your boyfriend probably involves a more interpersonal kind of anger in which you very much are a key player. Quite often, at least some of the anger is caused by your inability to see how you're responsible for what happened. You want everything to be his fault, and you're pissed off that such is not the case. So you try and try to avoid facing your own imperfections and responsibility for what went wrong.

You'll feel less angry and heal more quickly if you can take a deep breath and say, "I messed up, too." Some of the questions you might want to ask yourself are:

- Did you often not tell your boyfriend how you really felt—about sex, about what to have for dinner, about what you thought of him?
- Was there often a gap between what you knew was the right thing to say or do and what you actually said or did?
- Were you probably often difficult to reach—were you moody or withdrawn or not being honest about how you felt?
- Did you ever assume that you knew exactly why your boyfriend said or did certain things, without bothering to ask for his version of the story?
- In the relationship, were your decisions often based on pride or saving face, or making sure that you got to hurt him before he got to hurt you, rather than risking intimacy?
- How can you learn from this experience, so that next time you are better equipped to pick a suitable partner, and to treat him—and yourself—with honesty and respect?
- What concrete steps can you take to change your self-defeating patterns when it comes to relationships?

If all you do is feel hurt and angry and reach for the nearest bottle or pill or new lover that will numb the pain, you're likely to make the same mistakes all over again. But it might be even worse next time, because you'll be rendered that much more disappointed and cynical. Or you can try to make things happen in a new and positive way.

FINAL THOUGHTS

■ ■ ■

BEING A GAY MAN IN TODAY'S WORLD
is complicated. We're still men and have a lot of the same intimacy
issues that straight men have. Yet we often adopt subversive and
secretive ways of expressing our needs and fears that are more associated with women and other marginalized persons. In this book,
I've attempted to describe some of the specific patterns this somewhat veiled avoidance of intimacy can take through the twelve
OWTAs. I've also tried to talk about some of the general intimacy
issues that affect all gay men as male members of the species. I've
learned a lot by writing this book—about myself, and also about
the gay men I've encountered as friends and lovers. My hope is that
you've learned something, too.

Over the past thirty years, tremendous progress has been made
toward making U.S. society safe for gay people. Yet the innumerable
antigay laws and social policies still on the books, and the plethora
of hate crimes against gays, indicate that the struggle is far from over.
Just being brave enough to come out counts for an awful lot. But
maybe we can also remember that coming out doesn't change *everything* about us. We might still deceive the men we encounter and
be afraid of the very intimacy we claim that we want. Gay men
don't always have to like each other or agree with each other (and
in any case, we simply won't). But when attempting to love each
other, we can start to create new behavioral patterns—in our own

lives, and by extension, in the collective life of the gay community. We don't have to settle for mediocrity.

We need to live in a world where it's safe to love another man. But even when that battle is won, it has been my observation that gay men often know little about how to actually love another man. Gaining the civil rights to do so solves much of the problem, but not all of it. As we continue to fight and struggle for the rights we are due, let us not forget that underneath it all, we want the right to be close to another man. And that may well take more effort than our rather limited frames of reference can deal with.

The gay rights movement is simply still too new for there to be long-standing traditions, norms, or role models to fall back on. And as I have tried to explain in this book, men in general are not trained to deal with intimacy. So we are doubly cursed, so to speak. Perhaps this is why gay male partnerships tend to be of shorter duration than straight or lesbian ones. I do not advocate monogamy for gay men; I see this as a personal choice. But however we choose to express our attraction for men, there might just be more honest, creative, and fully integrated ways of doing so. We might be able to be more honest with ourselves and the men we encounter and learn not to fall back on the same old limiting patterns.

Good luck to us all.